D0152318

The Boulanger Affair
Reconsidered

The Boulanger Affair
Reconsidered

Royalism, Boulangism, and the
Origins of the Radical Right in France

William D. Irvine

NEW YORK   OXFORD
OXFORD UNIVERSITY PRESS
1989

Oxford University Press

Oxford New York Toronto
Delhi Bombay Calcutta Madras Karachi
Petaling Jaya Singapore Hong Kong Tokyo
Nairobi Dar es Salaam Cape Town
Melbourne Auckland

and associated companies in
Berlin Ibadan

Copyright © 1989 by Oxford University Press, Inc.

Published by Oxford University Press, Inc.,
200 Madison Avenue, New York, New York 10016

Library of Congress Cataloging-in-Publication Data

Irvine, William D., 1944–
The Boulanger Affair reconsidered : royalism, Boulangism, and the
origins of the radical right in France / William D. Irvine.
p. cm.
Bibliography: p.
Includes index.
ISBN 0-19-505334-6 (alk. paper)
1. Boulanger, Georges-Ernest-Jean-Marie, 1837–1891. 2. France—
Politics and government—1870–1940. 3. Generals—France—
Biography. 4. France. Armée—Biography. 5. Statesmen—France—
Biography. I. Title.
DC342.8.B7178 1989
944.081′092′4—dc 19 [B] 88-5177 CIP

2 4 6 8 10 9 7 5 3 1

Printed in the United States of America
on acid-free paper

To William Thomas Irvine
1911–1981

ACKNOWLEDGEMENTS

During the dozen years I worked on this book I was generously supported by a large number of individuals. My former teacher, Arno Mayer, has for the past two decades subjected my work to rigorous scrutiny and provided me with much-appreciated support and encouragement. A host of scholars read versions of this book, in whole or in part, and both it and I benefited from the resulting comments, criticisms, and, above all, moral support. They include: Oscar Arnal, Stewart Doty, Geoff Eley, Steven Englund, Adrienne Harris, Patrick Hutton, Lynn Hunt, Thomas Laqueur, Phil Nord, Karen Offen, and Robert Soucy.

During my many research trips in France, many librarians and archivists—too numerous to name—made their resources available to me, suggested possible sources and avenues of investigation, and politely overlooked the fact that I was making what appeared to be a "smash and grab" raid on their collections. One who cannot go unnamed is Mme Suzanne d'Huart, who facilitated access to the Archives de la Maison de France and, in the summer of 1981, responded to my lamentations about the inconvenience of the summer closing of the Archives Nationales by permitting me to work in her private office. I should also like to express my thanks to the current Count of Paris for granting me access to the archives of his family.

I should also like to acknowledge my typists—Dierdre MacLean, Chris Monteith, and Marina Sakuta—my research assistants—Dr. Donald Wileman and Howard Margolian—and the editorial staff of Oxford University Press, notably Henry Krawitz and Clifford Browder. I would like to thank *French Historical Studies* for permission to quote from my article, "French Royalists and Boulangism," *French Historical Studies,* XV (Spring 1988), 395–406. A Glendon College Research Fellowship in 1983–84 permitted me to complete the writing of this book. The many visits to France were made possible by research grants from the Social Sciences and Humanities Research Council (1979 and 1981) and Glendon College Research Grants (1978, 1980, 1982, and 1984). Of course, the real burden of my research trips was borne by my wife,

Marion Lane, and my sons, Carl and Benjamin, who settled for post-cards and phone calls when they were entitled to more.

This book is dedicated to my father. Although a geological engineer by profession, he read a book of history or biography every day of his adult life. I grew up watching him reconstruct the Battle of Waterloo with knives and forks at the dining room table. Of course, he had his own ideas as to how history should be written and considered the work of most academic historians—his son included—hopelessly pedantic. I do know that he never got beyond page 77 in my first book and rather doubt that he would have gotten much further in this one. For all that, every page of it is dedicated to his memory.

Toronto   W.D.I.
June 1988

CONTENTS

The Boulanger Affair
Reconsidered

Introduction

In the summer of 1888 the disgruntled editor of a provincial royalist newspaper was reflecting on France's latest political sensation: General Georges Boulanger. The new phenomenon of "Boulangism," he observed, would "provide material for the astonishment of future French historians when they are forced to explain why, in the year 1888, monarchists so ardently supported a republican."[1] What prompted this dyspeptic outburst was the growing evidence that French royalists were covertly in league with the general and playing a central role in what would later be known as the Boulanger affair.

Between 1886 and 1889 General Boulanger occupied the center of French political life. Although he had once affected a conventional piety and a corresponding preference for the monarchy, the ambitious young general found it expedient to adopt a heartily republican stance following the consolidation of the Third French Republic in the early 1880s. His professions of republicanism—then relatively rare in the French officer corps—brought Boulanger to the attention of left-wing republicans, the Radicals. Their leader, Georges Clemenceau, obtained for him the post of minister of war in January 1886. During his eighteen months in office Boulanger became the most talked-about figure in France. His phenomenal popularity owed something to his striking good looks and dashing manner, rather more to his considerable gift for self-advertising, and a great deal indeed to his belligerent anti-German nationalism. "Le général Revanche" soon became the idol of the Parisian crowds. A minor song-writing industry arose to satisfy music halls that wanted ever more odes to the popular general.

Conservative republicans were less enamored of the bellicose general and combined with royalists to remove him from office in the spring of

1887. Life in the barracks did not appeal to Boulanger, who was soon conspiring to renew his political career. After a series of abortive backroom plots, he began to run for office in the early spring of 1888, mounting a personal plebiscite. Although he was expelled from the army for political activity, his popular appeal was in no way diminished. His platform was characteristically vague: restoration of French national grandeur, cleansing of French political life, and defense of the "exploited" against the "exploiters." Nonetheless it attracted votes from across the political spectrum, including members of the working classes who had previously voted for candidates of the extreme Left. He was elected repeatedly, often with huge majorities. Once elected, he would resign to run elsewhere. In January 1889 he won a resounding electoral victory in Paris, hitherto the bastion of left-wing republicanism. Observers everywhere were predicting an imminent Boulganist dictatorship.

Boulanger, however, had neither the acumen nor the nerve to deal with a tenacious republican regime. When the government of the day leaked rumors of his impending arrest, Boulanger responded by fleeing abroad. Despite this, Boulangism did not immediately die; by 1889 a substantial and well-financed movement had sprung up around the general, and his followers continued to strive for power. In the elections held that year Boulangists waged an imposing struggle and scored some impressive successes. Nonetheless Boulanger's continued exile and the ruthless campaign of the government militated against any major electoral breakthrough; the handful of successful Boulangist candidates constituted little more than a noisy rump in parliament. When Boulanger shot himself in 1891, Boulangism had already been dead for over a year.

Although he mounted a major assault against the fledgling democratic republic, Boulanger was to all appearances a man of the Left, not of the Right. There was, as the unhappy royalist editor had noted, little about him that was appealing to the traditional conservative Right: the dynastic opposition represented by royalists and Bonapartists.[2] Certainly his every action as minister of war had been calculated to offend royalists. He had threatened to republicanize an army where monarchist sentiment remained strong. He had gratuitously expelled the royal princes from the army despite the fact that, a decade earlier, he had assiduously cultivated the friendship of one of them, the Duc d'Aumale. The brash minister of war then compounded that offense by gracelessly and unsuccessfully lying about the matter. He had sponsored a military reform bill which, by depriving seminarians of their exemption from military service, had outraged Catholic conservatives. During the widely publicized strike at Décazeville, he had blissfully assured the Chamber of Deputies that the

French troops sent to the scene were currently sharing their bread and soup with hungry strikers, thus inflaming royalists, who felt that the army might more appropriately repress than feed revolutionary malcontents. Boulanger quickly adopted the banner of patriotic nationalism, seeking revenge against the German Empire. The provocative saber rattling of "le général Revanche" frightened a French Right which, still traumatized by the Paris Commune, equated foreign war with domestic social upheaval and revolution. Boulanger's dismissal as war minister in the spring of 1887 had been, in large measure, the work of royalists in the Chamber of Deputies who were prepared to make substantial concessions to the ruling republicans in order to be rid of a man they freely denounced as a Communard.

If Boulanger had little appeal for French royalists, his friends had even less. He was the darling of the revolutionary masses of Paris, and his initial supporters were almost exclusively from the radical Left. Boulanger's entourage read like a list of those most feared and despised by conservative Frenchmen: Henri de Rochefort, a brilliant journalist, former Communard, ferocious anticlerical, and arguably the most accomplished blasphemer of the nineteenth century; Alfred Naquet, a Jew, champion of the graduated income tax, and author of the 1884 law liberalizing divorce; Georges Laguerre, former secretary of the socialist Louis Blanc and a lawyer who specialized in defending revolutionaries; Paul de Susini, whose maiden speech in the Chamber represented an impassioned call for the immediate expulsion of the monarchist pretenders; Charles-Ange Laisant, deputy of the extreme Left and political counselor of Georges Clemenceau; Francis Laur, Radical republican and advocate of cooperative socialism; Paul Déroulède, leader of the republican revanchist Ligue des Patriotes; and Henri Michelin, the Radical deputy who rendered the right flank of the Chamber of Deputies apoplectic by observing that the principal shortcoming of the French Revolution had been its failure to guillotine enough aristocrats. Boulangists, in short, seemed to be drawn exclusively from the revolutionary rabble, and Boulangism appeared as a reincarnation of the Commune.

In the end Boulanger's appeal proved a good deal more eclectic, but he undeniably exercised considerable charm in winning over important segments of the nascent French socialist movement. In the spring of 1888 the old revolutionary socialist Emile Eudes found himself in secret conversations with Boulanger. A good half of his fellow Blanquist socialists later endorsed Boulangism. Even Marx's son-in-law, Paul Lafargue, was momentarily tempted. The most famous convert to Boulangism, Maurice Barrès, became for a number of years a prominent

French socialist. Antoine Jourde, later one of the leaders of France's first Marxist socialist party, began his political career in the ranks of the Boulangists.

To be sure, Boulanger's plebiscitary and antiparliamentary political style was more than a little reminiscent of the Napoleonic tradition, a point that did not escape the remaining French Bonapartists. That very fact, however, rendered Boulangism even less palatable to the far more powerful royalists. For Orleanists, principled partisans of parliamentarianism, plebiscitarianism was reminiscent of the worst and most dangerously demagogic features of the Second Empire. For legitimists, whose pretender had died in exile rather than accept the tricolor, the plebiscite was a frankly revolutionary instrument, the very antithesis of dynastic principles. As countless royalist editorials noted, Boulangism was the enemy.

Yet in 1888 the royalist leadership was behaving as if none of this mattered. The bewildered provincial editor saw signs everywhere that royalists, far from opposing Boulanger's ambitions, were giving him indispensable electoral assistance. Increasingly he heard rumors that the fabulous sums Boulanger and his entourage were spending came from royalist coffers. Just as disquieting were the ambiguous pronouncements emanating from royalist headquarters and, worse still, the gentle hints reaching his editorial office that the standard anti-Boulangist diatribes were no longer appropriate fare for royalist readers. It is little wonder that the perplexed editor would appeal to future historians to explain this bizarre transformation of the royalist Right.

For the most part historians have not done so. That royalists played a role in the Boulanger affair has never been at issue. Contemporaries were vaguely aware of it and many of the details of the royalist-Boulangist alliance were authoritatively documented in 1890 in *Les Coulisses du Boulangisme*, written by Gabriel Terrail, a disillusioned former Boulangist.[3] Adrien Dansette's 1946 account of Boulangism, drawing on private royalist papers, confirmed and reinforced Terrail's account.[4] Nonetheless subsequent histories, while conceding the fact of royalist involvement, invariably gloss over its ramifications.[5] Michael Burns's recent examination of grass-roots Boulangism, for example, concedes only obliquely and inconsistently that the decisive determinant of Boulanger's electoral support was the attitude of local conservative elites.[6]

Most historians would appear to agree that Boulanger's secret royalist allies do not adequately explain his phenomenal electoral success, nor does their support prevent Boulangism from being a fundamentally left-wing phenomenon. One of the most accomplished students of Boulangism, Patrick Hutton, has recently described it in the following terms: "The Boulangist movement . . . was an expression of Jacobin discontent which drew together the constituent elements of the revolutionary tradition. Radicals, populists and Blanquists were all enticed into General Boulanger's cause. The Boulangists were committed to constitutional revision, and their propaganda about creating a more open, democratic republic evoked longings similar to those which had perpetuated the myth of the Commune." Boulangism is repeatedly depicted by him as "a restatement of Jacobin values," an attempt "to rekindle revolutionary fervor by restating Jacobin values in populist idiom," "a genuine expression of popular discontent with Opportunist political oppression," "a means of challenging the elitist style of parliamentary politics which had so long frustrated the ambitions of the revolutionary movement," and "a configuration of protest not unlike those which had preceded the revolutions of 1830 and 1848." Considered in isolation, such quotations are not an entirely fair representation of the author's position, yet he explicitly challenges those historians who have accepted "uncritically . . . this interpretation of Boulangism as a right-wing conspiracy," noting that "recent scholarship has . . . called into question . . . the interpretation of the Boulangist movement as a monarchist front," and has demonstrated that the popular movement behind Boulanger was "one of left-wing protest against the failings of the moderate republican regime."[7]

Hutton is on undeniably strong historiographical grounds, for a host of scholars have emphasized the leftist dimensions of the Boulangist phenomenon. The starting point for this reading was Jacques Néré's monumental thesis on Boulangism.[8] Néré demonstrated that after 1882 there was a sustained economic crisis in France which, while largely unnoticed by contemporary observers, led to high unemployment, low wages, and economic misery among the popular classes. Faced with the ruling republicans' ignorance of and indifference to their plight, and the absence of a significant socialist movement, the French working classes found in Boulanger and Boulangism an appropriate outlet for their grievances. There was, in short, a determining link between "working-class misery and Boulangism."[9] Boulanger's campaign greatly appealed to the popular classes because they saw it as "the sole means of putting an end to parliamentary impotence and, as a consequence, of bringing about the social reforms, so long promised, which would end their suffering."[10] So desperate were the working masses, and so insensitive to their condition was the government, that "it is hardly astonishing that they became more and more engaged in Boulangism without being deterred by the support, increasingly difficult to hide, that the majority of the conservative right was giving to Boulanger."[11] Although Néré's able dissection of the industrial and social crisis is a good deal more convincing than his explanation of Boulangism, most historians have accepted the broad outlines of his thesis.[12]

The leading English historian of the Third Republic, Theodore Zeldin, has chided Jules Ferry for dismissing Boulangism as the work of the monarchists and for failing to understand the true nature of the movement. According to Zeldin, "it was the socialists who became the backbone of Boulangism. . . . They defined it clearly as a movement for social reform, for action to meet the economic crisis, with constitutional revision as the means. Boulangism survived . . . to become one of the elements in a reinvigorated socialism." By crushing Boulangism the republicans demonstrated that they were the true conservatives.[13] Zeev Sternhell, one of the foremost French authorities on the subject, has focused almost exclusively on "popular authoritarian, antibourgeois and antiparliamentary Boulangism, the Boulangism of the Radicals, of the Blanquists and of the Guesdists, the Boulangism of the miners of the Nord and the common people of Belleville." For him Boulangism represents "the revolt of the new social classes, in particular those of the big cities and industrial centers . . . which prepared the terrain for the growth of the workers' movement in the region of Paris and the industrial north, east, and southwest." As a consequence the Boulangist flirtations of some French socialists were hardly the betrayal that Friedrich Engels imagined. French Marxists recognized Boulangism as "a revolt against bourgeois society" and "a popular movement fulfilling a function of which the workers' party was as yet incapable." It was therefore entirely appropriate for socialists to "support Boulangism in its destruction of the established order."[14] Since Boulangism is treated as the handmaiden of socialism, the active participation of Maurice Barrès in the movement is but the logical springboard for his 1890s socialism.[15] All these writers recognize a disquieting undercurrent of xenophobia, racism, irrationalism, and authoritarianism in Boulangism, but they insist that these arise directly from the less savory dimensions of the Jacobin and socialist traditions and are, if anything, proof of the distinctly leftist valence of Boulangism. This reading is oddly congruent with the anti-Boulangist diatribes of royalists in 1886 and 1887. The subsequent royalist involvement—invariably acknowledged—is dismissed as a rather bizarre sideshow: the desperate, unsuccessful, and ultimately uninteresting intrigue of a dying political force.

Yet the royalist role in the Boulanger affair was anything but peripheral. True, Boulanger was always lionized by the popular classes of

Paris, but he became an imposing political force because he won a series of provincial by-elections in 1888. In these elections Boulanger invariably ran in conservative departments, always replaced a recently deceased conservative deputy, never faced a conservative opponent, and in every instance obtained the great majority of his votes from those who usually voted for conservatives. Indeed, these were necessary preconditions for his successes, explicitly requested by Boulanger. In June 1888, when Paul Déroulède attempted to run as Boulanger's personal candidate against a conservative in the Charente, he came in third. When royalists remained neutral, as they did in the Ardèche in July 1888, Boulanger lost. Whenever Boulanger resigned a recently won seat in order to run elsewhere, he was replaced by a royalist or Bonapartist in subsequent by-elections. Only once—in Paris in January 1889—was this pattern broken, when he received a majority of his votes from the Left in a thoroughly republican constituency. Even here, however, he obtained the quasi totality of the capital's conservative vote, which, had it gone elsewhere, might well have cost him the election.

Boulanger's electoral campaigns were without precedent in French history. They were also financed by unprecedented sums of money, all of which came from royalist coffers. Boulanger and the Boulangists almost always had at their disposal the royalist electoral machine and the royalist printing presses. For a while some part of the royalist press proved refractory (although the fulminations of editors were always a poor guide to their back-room behavior), but when its support counted and it was ordered to comply, the press also swung behind Boulanger. Royalists were not, as is often suggested, mere backdoor conspirators and credulous paymasters. They actively orchestrated Boulanger's campaigns at almost all levels. Without their active intervention there would have been no Boulanger affair.

Boulanger's contacts with royalists were far more consequential than his dalliances with the Left. The discussions between Boulanger and the Radicals, the famous "nuits historiques" of November 1887, were subsequently highly embarrassing for the latter, but nothing came of them. By contrast, Boulanger's simultaneous meetings with the royalists Mackau and Martimprey established the basis for two years of active collaboration. The secret meeting between Boulanger and Emile Eudes, the ex-Communard leader of the Blanquists, is no doubt a commentary on the ambivalent nature of Blanquist socialism (as well as on Boulanger's duplicity), but its overall significance pales in comparison with the repeated contacts between the general and the royalist leadership. Friedrich Engels's profound irritation at Paul Lafargue's momentary temptation and Guesdist irresolution in the face of Boulangism is well (and often) documented, but the political consequences of such flirtations were minimal compared to the resolute action of the royalists. Although royalist leadership was also divided on the question of Boulanger, the most skeptical of them showed less hesitation than did a man like Lafargue. It is significant that five Blanquist candidates in 1889 were supported by the Boulangist Republican National Committee, but surely less important than the fact that the great majority of candidates endorsed by that committee were in fact royalists or Bonapartists. There is no denying that Boulangism attracted some fraction of the extreme Left, but it was precisely that fact which made Boulanger so attractive to the royalists. By discounting the relevance of royalist support for Boulanger, historians are no closer to resolving the question posed by the bemused royalist editor in 1888.

Why have most historians minimized the significance of the royalist role in the Boulanger affair? One reason is that the royalist gambit failed and, having failed, appears in retrospect to have been hopeless, desperate, and perhaps even frivolous. As one disgusted royalist later observed, the calculations of the monarchist leaders "would have been the ultimate in Machiavellianism had they not been the height of stupidity." Charles Dupuy, editor of *La Gazette de France* and one of the few consistent royalist opponents of Boulanger, once complained that when he asked a prominent royalist why he had invited Boulanger to dinner, he received the disarming reply, "Mon cher, boulangisme, c'est du sport." Among some royalists, Dupuy remarked, Boulangism enjoyed "un certain côté du snobisme et du chic."[16] Weary of defending royalist principles and bored with dynastic politics, too many royalists supported Boulangism for its nuisance value or its potential for amusement. With few remaining political options but plenty of wealth, royalists could easily toss a few million francs after the disruptive general. Given the fact that the best-known (although not the most important) source of royalist funds for Boulanger was the Duchesse d'Uzès, whose naiveté was as great as her fortune, the hypothesis has a superficial plausibility. Yet the entire campaign was underwritten by the royalist pretender, the Count of Paris, a man not temperamentally disposed to rash actions or rash expenditures. There were certainly some quixotic elements in the royalist party, but Albert de Mun, Jacques Piou, the Baron de Mackau, the Marquis de Breteuil, the Marquis de Beauvoir, and Edouard Bocher were seasoned veterans of political struggles, entirely immune to the seductive charms that so endeared the general to the benevolent duchess. That they, albeit with varying degrees of enthusiasm, should have endorsed the Boulangist strategy suggests that it was something more than a *divertissement*.

A second reason for the inattention to the right-wing dimensions of Boulangism is the enduring influence of the interpretive framework established by Néré. Once it is accepted that Boulangism is a radical republican phenomenon, the activities of those who are neither radical nor republican become, almost by definition, of secondary importance. In his analysis of the contemporary press, Néré asserts that the question of Boulanger "leaves few traces in the royalist press. . . . Conservative newspapers by and large preferred to speak as little as possible about Boulangism." In fact the royalist press, be it Parisian or provincial, was absolutely obsessed by Boulangism, talked about little else for months, and openly debated the merits of the alliance throughout 1888 and 1889. These debates make little impression on Néré because he has already dismissed royalist relations with Boulanger as "an unnatural alliance."[17] Odile Rudelle's excellent analysis of the 1889 elections is marred by the arbitrariness of her designation of Boulangists. For her they are by definition republicans of the kind who object to the "odious persecution" of Boulanger (although the example she cites is, inconveniently, a Bonapartist). Socialists, except where overtly and explicitly hostile to Boulanger, are automatically included among the ranks of Boulangists "in order to give Boulangism its exact dimensions." Royalists and Bonapartists, by contrast, are automatically excluded, even when they enjoy the formal endorsement of the Boulangist headquarters or even Boulanger himself. Maurice Barrès is a "true Boulangist candidate," as opposed to the Bonapartist Paul de Cassagnac, who, despite his intimate collaboration with the royalists in the entire Boulangist enterprise, is merely a "false revisionist."[18] Since it has become virtually an article of faith that being a Boulangist meant being on the political Left, the many ultraconservative Boulangists are usually either ignored or misidentified. The quest for "genuine" Boulangists of unsullied republicanism can color the findings of the most acute observer. In his classic study of the west of France, André Siegfried managed to identify four "pure" Boulangists, one of whom was in fact a royalist, one a Bonapartist, and one an exroyalist. The fourth, while admittedly a republican of long standing, was prepared to drop the word "republican" from his campaign posters in deference to local royalists.[19]

Undeniably the nebulous program of Boulangism admits of a multitude of interpretations. Denouncing the moderate republic as the "regime of persecution and exploitation" sounds healthily radical, but royalists could and did bandy about similar epithets. Of course their target was

not the social conservatism of the Opportunist republic but its anticlerical legislation and the republican zeal of its administrators. Royalists
despised Jules Ferry as intensely as did the Radicals, albeit usually for
quite different reasons. The demand for the revision of the 1875 constitution was the classic platform of those who sought a more thoroughly
democratic political system. But since, as of 1887, royalists hoped to restore the monarchy by means of a constitutional revision, they could as
easily claim to be revisionists. Some Boulangists did espouse socialist
doctrines, but so did some royalists. Presumably these were different
kinds of socialism, but the respective contours remained vague. Boulangists like Alfred Gabriel and Maurice Barrès certainly had kind words
for the socialism of royalists like Albert de Mun and even of the German emperor. A socialism thoroughly infused with anti-Semitism was
not unwelcome in some royalist quarters, and there were plenty of royalists who believed that the Boulangist variety of socialist could be
domesticated for their purposes. The ambiguity of the prevailing rhetoric
therefore permitted all kinds of "unnatural alliances."

Most historians of Boulangism, however, dismiss the alliance with the
royalists as a purely tactical one while simultaneously insisting that the adhesion to Boulangism by some part of the radical Left speaks to the
very essence of the phenomenon. The assumptions behind this argument
are at best highly problematic. The great majority of the Radicals, after
all, did not endorse Boulangism. Their qualified enthusiasm for Boulanger in 1886 and 1887 is hardly more significant than their hostility
by 1888. His principal parliamentary antagonist in that year was the
Radical premier Charles Floquet. The latter was perhaps a pretty tepid
Radical, but the uncontested leaders of the left wing of Radicalism,
Camille Pelletan and Georges Clemenceau, were equally outspoken in
their denunciations of "le brav' général." It might be objected that the
rejection of Boulanger by most Radicals is proof of their growing conservatism; certainly on most accounts the years 1888–89 mark the acceptance by the Radicals of the existing parliamentary regime. Yet the
subsequent rightward evolution of Georges Clemenceau is far less pronounced than that of "radical" Boulangists like Maurice Barrès and Paul
Déroulède. Radicals rejected Boulangism not because they were frightened by its socialist dimensions but, as they claimed, because it was reactionary.

By stressing the "tactical" nature of the Boulangist alliance with royalists, it is implicitly assumed that the radical Boulangists were prepared
to spend royalist money, attract royalist votes, permit their campaign to
be orchestrated by royalists and, where called upon, vote for royalists

while remaining faithful throughout to their revolutionary past. According to this reading, the Boulangist "use" of royalists did not undermine their sincere commitment to their radical goals. But the question of political sincerity poses some awkward questions. Is Georges Laguerre's status as the former secretary to Louis Blanc ultimately more important than his willingness to permit his newspaper to be subsidized and later owned outright by royalists? Was Paul de Susini's declaration that he had, since 1885, "flown the true flag of socialism" undermined when he assured the Count of Paris of his family's royalist past in order to obtain 25,000 francs? Were Maurice Barrès's assertions of socialism in *Le Courrier de l'Est* at all vitiated by his continued contacts with the royalists of Nancy? In the end, are electoral declarations and newspaper articles more important than what transpires in the smoke-filled rooms? The question must remain open, although the subsequent political trajectory of many of the radical Boulangists does suggest that by 1888 their past was already behind them.

Nonetheless the royalist-Boulangist relationship was, by any standard, a *mésalliance,* an "unnatural" association of fundamentally incongruous political philosophies. Nor would it be the last. In the half century following the Boulanger affair European conservatives would often find themselves allied to movements which appeared to share few of their basic values. Indeed, many of the issues raised by the Boulangist episode have reappeared in the ongoing debate about twentieth-century fascism. Because the classic models of fascism arose as a reaction to the reformist and revolutionary Left, many scholars have stressed its affinity with the conservative Right, even suggesting that fascism amounts to a radical version of conservatism.[20] No one of course contends that fascism is the *same* as conservatism, for there are important elements in the doctrine and practice of the former which are alien to the conservative tradition and which, in fact, are borrowed from the traditional Left.

In his classic study Ernst Nolte defined fascism as "anti-Marxism which seeks to destroy the enemy by the evolvement of a radically opposed and yet related ideology and by the use of almost identical and yet typically modified methods, always, however, within the unyielding framework of national self-assertion and autonomy."[21] Although cumbersome, Nolte's definition accurately captures the central tension within fascism: Its enemies are clearly the parties of the classic political Left, but its means of combating them bear striking similarities to the means employed by the Left. Many of the best-known fascist leaders served their political apprenticeships in parties of the extreme Left: Benito Mussolini in the revolutionary wing of prewar Italian socialism and Jacques Doriot in the French Communist Party. Hitler's party chose to call itself the "National Socialists" (a term coined in the 1890s by the onetime French socialist and Boulangist Maurice Barrès). Just as Italian Fascists made much use of the vocabulary of revolutionary syndicalism, so the early program of the National Socialists was replete with anti-capitalist rhetoric. Moreover, the "methods" of the fascists were far closer to those of the revolutionary Left than to those of traditional con-servatives. They were, or purported to be, "popular" movements with a mass base and support among the lower classes of society—elements for which conservatives had rarely had any appeal. Furthermore, theirs was the politics "of the street," involving direct and violent action against political enemies and selected targets among the established political order. By descending into the piazza they appeared to emulate the revo-lutionary forces of the nineteenth century. Even when they engaged in electoral politics, they did so with an energy, vigor, and attention to mass propaganda which had heretofore been the exclusive preserve of the Left. Like the Socialists and communists, fascists formed mass-based parties that excelled in the techniques of mass politics.

As a consequence, students of fascism have long been fascinated by its affinities with the revolutionary Left. During the 1940s and 1950s, fascism and communism were frequently lumped together under the general rubric of "totalitarianism."[22] With the end of the Cold War and the correspondingly reduced appeal of a theory identifying communism with the Nazis, the totalitarianism thesis lost much of its attractiveness. Nonetheless an important current of scholarship continues to emphasize the fundamental affinity between fascism and the revolutionary Left. In a major study of Fascist Italy, A. James Gregor identifies "Fascism as a member of a class of regimes that include Bolshevism, Maoism [and] Castroism" and assigns it the status of "the first revolutionary socialist heresy."[23] In a provocative interview a leading scholar of the subject, Renzo de Felice, after correctly identifying mass mobilization as a salient feature of fascism, insisted that this placed the phenomenon in the revo-lutionary tradition.[24] A seminal article by Eugen Weber contends that, far from being a species of "counterrevolution," fascism represents an "alternate revolution." In his account, most of the distinguishing features of this "alternate revolution" suggest compelling parallels with the revo-lutions of the classic Left.[25] In the same spirit, the concluding volume of Zeev Sternhell's trilogy on fascism in France, *Ni droite ni gauche,* treats the subject as "one more stage in the revision of Marxism."[26]

The radical aspects of the fascist program were, however, the first casualty of the transition from fascist movement to fascist regime. "Seizure" and consolidation of power necessitated the support—overt or covert—of traditional elites: political, military, bureaucratic, ecclesiastical, industrial, and agrarian. Consequently, as fascist movements drew closer to power, the more radical of their platforms were quietly shelved and a host of accommodations were struck with prefascist elites. The various appeals for "a second revolution," emanating from fascists of the first hour, went unheard; the Farinaccis and Rossonis were tamed; the Strassers and Roehms were shot. There ensued a period of "partial fascistization"[27] during which fascists exercised an effective monopoly over the political process while leaving the direction of military, economic, and religious affairs to traditional incumbents. Although recent scholarship has sought to minimize elite complicity in fascist seizures of power (most notably the role of industrialists) and to emphasize fascist encroachments on extrapolitical spheres, no one denies that fascist society rarely corresponded to the radical vision of fascist ideology. Nonetheless many historians treat such compromises as tactical and temporary concessions, destined to disappear with the final consolidation of fascist rule. What appeared to so many contemporary observers as the dictatorship of the possessing classes is now seen as a mere interlude preparatory to wars of foreign conquest, which were "the decisive prerequisite for a revolution at home that would sweep away inherited institutions and values, Piedmontese-Italian and Prusso-German military castes, the churches . . . and . . . the putatively decadent and cowardly upper-middle classes."[28]

By contrast with the Italian and German experience, fascism in France never took power or even came very close. Consequently the authenticity of its radicalism was never tested. For some historians this renders France a particularly fruitful testing ground for an analysis of fascism. A leading student of French fascism, Zeev Sternhell, has noted: "France offers particularly favorable conditions for [a study of fascism]: the fascist era there was one of movements and ideologies and not that of a regime. It is prior to the conquest of power and before pressures and compromises transform them into governmental groups like others that movements and ideas present their most faithful image. The nature of a political ideology is always clearer in its aspirations than in its application."[29] To be sure, even granting the greater significance of "aspirations" as opposed to "application" (a proposition which is at least moot), it has been forcefully argued that, even taken at face value, French fascism is closer to the political Right than to anything approaching the socialist Left.[30]

For Sternhell, however, fascism represents "the conjunction of the nationalist, antiliberal and antibourgeois Right and the socialist and quasi-socialist Left . . . a synthesis made possible only by a continual process of the revision of Marxism."[31] Far from having anything in common with conservatism, fascism is fundamentally antagonistic. Its attitude is epitomized by Thierry Maulnier's celebrated phrase, "conservateur: voilà un mot qui commence bien mal." Those political movements that did display a certain intimacy with the traditional Right, such as the leagues of the 1920s and 1930s, are by definition simply not fascist. Historians who persist in so designating them Sternhell roundly scolds for uncritically adopting the partisan label-mongering of the contemporary Left. Nor was the French Right tempted by fascism.

> In France the strength of the traditional Right was such that it never permitted the revolutionaries to triumph over it and never found itself in the extreme situation of conservatives elsewhere, who were driven to place themselves in the hands of the fascists. It is precisely that long struggle between the Right and fascism—all Rights and all fascisms— which constitutes one of the most striking—as well as one of the least known—chapters in French politics.[32]

The starting point for Sternhell's analysis of fascism in France is the late 1880s. "It was then that the critical symptoms of an intellectual evolution first appeared, without which fascism could never have taken form; it was then that for the first time that synthesis of a new type of nationalism and a certain form of socialism was created."[33] What precipitated the formation of this "synthesis" was the Boulanger affair. By insisting that fascism in France can be traced back to the latter and that Boulangism was primarily a left-wing phenomenon, scholars like Sternhell seek to reinforce their overall interpretation of fascism. If, as Sternhell asserts, the Boulangists were the "legitimate sons of the Third Estate,"[34] so too by extension can fascism be comfortably situated within the revolutionary tradition.

But the transformation and/or vacillation of a fraction of the revolutionary Left is not the whole story of Boulangism, nor indeed its most significant dimension. The central development of the Boulanger affair was the profound transformation of the traditional, conservative Right. The royalist involvement with Boulanger was part of a desperate strategy of elitist conservatives to confront mass society and political democracy. The social and political transformations of post-1870 Europe threatened conservatives everywhere. An increasingly urban, secular, literate, and democratic society gradually eroded the political influence of the conservative elite. With traditional agencies of legitimation—notably the

Church—in decline, conservative economic, social, and cultural predominance—also waning—could no longer ensure political control. The politics of deference gradually gave way to mass politics.

Conservatives recognized that, to survive, they had to appeal directly to constituents whose subservient support had heretofore been taken for granted. Everywhere there were calls for organized, mass-based, popular conservative parties which might attract the newly emancipated masses and insulate them from subversive new political forces. Yet such calls were rarely answered precisely because mass-based parties ran against the grain for most *notables, notabile,* or *Honoratioren.* Hostile toward and suspicious of the lower classes, conservatives could not—and usually did not want to—emulate the political style of their democratic challengers. They were as uncomfortable on the hustings as they were implausible and ineffective. As conservative political influence stagnated or declined, a host of popular movements arose to challenge the existing social and political order.[35]

Yet not all the newly emergent popular movements represented an equal challenge to beleaguered conservatives. The decades before 1914 were a time of flux, and within movements of the Left there were a number of undercurrents that could, under the proper circumstances, be adapted for conservative purposes. The legacy of the nineteenth-century Left was an ambiguous one. The Jacobin tradition evoked memories of the Great Revolution but also contained an undercurrent of authoritarianism and antiparliamentarianism. Anticlericalism and hostility to plutocratic wealth led some on the Left to espouse a primitive anti-Semitism. Throughout much of the nineteenth century the Left had been the repository of revolutionary nationalism. After 1890, however, much of this political baggage became outdated as the democratic socialists of the Second International gained the ascendancy within the Left. Socialists embraced internationalism, shunning nationalism as a manipulative tool of capitalists. They likewise distanced themselves from anti-Semitism, now scorned as "the socialism of the imbecile." In practice, if not always in theory, socialists reconciled themselves to bourgeois parliamentary democracy. But not all men of the Left accepted this evolution gracefully, and some found themselves looking for a new political home.

This point did not escape the more astute conservatives. However distrustful they might have been of the dissident Left, conservatives could not fail to notice potentially useful traits in the latter. Nationalists, anti-Semites, and Boulangists all evoked populist symbols and utilized a radical rhetoric in a manner which conservatives could not or would not emulate. Moreover, these groups consciously strove to create a popular political organization far closer to parties and movements of the far Left than to the elitist formations of the Right. Were their already ambivalent political reflexes to be subtly redirected, the energies of such groups could be harnessed for the benefit of the conservative Right. By appropriating the dynamism and populism of the disillusioned Left, conservatives could forge a "new Right."[36]

The project was always problematic. Conservatives never lost their distrust of the latent radicalism in their putative allies, the more so since leaders of the new Right retained a persistent antagonism to the older elite and often found it politically expedient to pose as enemies—or at least challengers—of the traditional Right. Although these disquieting characteristics were what gave such movements their popular appeal, they ensured a permanent strain between conservatives and their partners. Still, all kinds of mutual accommodations were possible. Conservatives, once profoundly hostile to the patriotism of 1793, of Mazzini, or of the Nationalverein, had by the end of the century virtually monopolized the label *nationalist*. Shorn of its dangerous social dimensions, anti-Semitism became a common plank in the conservative platform. Words like *democratic, social,* and *people* became an indispensable part of the names of conservative parties.[37]

In turn, the radical rhetoric of the new Right often masked an innocuous content fully susceptible to safely conservative applications. The provocative Boulangist couplet "exploiters and exploited" lost its latent menace when royalists succeeded in identifying the "exploiters" with the existing republican regime. The distinction between "creative capital" and "rapacious capital" inoculated the German elite against the consequences of the anticapitalist rhetoric of their "radical" partners. Maurice Barrès's discovery that many royalists (to say nothing of the German emperor) were in fact socialists was as comforting to conservatives as was Mussolini's declaration that the working classes included not just "those with sweat on their brow and those who build up those famous calluses on their hands," but also the worthy *padroni* of the Confindustria.[38] The discovery by a Boulangist deputy that the real solution to unemployment was not the eight-hour day but *revanche* was wholly analogous to Enrico Corradini's recognition that it was not the Italian bourgeoisie against whom the Italian proletariat must wage war, but "plutocratic" England and France.[39] As nationalism and anti-Semitism crossed the political divide, what had once been dangerous demagogy became a staple of conservative political discourse. The ideological gulf that supposedly separates conservatives and fascists is most plausible if conservatism is identified with Burke, Tocqueville, and

Ortega. But by the late nineteenth century conservative politicians had abandoned the niceties of traditional conservative political theory in favor of more "modern" forms. In practice the cleavages between the new and old were often superficial, and the social radicalism of the political parvenus was more apparent than real, being directed at trivial or "safe" targets and constructed so as to obfuscate the nature of social and economic realities.

It need not follow that the leaders of the new Right were merely fools, scoundrels, or thinly disguised reactionaries (although General Boulanger was arguably all three). The sincerity of their early radicalism was often beyond dispute. Nonetheless they were temperamentally unsuited to a changing democratic Left and, feeling disillusioned and betrayed, were prepared to consort, however provisionally, with the conservative Right. Nor does this imply any crude agency theory (although, once again, in the case of Boulangism such a construct may not be altogether inappropriate). Far from being simply the products of conservative manipulation, the new formations had their own potent dynamic.[40] They usually had independent origins, stemming from the deep social, economic, and cultural discontent of the popular and intermediate strata of society. Their political organization and propaganda techniques resembled those of the extreme Left, not the Right. Indeed, both the German Agrarian League of the 1890s and the Parti Social Français of the 1930s, for example, explicitly claimed to adopt the organizational model of their respective socialist enemies.[41] Much the same can be said for the form, if not the substance, of their political rhetoric. But all this merely facilitated a symbiotic relationship with the conservative elite.

This point often escapes students of the new Right and fascism. By exclusively stressing the differences that separated fascist and protofascist movements from conservatives, they effectively ignored frequent instances of intimate cooperation. When the points of convergence between new movements and traditional conservatives are too numerous to be overlooked, scholars tend to respond by excluding the former from the fascist chapel (much as conservative Boulangists are stripped of their Boulangist credentials). The suggestion that movements like the Croix de Feu of interwar France might have had some fascist characteristics now earns a dismissive rebuke.[42] By virtue of its close links with traditional conservatives, the Croix de Feu cannot be "ni droite ni gauche" and therefore cannot be fascist. Consequently the Croix de Feu, with its imposing mass base, is ignored in favor of obscure groupings whose effective political impact was very nearly nil. Yet the Croix de Feu, whose favorite slogan happened to be "ni à droite ni à gauche," postured as a genuinely radical alternative and openly copied the techniques of mass mobilization of the political Left. It attracted conservatives because they hoped that it might—far better than the musty formations of the Right—parry the threat of social and political democratization.

The conservative strategy of allying with the délassé radicals of the new Right was neither certain nor safe. Their combined strength was not always sufficient to dislodge a democratic regime, as the French example attests. Even when victorious, the alliance could be unequal; the fascist destruction of German democracy did not lead to the restoration of conservative political predominance. Yet in all cases conservatives believed fascists, or their forerunners, to be useful vehicles for dealing with mass politics. An Italian conservative put it succinctly when he asserted that "fascism is the liberalism of the age of the masses."[43] Since in Italy, as in France, "liberalism" referred to what is generally meant by "conservatism," he had acutely identified the central attraction of fascism for threatened conservative elites.

Scholars like Sternhell are certainly correct in tracing the roots of French fascism back to the Boulanger affair. They err, however, in their assessment of the affair and, by extension, in their analysis of fascism in France and elsewhere. What made the Boulanger affair possible was not the radical dynamism of the Boulangists—although that was real enough—but the active involvement of the royalists. Unable to adapt either their rudimentary political organization or their shopworn image to the realities of mass politics, royalists desperately needed auxiliaries. As it turned out, so did Boulangists. Their disparate origins notwithstanding, they jointly launched a massive assault on the democratic republic. The strategy failed, but it would be repeated in the twentieth century by conservatives in France as elsewhere whose role in the rise of fascism was, current historiographical revisions notwithstanding, decisive.

I

Royalists and the Third Republic

When France became a republic in 1870 there was good reason to believe that the new regime would last no longer than the two previous republics. The declaration of the Third Republic had been the work of Paris alone; in much of the rest of France the population remained hostile to, or at least skeptical of, republican experiments. With Bonapartism discredited by France's crushing defeat in the Franco-Prussian War, the logical successor to the republic was the monarchy. In the elections to the National Assembly in February 1871, monarchists won 400 of the 645 seats. After 1873 a monarchist, Marshal MacMahon, was head of state, and his first three governments were dominated by royalists. It seemed only a matter of time before the provisional republican regime would be replaced by one headed by a king.

Chances of an immediate restoration were dashed by the severe rift between the two branches of French royalism: Orleanists and legitimists. Legitimists, clinging to religious piety, outdated political principles, and caste prerogatives, distrusted their more worldly Orleanist cousins with their Voltairean world view and their obsession with parliamentary government. Dedicated legitimists could not forget that the namesake of the junior branch of the monarchy, the Duc d'Orléans, had become the Jacobin Philippe Egalité, or that his descendants had overturned the last legitimate king in 1830. Not a few of them had welcomed the collapse of the Orleanist monarchy in 1848. Yet in truth these were family quarrels; much united the two royalist camps, notably a shared concern for the preservation of the traditional social order.[1] Enough rancor remained, however, to move legitimists to vote periodically with the extreme Left rather than support the Orleanists in the early Third Republic.

In an attempt to unify royalist forces the head of the Orleanist branch, the Count of Paris, formally recognized the authority of the legitimist pretender, the Count of Chambord, in August 1873. The "fusion" did not have the desired consequences because Chambord remained spiritually anchored in the world of the ancien régime; his refusal to accommodate the France of the nineteenth century, symbolized by his rejection of the tricolor, made his restoration impossible. Consequently, most moderate royalists took refuge in a highly conservative republican constitution, hoping that a conservative President and Senate would restrain the democratically elected Chamber of Deputies until an acceptable monarchist solution could be found. No previous republican regime (nor for that matter any regime) had endured. Chambord was aging and without heir. The Republican constitution of 1875 did not seem to be a permanent fixture.

Hopes that the republic would be but a transitional regime foundered as republicans strengthened their grip on a majority of the electorate. The monarchist victory of February 1871 had owed more to the near universal desire for peace than to any widespread longing for a monarchy. By successfully identifying all republicans with Léon Gambetta's passionate desire to continue the war with Prussia, monarchists could pose as the party of peace. With the signing of the peace treaty, that electoral advantage evaporated and republicans could now point to the clamoring of ultramontane Catholics for French intervention in Italy to restore the temporal power of the papacy. In the 174 by-elections held between the summer of 1871 and January 1876, republicans won 143 seats and the newly resurgent Bonapartists nearly half of the remainder.[2] Even the active intervention of a still predominantly conservative administration could not prevent the erosion of royalist electoral support. In the first elections to the Chamber of Deputies in February 1876, monarchists and Bonapartists together elected only 153 deputies out of 514. Moreover the republican-dominated Chamber began vigorously to assert itself against the other two branches of government. In a major constitutional confrontation in 1877, the Chamber successfully defied President MacMahon and the monarchist majority in the Senate and established its preponderance in French government. So efficient had the republican political machine become that even the extreme administrative measures taken by MacMahon to influence the outcome of the 1877 elections could not prevent 323 republicans from being returned, as compared to only 208 royalists and Bonapartists.[3]

The subsequent "republicanization" of the administration guaranteed that electoral circumstances would not again be as favorable for conservatives as they had been in 1877. The election of 70 conservatives was invalidated because of administrative or clerical interference, and few regained their seats in the following by-elections. By 1881 conservatives were so discouraged that they contested only slightly better than half the 541 seats and abstained in large numbers. Their share of the popular vote dropped from 44 to 25 percent and their total number of seats to 90. The 1881 elections were, of course, something of an anomaly, reflecting conservative demoralization as much as loss of electoral appeal.[4] Yet there were other indices of the decline of conservative strength. In 1874 a bare majority of the 3,000 members of the departmental General Councils were conservatives. By 1877 the figure was 46 percent; by 1880, 33 percent; and by 1883, less than 27 percent. The waning influence of conservatives in local government was reflected in senatorial elections. When the first third of the Senate was renewed in January 1879, conservatives won only 16 of 82 seats, giving republicans for the first time a majority in the upper house. In 1882 conservatives won only 14 of 80 senatorial elections, and in 1885 only 20 of 87, with 22 of the 42 incumbent conservative senators losing their seats. Republicans had gradually triumphed at all levels of government, and the depleted ranks of the conservatives were reduced to an increasingly ineffective opposition.

Nearly as disquieting for royalists was the fact that fully half the conservative deputies elected in 1876, 1877, and 1881 were Bonapartists. Owing to the stigma of Sedan, Bonapartism had been a negligible force in 1871, but its recrudescence after 1873 marked it as a plausible alternative to the republic. Bonapartism commanded a political popularity which royalists could rarely match. The Empire was a less distant memory than the July Monarchy, and as the trauma of 1870 faded from the popular imagination, Bonapartists could exploit the positive achievements of the imperial regime. The Bonapartist claim to reconcile order with progress contrasted sharply with the Count of Chambord's apparent desire to restore the world of the old regime. After the post-1882 economic depression, Bonapartists could effectively evoke the comparative industrial and agricultural prosperity of the Empire. Ideologically, Bonapartists were a good deal closer to the republic and far more at ease with universal suffrage than were royalists.[5] Government agents and royalist observers generally conceded that whereas Bonapartists successfully cultivated the more modest agricultural classes, the typical royalist was likely to be "the candidate of the château, which is to his credit socially, but from the electoral perspective is the worst of recommendations."[6]

In theory a significant ideological gulf divided royalists from Bona-partists. For legitimists the line separating the Bonapartist from the Jacobin tradition was exceedingly fine. Both were heirs of the Revolu-tion, and Bonapartism, "the party of three invasions," was nearly as great a menace to France. Orleanists, having defended parliamentarian-ism under the Empire, retained their suspicions of Bonapartism under the republic. The resurgence of Bonapartism in 1873 had moved some Orleanists to vote for the 1875 republican constitution. Nonetheless, fine points of doctrine were less important than the vigorous defense of the social order, and there was always considerable migration, in both direc-tions, between the royalist party and the Bonapartists. Three of the Count of Paris's most influential counselors, the Marquis de Breteuil, the Baron de Mackau, and the Comte de Martimprey, were former Bonapartists.

The growing appeal of royalism to many Bonapartists reflected the chief defect of the imperialist party: the absence of an authoritative leader. Napoleon III had died in 1873 and his son and heir, the Prince Imperial, in 1879. The dynastic succession fell to Napoleon's cousin, Prince Jerome Napoleon. Jerome—or "Plon-Plon," as he was unaffec-tionately known—was a Jacobin rather than a Bonapartist. Even under the Empire most Bonapartists had detested him, and in 1877 the future pretender had been among the famous 363 republicans who had chal-lenged President MacMahon. In the end, the Jeromist brand of Bona-partism meant no more than a desire for the democratic election of the President and senators. Alert to the aberrant political views of his cousin, the Prince Imperial had added a codicil to his will naming Jerome's son Victor as his true successor. Prince Victor, while far more conservative than his father, was only seventeen and in no position to accept the suc-cession. Most Bonapartists rallied unenthusiastically to Jerome in the hopes that he would alter his views. He did not, and was soon endorsing the anticlerical measures of the government. Most of Jerome's personal supporters were defeated in 1881, and the remaining Bonapartists began actively cultivating his son. After a prolonged, public, bitter intrafamily feud, by the summer of 1884 Victor was the acknowledged leader of the majority of French Bonapartists. Yet the open display of internal discord did not end in 1884 and Prince Victor never enjoyed the stature or, even more important, the financial resources of his royalist counterpart.[7]

While the Bonapartists feuded among themselves, the royalist party at last achieved a unified and effective leadership. The Count of Cham-bord, symbol of royalist futility, died without heir in 1883, and the leadership of the royalist party devolved upon the Count of Paris.

Whereas the Count of Chambord had signified for many Frenchmen the world of "the seigneur and the curé," his Orleanist successor was to all appearances a man of his times. Intelligent, learned, hard-working, the young Count of Paris strove to be "a modern prince." A staid, sober individual with a very un-Orleanist commitment to marital fidelity, he inspired little passion among his followers. But he took seriously the role of pretender, possessed a comprehensive grasp of French political realities, and genuinely wanted to become king. The great-grandson of a regicide, he evoked not the old regime but the sensible and cautious conservatism of the July Monarchy. The vast majority of legitimists rallied, with varying degrees of enthusiasm, to the new pretender, bringing with them their political organization and their newspapers.[8] The Count of Paris began a concerted campaign to reconstitute royalist committees, integrating legitimist and Orleanist notables. Within a year most of the committees had been reconstructed, and ample royalist subsidies (sometimes but not always from the pretender's considerable personal fortune) began to flow to royalist electoral agents and royalist newspapers.

The royalist party in France was directed by four individuals. The nominal head of the propaganda organization was Charles Lambert de Sainte-Croix, responsible for both the local committees and the press. He began his career in the diplomatic service of Louis-Philippe, sat in the National Assembly in 1871, and was elected senator from the Landes in 1876. After flirting with Bonapartism in the late 1870s, Lambert de Sainte-Croix rallied to the Count of Paris and played a central role in organizing the 1885 elections. After 1886, however, his authority within the royalist leadership began to diminish. Aging and ailing, deeply embittered by his failure to be reelected as either senator or deputy, Lambert tended to prefer doctrinaire posturing to concerted organizational activity. Forgetting his own dalliances with the imperialists, he saw Bonapartist plots everywhere and was increasingly out of step with the more flexible thinking of the pretender.[9] By 1887 most of his functions were in fact being performed by his subordinate, the younger, more energetic, and more open-minded Eugène Dufeuille. Dufeuille, a former journalist and local royalist organizer, was the real workhorse of the party and the effective link between the exiled pretender and the local royalist committees. An indefatigable correspondent, he wrote at length to the Count of Paris, displaying an acute sense of contemporary political realities and of the degree to which they seemed to have escaped most French royalists.

Financial matters were the responsibility of the senator from the Orne,

Edouard Bocher. A prefect under the July Monarchy and friend of Louis-Philippe, Bocher was the elder statesman of the Orleanist party. In his management of the financial affairs of the family of Orléans he displayed a parsimony that exceeded that of the prince himself. Finally, the Count of Paris's personal secretary was Marquis Ludovic de Beauvoir. Beauvoir's father had accompanied Louis-Philippe into exile and had been an intimate counselor of the royal family. His son had entered the diplomatic service in the 1870s and had been an undersecretary of his father-in-law, the foreign minister, Duc Decazes. Moving easily in aristocratic circles, possessed of a sharp mind and a delightful wit, he was the pretender's closest counselor and undertook the most delicate negotiations on his behalf.[10]

The unity and newfound energy within royalist ranks did not escape the attention of some Bonapartists, the most notable of whom was Paul de Cassagnac. Cassagnac, deputy from the Gers, was one of the ablest and most dynamic representatives of the Bonapartist tradition. Initially a supporter of Prince Victor, he was quickly disillusioned by the inactivity of the young pretender and genuinely impressed by the Count of Paris, whom he had known since 1882. He soon declared that conservatives ought to unite behind any monarch, Bonapartist or royalist, who took the initiative in rescuing France from the republic. "Solutionisme" or "n'importequisme," as this approach was soon called, could only mean a Bonapartist reconciliation with royalism, since Prince Victor's chances of attracting royalist support were nil. Royalists certainly thought Cassagnac a fine catch; he was an excellent journalist and his *L'Autorité,* which they supported financially, was by far the most readable of the major conservative newspapers.[11] Contemporaries often contended that personal venality had attracted Cassagnac to the monarchy, but the charge remains unproven and he always insisted that he was not a royalist. Nevertheless in private and in public Cassagnac made no secret of his deep admiration for the Count of Paris, a sentiment he notoriously did not extend to Prince Victor.[12] Few other prominent Bonapartists were as enamored of the Count of Paris, but in the years that followed there were persistent reports of Bonapartists who (usually privately) were shifting their allegiance.[13] Royalists encouraged this evolution, using money as an inducement as always. Typically they subventioned the popular "solutionist" Bonapartist daily *Le Petit Corporal* and bought outright a number of other major Bonapartist newspapers.[14]

By the late 1880s there was a logic to the effective unification of the two conservative parties, since their respective strengths and deficiencies were complementary. As a royalist from the Loir-et-Cher noted at the end of the decade: "The royalist party recruits only from the higher ranks of society and is without influence . . . ; the imperialist party still has a number of supporters in the countryside [but] is without leadership."[15] He delicately omitted mentioning that Bonapartists were usually without money as well. This suited the immeasurably wealthy royalists, since it permitted them to claim the lion's share of seats. As a disgruntled Bonapartist caustically observed, an alliance in which royalists provided the money and Bonapartists the voters usually resulted in a royalist candidate.[16]

Bonapartists and royalists did unite prior to the 1885 elections in a "conservative union." The union allowed both royalists and Bonapartists to disguise electorally disadvantageous dynastic labels under the ambiguous designation "conservative." Instead of directly challenging the form of government, the "conservateurs" could concentrate on the disastrous foreign and domestic policy of the regime. This strategy offended purists in both camps (notably the legitimists) who feared that discounting monarchist principles could lead to an accommodation with the republic. Of course it also meant that conservatives might ally themselves in the future with any movement hostile to the existing regime, including (although no one would have guessed it in 1885) the followers of General Boulanger. In the short run, however, the conservative union would reap significant electoral dividends. The 1885 election was to be held under the *scrutin de liste,* an exceedingly complex system in which the electoral unit was the department and competing parties submitted lists containing as many names as there were deputies to be elected from any given department.[17] Competing lists of royalists and Bonapartists meant certain defeat; by contrast, given the disunion within the republican camp, a unified list promised real gains. Although it required extensive negotiations which left both parties mildly dissatisfied, common lists were ultimately achieved in all but four departments.[18]

For the first time since 1877 conservatives entered the election under advantageous circumstances. Although the two-year government of Jules Ferry had achieved some significant successes at home and abroad, public attention focused on its ill-fated Far East policy. Few Frenchman appreciated the acquisition of Cochin China and Tonkin. For Radicals, Ferry's colonial ambitions merely served to direct French eyes away from where they properly belonged: Alsace-Lorraine and the "blue line of the Vosges." For everyone else the Far Eastern campaign was ruinously expensive, militarily unsuccessful, and disingenuously presented. News of the military disaster of Lang-Son at the end of March 1885 brought the downfall of the Ferry government, effectively ruined the career of the man who was known henceforth as "Ferry-Tonkin," and doomed his supporters among the moderate republicans, the Opportunists, to electoral defeat. On the first ballot conservatives scored a resounding victory, electing 177 deputies compared to only 124 republicans. Moreover, they gained nearly 1.7 million more votes than in 1881, doubling their share of the popular vote, which now stood at 44 percent of the total. The prospect of an antirepublican victory, prematurely announced by some conservatives, forced the divided republicans to close ranks on the second ballot, when they won 241 seats compared to only 26 for conservatives. The victorious republicans invalidated 22 successful conservatives, only 4 of whom regained their seats in the subsequent by-elections.

Nonetheless, even as amended, the election marked a dramatic change in conservative fortunes. Conventional wisdom treated the election as a victory for the political extremes, because conservatives and Radicals gained greatly at the expense of the moderate Opportunists. A recent detailed analysis of the elections suggests that the final results were an inaccurate reflection of the wishes of a generally moderate electorate.[19] The Radicals increased their representation in the Chamber out of all proportion to their increase in popular vote, and conservatives made substantial gains because of dissatisfaction with Ferry among a segment of moderate republicans. To read the 1885 elections as the work of an electorate seeking to confirm the moderate republic, however, requires a sophisticated analysis of the complexities of the electoral system, the significance of *voix panachées,* and the workings of the Condorcet paradox, all of which escaped contemporaries. For conservatives the critical facts were that their decline had been reversed and they were now separated from the republicans by fewer than a million votes. A shift of 500,000 votes or 6 percent of the participating electorate would produce a conservative majority. To be sure, calculations based on popular vote, which mesmerized conservatives for the next four years, actually meant little in terms of parliamentary representation. Nonetheless conservative momentum seemed incontestable. The future Chamber, divided about equally between Radicals, conservatives, and Opportunists, would be ungovernable and unlikely to last until 1889. Since Opportunism appeared to have been decisively rebuffed by the nation and a Radical majority was unthinkable, the plausible outcome of a future dissolution was a conservative parliamentary victory after which everything seemed possible.

For conservatives a victory meant more than a change in the form of government. It would be the occasion to eradicate the corrosive forces that thrived under the republic. In some respects it seems ironic that the intransigent opponents of the Third Republic should have labeled themselves "conservatives." The regime was, in any meaningful sense of the word, a conservative one founded by men who believed a republic to be the best means for ensuring social harmony, and dominated by individuals who had proven their social conservatism by their ferocious repression of the Paris Commune.[20] Apart from a few large towns, there was as yet no significant socialist movement; the extreme Left was represented by the Radicals, whose belief in private property was unshakable. Labor unions were still in their infancy, and while the incidence of strikes did increase in the late 1880s, serious labor unrest was still relatively rare. Objectively, France in the 1880s was as free from the threat of social upheaval and revolutionary change as it ever had been or ever would be.

French conservatives, however, were unimpressed by the essential moderation of the republican regime and unconvinced of its ability, or willingness, to preserve France from revolutionary chaos. The clearest evidence of the dangerous radicalism of even moderate republicans was their persistent attacks on the rights and prerogatives of the French Church. A contemporary royalist put it about right when he observed that his colleagues were "more Catholic than monarchist and more conservative than Catholic."[21] For many conservatives, preservation of the social influence of the Church was more important than the restoration of a monarch. To be sure, many Orleanists remained uncomfortable with the ultramontane extravagances of some Catholics. Nonetheless they too agreed that the Church was a vital component of the French national fabric and an essential precondition for social stability.

It was precisely this preponderant influence that republicans were determined to break. Believing that "clericalism is the enemy" and infused with a generation of positivist thinking, even moderate republicans set out to laicize French society. As they watched divorce legalized, public prayer abolished, and lay funerals encouraged, conservatives believed they were witnessing the dismantling of a stable and secure France. Public education, long the preserve of the Church, was the obvious target of anticlerical republicans, while the famous trilogy of laic, compulsory, free education provoked conservative wrath. Henceforth only the relatively affluent could afford to obtain a Catholic education for their children; they were, as conservatives reminded everyone, paying twice: once to the school and once, in the form of crippling taxes, to the state. The devout poor had little choice but to send their offspring to the free public schools, the "école sans Dieu" where, conservatives believed, the presumptuous products of the *écoles normales* would undermine parental teachings with subversive doctrines. Jules Ferry's notorious article 7, dissolving most Catholic teaching congregations, was but the worst of a series of measures designed to weaken Catholic moral and educational influence. The least of the problems with the proliferating public schools was that they were ruinously and unnecessarily expensive. Father was being set against son, and the religious beliefs of humble Frenchmen scorned and mocked. If religious devotion was the basis of all well-ordered societies, the anticlerical crusade of the republic was a systematic assault on the moral fiber of the nation and presaged wholesale societal collapse.

Republican rhetoric about liberty rang hollow to conservatives, who considered the republic to be "the regime of persecutions." After 1877, republicans sought to purge the public service of avowed enemies of the existing government and dismissed large numbers of conservatives from the administration and the judiciary. Republican claims of legitimate self-defense seemed but a transparent excuse for satisfying the incessant demands of a new breed of parvenus for "toutes les places et tout de suite." At best the expanding army of civil servants, the famous "budgétivores," simply wrecked French finances. More often they waged unceasing war on the conservatives. A new generation of administrators vengefully troubled the lives of private citizens, incessantly badgering all those whose allegiance to the new regime was less than enthusiastic. Not only was a natural elite being displaced by newcomers whose only credentials were their republican contacts, but even the most modest Frenchman was now subject to the arbitrary spite of republican officialdom. An incautious remark by a curé could earn him a year's suspension of salary; a forest warden whose religious devotion was too public might lose his job. The *épurations* became a symbol of republican tyranny, just as revoked subprefects and magistrates became the corporals of the conservative army.

It did not matter very much to conservatives that the governmental republicans of the early 1880s sought to moderate the more zealous reflexes of republican purists, their very name, Opportunists, being a symbol of their flexibility. Nor was it important that some of the more radical measures, including article 7, were blocked by conservative republicans. For every conciliatory gesture on the part of the Opportunists, conservatives could cite an outlandish demand emanating from the Radicals. The very presence of the Radicals on the left flank of the government was proof to conservatives that a "conservative republic" was impossible. Just as 1789 had led inevitably to 1793, the regime of the moderate republicans like Jules Ferry and Jules Grévy would spawn one headed by Radicals like Georges Clemenceau and Henri de Rochefort. The *essai loyal* proposed by Adolphe Thiers in the early 1870s had obviously failed and had served no purpose save to immobilize conservatives while republicans pursued their relentless war on French society.

The Radicals were a symbol, of course, rather than a tangible threat. They had received less than 10 percent of the vote cast in 1881 and only about a third more in 1885, in spite of their substantial representation in parliament. Nor were Radicals, whose name has always struck Anglo-Saxons as a Gallic misnomer, very radical. A good half of their leaders, the Floquets, Brissons, Lockroys, and Allain-Targés, were increasingly separated from the Opportunists only by their exclusion from government, their radical postures tending to crumble at the offer of a ministerial portfolio. The Clemenceau wing of the party was firmer but even Clemenceau, when challenged by the fledgling socialist movement in 1884, loudly denounced the collectivism and dogmatism of the latter. Nevertheless the high Radical profile in major urban centers, notably Paris, obsessed conservatives, who had not forgotten the civil war of 1871. *Le Salut public* in Lyons, faithfully monitoring each new outrage of the Parisian Radicals, complained: "An engineer cannot be assassinated, a church cannot be closed, a freethinker not buried . . . , a statue not erected to a regicide or pornographer, no revolution or assassination take place in Europe, Asia, Africa, America, or the South Seas, without the municipal council of Paris immediately giving its blessing."[22] The flamboyant rhetoric of many Radical leaders did mask their essentially moderate reflexes. Moreover there was much in their platform that the conservatives of the 1880s could not ignore. Radicals found Jules Ferry to be soft on religion and demanded the separation of Church and State. Not content to burden the budget with an expensive lay school system and a crassly partisan corps of civil servants, the Radicals advocated paying for them by an income tax. Like conservatives they denounced Ferry's imperialist policy in the Far East, not because it was an expensive venture serving no purpose but to create posts for republican appointees, but because it distracted France from her proper mission, a war of revenge against Germany.

That the most passionate partisans of *revanche* were on the extreme Left was a source of considerable anxiety for most conservatives, especially royalists. The connection between domestic and foreign policy was never very far from their minds, nor were the lessons of 1792–93 and 1870–71. With varying degrees of consistency royalists made three assumptions about the consequences of war in the 1880s. First, they feared that the war which Radicals seemed to want would likely end in defeat. Republican France was a renegade state in monarchical Europe, universally distrusted and diplomatically isolated. Her unstable governments, depleted treasury, and low morale all contrasted so sharply with the situation of her hereditary enemy as to render military victory improbable. Second, a defeated France, they assumed, would once again be convulsed by civil war and revolution. Given the steady erosion of public order under the republic, the impending revolution would be far more terrible than the Paris Commune. Finally, conservatives assumed that the Radical Left, or at least some of it, deliberately sought war precisely because revolution would result. Had not the Brissotin Left in 1792 deliberately sought a war in order to radicalize the revolution? And had not Louis XVI lost his throne and his head for having, albeit for quite different reasons, abetted the war party? More recently, had it not been radical republicans like the "furious fool" Gambetta who demanded "guerre à l'outrance" in 1870, and had not patriotism been the pretext for the odious insurrection in Paris in 1871? Of course conservatives conceded nothing to republicans when it came to patriotism; they too wanted *revanche,* but theirs would be "la revanche du bon sens ou plutôt de la Providence."[23] Like the Feuillants of 1792, the *droite capitularde* of 1870, and the parliamentary Right of the 1930s, the royalists of the 1880s insisted that, given a potentially revolutionary situation at home, peace, even a humiliating one, was preferable to war with its attendant consequences.

Newspapers like the influential legitimist organ *L'Espérance du peuple* in Nantes assiduously scoured the left-wing press for evidence of dangerously warlike sentiments. In 1886 it noted with alarm a column in the socialist *Cri du peuple* which suggested that "the next international conflagration must be the struggle between Reaction and Revolution—on the one side Bismarck, on the other side France." These, *L'Espérance* insisted, were the ruminations of "furious fools" or, more likely, "criminal charlatans." "The socialists provoke universal war," it continued, "in order to seize power in the midst of the general confusion, just like their ancestors in '92." Those who, like the Radical Henri de Rochefort, preached *revanche* were motivated exclusively, it insisted, by "the domestic question" and were interested only in "a future Commune." During the war scare of 1887 the same newspaper argued that "the return of the Commune is impossible in the face of the French army. . . . These republicans know it and reason as follows: it is essential to get rid of the army by occupying it elsewhere. War with Germany serves the purpose perfectly. Our soldiers will rush to the frontier and Paris will fall prey to the insurgents."[24]

This fascination with the war-revolution nexus was a commonplace among contemporary conservatives. In Marseilles the *Soleil du Midi* solemnly warned: "The domestic revolutionaries who now govern us profited from the war of 1870 to overthrow the government and seize power. Why should we believe that the socialists and anarchists will not follow that example, should war break out?"[25] *Le Messager de Toulouse,* a powerful and usually sober royalist newspaper, grimly announced: "When our attention and our material and moral forces are turned toward the foreign enemy . . . dare we assume that there will not be some terrible explosion? The new Commune will bear the same relationship to that of 1871 that dynamite does to gasoline."[26] France, *Le Moniteur de Calvados* warned its readers, was beset by elements who were "disposed to play into the hands of foreigners by making a revolution in the face of the enemy, just as in 1870. The socialist party will once again, in the event of war, provide a powerful auxiliary for our enemies." Germany enjoyed "in the very heart of France allies ready to set Paris and France on fire as they did in 1870 and let blood flow the minute the armed forces no longer protect our social institutions."[27]

Warnings about imminent war and revolution seem singularly implausible in the real political context of the 1880s. The revolutionary Left was hardly a politically significant force, and violent social upheaval seemed unlikely. The dour predictions of royalists therefore appeared at best paranoid and at worst insincere. Probably it was a bit of both. The electoral utility of equating republicans with war had been amply demonstrated as early as 1871 and remained a useful component of the antirepublican lexicon. Still, the association of a neo-Jacobin Left with war and revolution was hardly unique to the French Right of the 1880s. Conservatives in the 1930s abruptly adopted a neopacifism which in all critical respects replicated that of their forebears of the 1880s.[28] To be sure, the domestic situation was considerably more tense in the 1930s, and France was haunted by the specter of the Bolshevik Revolution. Yet the Popular Front, which prompted the dramatic *revirement* of the French Right of the period, was in the end neither very bellicose nor very revolutionary. If the 1880s was a decade of comparative social peace, memories of real civil war were a good deal fresher.

The Paris Commune, to judge by the numerous allusions to it, was still a vivid specter among the *bien pensants*. The most innocuous gesture of the Radical-dominated city council of Paris prompted a flurry of extravagant editorials announcing an imminent return to 1871, if not to 1793. Moreover the distinction between radical reform and revolution was, in the 1880s as in the 1930s, blurred in the distorted perspective of frightened conservatives. When *L'Espérance du peuple* insisted that war with Germany meant civil war at home, what it meant was that the "radical socialists will profit from the public misfortune to enact the social reforms they have so often advocated."[29] Furthermore, by 1886 there was a concrete basis for conservative anxiety about the link between domestic radicalism and aggressive nationalism. The most dramatic symbol of this connection was the political ascendancy of Gen. Georges Boulanger.

For most conservatives nothing so symbolized the degeneration and dangers of the republic as did General Boulanger's sixteen months as war minister.[30] That he should be chosen at all for the Opportunist ministry of Charles de Freycinet seemed a sad commentary. Boulanger was young, with no significant military record, and notable primarily for his amorous adventures and his considerable talent for self-promotion. True, he had been wounded while repressing the Paris Commune, but that fact had not prevented him from assiduously cultivating elements of the radical Left in Paris. He was a protégé of Georges Clemenceau, and his inclusion in Freycinet's ministry was deemed by conservatives to have been the price paid for the Radical leader's support. From the outset, then, the Boulanger ministry appeared to offer evidence of Radical efforts to politicize and tarnish one of France's few remaining proud institutions.

As war minister, Boulanger did little of lasting significance, but what he did accomplish invariably angered conservatives. Shortly after assuming his post he proposed a major reform of the army. This project, under consideration since the early 1880s, called for the reduction of military service from five to three years, and for a universal military obligation. A genuinely popular army, with its connotation of the *levée en masse,* had long been a demand of the Radicals and was, correspondingly, anathema to conservatives. Of particular prominence in the reform was the abolition of the existing exemption from service for seminarians. This struck conservatives as a gratuitous attack on the Church. Although Boulanger's bill was soon tabled, he was quickly identified by the Right with the "loi curé sac au dos." To the further outrage of royalists, the new minister ostentatiously relocated several cavalry units in the west whose officers had displayed too prominently their monarchist convictions.

Boulanger's republican ardor manifested itself most dramatically when he expelled the royal princes from the officer corps. A recent decree exiling the direct heirs of previous ruling dynasties had also forbidden other members of former royal families to enter the French army. Strictly speaking, the law said nothing about members of the royal family already serving in the army, but Boulanger chose to interpret the decree in its loosest sense and, on his own initiative, announced the expulsion of the pretender's uncle, the Duc d'Aumale, and his younger brother, the Duc de Chartres. Since Aumale's enthusiasm for the dynastic claims of his nephew was notoriously tepid, Freycinet was embarrassed by the rash actions of his colleague. But the decree had already been registered, and when Aumale rather provocatively protested to the President, the government expelled him from France. In response to Aumale's assertion that military rank could not be taken away by the government, Boulanger told the Chamber that the principle applied only to officers who had earned their rank. Aumale had been promoted to the rank of general at the age of twenty-one only because of his royal name and could hardly be compared to a general like himself who had earned his rank with war wounds.

Royalists were livid at Boulanger's snide baiting of Aumale. One of them, the Baron de Lareinty, senator from the Loire-Atlantique, challenged Boulanger to duel. Boulanger's pistol failed to go off, whereupon Lareinty fired in the air. Such ineptitude enchanted royalists: noting that three generals (Boulanger and his two seconds) had been unable to get a pistol to work, the irrepressible Beauvoir wondered how many generals it would now take to fire a cannon.[31] Furthermore royalists observed that Boulanger's own promotion to general owed less to his minor wounds than it did to the carefully cultivated support of his superior officer—who happened to be the Duc d'Aumale. As proof, the royalist press published copies of several unctuous letters sent by Boulanger to Aumale, including one, dated 1880, which fulsomely thanked the royalist for having recommended his promotion and concluded with the line, "Blessed be the day [béni sera le jour] when I may again serve under you." Characteristically, Boulanger formally denied authorship of the letter, a denial he gracelessly retracted when royalists presented him with photographs of the original. In the end he looked the complete fool, Radicals had momentary doubts about their erstwhile hero, and royalists dubbed him "Général Béni Sera Le Jour."

Boulanger was more than a bumptious insulter of royal princes. He was also a radical general in command of the final guarantor of French security, external and domestic. In January 1886 a violent strike broke out in the mining town of Decazeville in the Aveyron. During the strike a mining engineer named Watrin was murdered, and troops had to be sent to preserve order. The episode created a major sensation, and for some months the word "watriner" entered the French language as a transitive verb. In the Chamber, deputies of the extreme Left attacked Boulanger for using the army against the strikers. Boulanger assured them that working men had nothing to fear from the army, because at that very minute every soldier in Decazeville was sharing his rations with a hungry striker. The care and feeding of murderous strikers was not exactly the role conservatives envisaged for the army, and many wondered if under Boulanger the army would cease to be an instrument for preserving order. Bitterly noting that only in France did "soldiers and strikers eat from the same canteen," *L'Espérance du peuple* fumed, "Are the defenders of order confronting the strikers to contain the revolution or to enroll under its banner?" As *Le Salut public* in Lyons sarcastically quipped, every time a mob wanted to murder an engineer, rob a house, or smash a printing press, the chosen rallying cry was "Vive Boulanger!" The army would no longer intervene, because it was too busy searching for strikers to feed.[32]

Boulanger certainly was on his way to becoming the darling of the masses. The July 14 ceremonies of 1886 were the occasion for a massive celebration of Boulanger's phenomenal popularity. His picture appeared everywhere, his name inspired countless laudatory music-hall ditties. The most popular war minister in the history of France quickly became a symbol of Jacobin patriotism. Paul Déroulède, Henri de Rochefort, Alfred Naquet, Georges Laguerre, all men of the far Left, publicly adopted Boulanger as one of their own. A series of periodicals sprang up evoking two themes: *revanche* and Boulanger. Although, as a result of the Aumale affair, his public pronouncements were more subdued, Boulanger quietly encouraged the growth of "Boulangism."

Boulanger, for once reflecting the sentiments of his government, remained circumspect about France's relations with Germany, but both inside France and abroad he was regarded as a putative agent of *revanche*. René Goblet, whose government replaced that of Freycinet in December but did not significantly alter its political composition, advocated a very cautious foreign policy, but already France was alive with allusions to Louis Napoleon's coup of December 2, 1851, and the suggestions that a Boulanger dictatorship might be a precondition for, or a consequence of, a war with Germany. Taking advantage of Boulanger's popularity, Bismarck proposed a significant increase in the size of the German army. Faced with a refractory Reichstag, on January 11 he publicly evoked the threat to Germany represented by the popular and belligerent French minister. Despite the relative moderation of the current French government, he noted, the possibility of one led by Boulanger and intent on *revanche* was increasingly real. When the Reichstag continued to balk, Bismarck dissolved it and mounted an election campaign, the chief feature of which was the carefully cultivated fear of a war of revenge led by Boulanger. To enhance the artificially created war scare, Bismarck called up 72,000 reservists in February. Boulanger proposed similar measures for France but was overruled by Goblet and President Grévy, who sought to minimize tensions between the two powers. The elections were a triumph for Bismarck, whose military bill then passed comfortably. Having achieved his domestic goals, the German chancellor quickly put an end to the anti-French rhetoric of his government. Although international tensions soon subsided, patriotic sentiment in France had been inflamed by the war scare and Boulanger, seemingly the cause of so much German anxiety, became a symbol of French national pride.

Five weeks later another incident appeared to bring the two nations to the brink of war. On April 20 a French police official, Schnaebelé, was arrested by the Germans on the frontier and charged with espionage. As it was initially believed that Schnaebelé had been arrested on the French side of the border, the French government prepared a strongly worded ultimatum to Germany, and Boulanger proposed a partial mobilization. War would likely have resulted, had not President Grévy urged his ministers to postpone these measures until the German government could provide an explanation for its actions. Schnaebelé had in fact been engaged in espionage, at the express request of Boulanger, but the French government established that he had been invited onto German territory by his German counterpart. Because such an invitation amounted to a guarantee of safe-conduct, Schnaebelé's arrest was juridically irregular and after ten days Bismarck agreed to his release. The new war scare quickly evaporated and Franco-German relations returned to normal. Public opinion treated Bismarck's retreat in the Schnaebelé affair as a major French diplomatic victory, attributable entirely to the dashing minister of war who could make the German empire tremble. In fact, Bismarck had backed down exclusively because of the circumstances surrounding the arrest of Schnaebelé, and informed opinion recognized that Boulanger's principal achievement had been carelessly to risk a war for which France was unprepared.

Conservatives shared the anxieties of Boulanger's Opportunist colleagues, and the royalist press relentlessly pursued the theme of war and revolution. Albert de Mun, the influential royalist deputy from the Morbihan, assured the Count of Paris that Boulanger represented a genuine danger of war which would be "the signal for the most serious developments domestically and, according to all indications, the creation in Paris of a Commune government."[33] General Humann, a confidant of the Count of Paris, assured the pretender that Boulanger was preparing for war and that men like Henri de Rochefort eagerly anticipated the proclamation of a second Commune.[34] Beauvoir, whose diplomatic connections had convinced him that Germany was prepared to go to war if Boulanger provided the pretext, felt it urgent that the general be removed.[35]

Still, the anxiety prompted by Boulanger was tempered by periodic reports that Boulanger could be "bought" for the cause of monarchy.[36] As minister of war, Boulanger controlled an imposing patronage machine which he used to ingratiate himself with royalist deputies. At least seventeen had obtained significant favors from the minister of war, and royalist insiders reported with regret that the right wing of the Chamber was reluctant to overturn Boulanger in spite of his offensive demeanor.[37]

Moreover, many royalists believed that Boulanger's apparent belligerence could redound to the advantage of the monarchy. For all their denunciations of republican bellicosity, it was widely acknowledged that the royalists' fears were not shared by Bismarck. The German chancellor greatly preferred a weak republican France to a strong monarchical one and feared that a monarchist restoration would be a prelude to a French military adventure. After the Schnaebelé affair, the Duc de La Ferronnays reported on his soundings of the diplomatic corps. The German embassy still thought that restoration meant war, but Boulanger's behavior had shaken that conviction somewhat. It was essential, the duke argued, that Germany be alerted to the fact that the real danger of war came from the republic and not the monarchy, and that the latter was not synonymous with *revanche*. He suggested further pacifistic utterances from the pretender as a counterpoint to the saber-rattling coming from the Rue Saint-Dominique. As Dufeuille noted, it was perhaps "good that Europe lose the idea that the republic is incapable of being bellicose." Beauvoir sought to use his international connections to encourage German newspapers to play up the warlike stance of Boulanger and the republic in general.[38]

Royalists sought to assure both France and Europe that only a monarchist restoration could achieve a peaceful accommodation with imperial Germany. A tireless proponent of this thesis was the former royalist deputy, Count Paul de Leusse. In the 1870s, he argued, it might have served German self-interest to have a republican regime in France, but the inevitable radicalization of the regime threatened the social order not just of France but of Europe. Germany would soon realize that only "a solidly reestablished monarchy [could] return France to the conservative tradition and prevent it from being a revolutionary *foyer* in the midst of monarchist Europe." The French and German crowns could then unite in "a mutual struggle against democracy, socialism, and the materialistic philosophy which produced them." A monarchist France would abandon its claims on Alsace and exchange Indo-China for Lorraine. Germany, unlike France, had a rapidly growing population and a corresponding need for colonies, so the arrangement seemed eminently possible.[39]

Similar ideas were common among royalists in the late 1880s. Early in 1888 the Comte de Martimprey, a confidant of the Count of Paris, suggested a secret meeting between the pretender and Bismarck to discuss an imminent restoration. He too thought that Germany would prefer a "Christian monarchy as a western neighbor instead of a socialist republic," and would cede the lost provinces in exchange for colonies and a monetary indemnity.[40] At the same time the Baron de Mackau contemplated a visit to Rome in the hopes of persuading the Pope to convince Bismarck that he should promise the restoration of Lorraine, should the monarchy be restored.[41] Such schemes were hopelessly quixotic. Beauvoir's skeptical assessment of Mackau's project was that it amounted to entering "a snail in the Derby." But even he had considerable faith in the utility of the royalist party ingratiating itself with the crowned heads of Europe. He passed along the bizarre proposal of a royalist from the Dordogne who had invented a special kind of dynamite which he thought the Count of Paris ought to present to the Czar of Russia. Apparently this dynamite would explode only under very special conditions which the Russian Nihilists would be technically unable to replicate.[42] Although such ideas had little to recommend them, they reflected the royalist perception that the common concern to prevent revolutionary disorder was more important than the diplomatic issues that separated European powers. A restoration in France, therefore, was the logical complement to the preservation of the European social order.

The substantial gains made by conservatives in the 1885 elections seemed to indicate that a growing number of Frenchmen shared the conservative indictment of the republic. The assumption was problematic, but the danger of a monarchist restoration sufficiently alarmed republicans that they took active measures against the leaders of the dynastic opposition. On 15 May 1886 the Count of Paris held a major reception in Paris to celebrate the marriage of his daughter to the heir to the Portuguese throne. Royalists unwisely sent invitations to all the major em-

bassies. Although most accredited foreign representatives quietly declined, there were enough foreign dignitaries, senior functionaries, and
French diplomats and generals present to suggest to the royalist and republican press that they were witnessing a dress rehearsal of the governing elite of a future monarchy. The government decided to implement
measures, long demanded by the Radicals, expelling the pretenders and
heirs of all dynasties having once ruled in France. The law was adopted
on June 23 and the Count of Paris left France for Great Britain. The
outrage of French royalists could not hide the fact that a prince in exile
lost credibility as a likely successor to the existing regime. Never capable
of generating much popular enthusiasm while in France, in exile the
Count of Paris increasingly appeared to Frenchmen as a scholarly rec-
luse, limiting himself to the periodic production of learned but opaque
manifestos.

Furthermore, the post-1885 elections indicated the real limits of conservative appeal. Prior to the 1886 cantonal elections many conservatives, anticipating a continuation of their electoral momentum, incau-
tiously declared the local voting to be a plebiscite on the regime. To
their dismay they gained only 17 seats, increasing their representation
from 432 to 449 as compared to 987 for the republicans. Although these
modest gains did arrest the steady erosion in local government dating
from 1874, even cautious royalists had anticipated more significant in-
creases.[43] Subsequent by-elections simply confirmed the conservative
stagnation. Conservatives discounted the political significance of by-
elections, which they usually lost, contending that when the fate of the
regime was not at stake, they were often not worth the cost of campaigning. Informed royalists knew better, however, and were clearly dismayed
by the consistency and magnitude of their losses. By March 1887 Beauvoir, reflecting on the combined effect of the expulsion and the electoral
defeats, was bemoaning the "distance between the hopes of '85 and the
reality of '87."[44]

A glance at the electoral map of France also suggested distinct limits
to any future conservative growth. A line running roughly from Lille to
Toulouse, gently curving westward in the center, divided conservative
France from republican France. West of that line—especially in the
north, Normandy, Brittany, Anjou, and the southwest fringe of the Massif Central—conservatives maintained solid roots. In 1889 twenty-eight
conservative deputies ran in these regions unopposed, compared to only
one Boulangist (a former western royalist at that) and eight republicans
in all of France. To the east, with the exceptions of the Aveyron, the
Lozère, and the Ardèche, conservatives were feeble. The center, the

northeast, the Mediterranean littoral, and especially the southeast were refractory to them. Intensity of religious devotion correlated imperfectly with conservative strength. Most areas dominated by conservatives were also areas of clerical influence, although parts of the southwest and Normandy were not. The east, powerfully religious, was still firmly in the control of republicans. Of concern to contemporary conservatives was the fact that the line of demarcation had remained remarkably stable over four elections. The relative improvement in conservative fortunes in the east in 1885 was due exclusively to their massive abstention there in 1881. Propitious circumstances and sound electoral tactics might allow conservatives to consolidate areas of latent strength, but the chances of making significant inroads in the other half of France seemed slender. Commenting on the 1885 elections, François Goguel has noted that conservatives "remain the prisoners of what appears to have been, since 1870, a rigid geographical determinism which condemns to failure their attempts to gain the confidence of the population of the eastern half of the country."[45]

The "hopes of '85" were also frustrated because the dramatic increase in conservative representation in the Chamber did not automatically yield any obvious political advantage. Conservative and Radical gains had cut in half the solid block of 400 Opportunist deputies of the previous Chamber. Yet the subsequent division of the Chamber into three roughly equal blocks also meant that no republican government could be formed without the support of the Radicals. As a result, France seemed doomed to chronic political instability relieved only by short-lived governments in which the Opportunists would inevitably be hostage to the Radicals. Certainly they would be, as long as conservatives retained their overt hostility to the regime. Only by dropping the dynastic question could conservatives hope to obtain a government that might make concessions to their social and religious preoccupations. Albert de Mun recognized this fact as early as November 1885. Always more concerned to defend conservative social and religious interests than to put an Orleanist pretender on the throne, this former legitimist had suggested the creation of a purely Catholic party, but the idea foundered on the opposition of the Pope.[46]

In March 1886, impressed by the essential moderation of the Freycinet ministry, a number of conservative deputies began informally to consider constituting a conservative parliamentary group which would not contest the republican form of government. The inspiration came from Edgar Raoul-Duval, deputy from the Eure. Raoul-Duval was a rather marginal Bonapartist who had flirted with Orleanism in the early 1870s. The notion of a partial rapprochement with moderate republicans temporarily lost most of its appeal when, shortly thereafter, the Freycinet government proceeded to expel the pretenders from France. But when conservatives failed to make significant gains in the cantonal elections of August 1886, Raoul-Duval formally proposed the creation of a *droite républicaine*. Except for the question of the regime, its program was essentially that of the royalists and Bonapartists, denouncing all the social, political, and religious abuses of past governments. He admitted that he and his followers had not lost their monarchist convictions, but announced that they were nonetheless now prepared to present themselves "on the terrain of the republic." The proposal was received with hostility by royalist newspapers and with skepticism by everyone else. It also attracted no support from the conservative deputies, only two of whom were prepared to associate with Raoul-Duval. The whole enterprise died before Raoul-Duval himself did in February 1887.[47]

In practice, however, royalists were increasingly behaving as Raoul-Duval had suggested. In September 1886 the Count of Paris had responded to Raoul-Duval's proposal in a note to French royalists which was published by the *Times* of London in December. He considered the new political formation a positive development only if it attracted republicans into the conservative camp, something which, quite obviously, the *droite républicaine* was not going to do. At the same time, however, the Count of Paris admonished his followers against evoking the monarchy only to abuse the republic. Instead of endlessly challenging the legitimacy of the existing regime, royalists in France ought to put their energies into fighting only on "conservative terrain and for conservative ideas." Like most of his pronouncements the document was ambiguous, and as always it irritated most of his representatives in France. Nonetheless it corresponded to the stance most royalist deputies would soon be taking.

After the war scare of 1887 most Opportunists were anxious to get rid of the belligerent minister of war, so they combined with the conservatives to defeat the Goblet government in May. As Radicals were adamant about retaining Boulanger, a government without him could be formed only with the support of the conservatives. During a prolonged ministerial crisis conservative leaders led by the Baron de Mackau met secretly with President Grévy. Baron Armand de Mackau, deputy from the Orne, was the effective leader of the conservative deputies. The son of the minister of the navy under Louis-Philippe, Mackau had been a Bonapartist in the 1870s but rallied to the Count of Paris after the death of the Prince Imperial. Mackau was a consummate political tactician, acutely aware that dogmatic posturing was a luxury that conservatives out of power could not afford. His correspondence is replete with angry comments about intransigent royalists who did little except articulate their cherished principles, confuse strategy with tactics, and remain unaware that the July Monarchy had disappeared some decades earlier. He was president of the Union des Droites, the largest of the three conservative parliamentary groups, uniting the more flexible royalists and Bonapartists. Mackau now promised loyally to support an Opportunist government, on condition that Boulanger be absent from it and that the application of anticlerical legislation be moderated. In the end, a majority of conservatives supported the new government of Maurice Rouvier, avoiding direct attacks on the republic in exchange for Rouvier's growing indifference to the "clerical menace."

The cooperative stance of the Right was heralded as a major step in the direction of conservative accommodation with the republic, but conservatives really had little choice. The alternative was either another Boulanger ministry or dissolution and elections for which they were manifestly unprepared. The tacit alliance was nonetheless always fragile because Rouvier was under constant attack from the Radicals, who were angered by the abandonment of Boulanger and the capitulation to the clericals. At the same time the more intransigent royalists denounced the alliance as unprincipled, complaining that the government's concessions on religious questions had been minimal. It required all of Mackau's considerable diplomatic skill to prevent them from toppling the government.[48]

Quite apart from the inherent difficulties in sustaining an effective entente with moderate republicans, the major problem with the arrangement was that, while it might ensure domestic and international peace, it got France no closer to the monarchy. In spite of his note to the *Times,* the Count of Paris did not wish France to forget the monarchy and settle for a moderately conservative republican government. Consequently he issued a major policy statement in September 1887. For once his instructions to the royalist party were bold and provocative—so much so, in fact, that Radicals spitefully wondered why the Rouvier government accepted allies whose leader indicated no intention of forgetting his dynastic claims. As several of the pretender's lieutenants complained, from the point of view of parliamentary politics and given the general desire to retain the Rouvier government, the timing of his manifesto could not have been less opportune.[49]

In his Instructions the Count of Paris praised the work of the conservative minority in parliament. Its disinterested and patriotic actions alone had rescued France from the chaos of the previous spring. Outside the Chamber, however, royalists had the larger duty of persuading Frenchmen that only the restoration of the monarchy could bring permanent domestic peace to France. Unfortunately, the experience of the last century had led many Frenchmen to believe that a change of regime could result only from violent social upheaval and civil war. If France were to lapse into total anarchy, the restoration of the monarchy would be inevitable, but any future breakdown of civil authority in France would be the work only of the republicans. Royalists were too patriotic to subject France to another revolutionary experience, nor would it be necessary. A change of regime could be wrought by perfectly peaceful and legal means. There was nothing sacrosanct about the 1875 constitution; "what one assembly has created another can undo." There were, in short, no procedural obstacles to a peaceful transition to the monarchy.[50]

The restoration, far from being merely a seizure of power, would receive the formal assent of the nation. Strictly speaking, of course, the monarchy needed no new legitimation because, since the days of the Capetians, the monarchy had always been "a true national compact." Nonetheless, after a century of revolution, the "historic tradition" needed to be revived "by a freely consented accord between the nation and the family which is the repository of that tradition." What form would that accord take? In the most controversial part of his manifesto, the pretender announced that "this pact of union will be implemented . . . either by a constituent assembly or by a popular vote." The latter he thought the "more solemn" and "most appropriate for an act which will not be repeated." Despite his hedging he was clearly talking about a plebiscite, although he had removed the word from an earlier draft at the insistence of his advisers.

A major reason for continued resistance to the monarchist idea in France, said the pretender, was the widespread misbelief that a restoration would represent "a step backward." It was therefore important to emphasize that the monarchy could and would be adapted to "modern institutions." Indeed the monarchy would bring "to our democratic society that authoritative [prépondérateur] element that is lacking under the republican regime." Royalists had no quarrel with universal suffrage, but when combined with a parliamentary regime it deprived France of a "strong government." A true parliamentary government such as that of the July Monarchy was "incompatible with an assembly elected by universal suffrage."

Although a popularly elected Chamber of Deputies would be retained under the monarchy, its power would be shared equally with the King and a Senate, representing the "major social interests," some but not all of whose members would be elected. Ministers of the government would no longer be responsible before the Chamber alone but before all three branches of government. In defense of his proposed elimination of responsible government, the pretender noted that once ministers could no longer be dismissed at the whim of a fleeting parliamentary majority, there would be a stability and order to public affairs. Moreover, he hinted, no ministry could remain insensitive to the combined dissatisfaction of both the Senate and the Chamber of Deputies. Even this vague assurance was undermined by his proposal to restrict parliamentary control over the budget. The budget would no longer be voted annually, but only once, thus having the status of an ordinary law. It could of course be amended, but only by the consent of the King and his two chambers. Consequently, the government could neither make new expenditures nor collect new taxes without the accord of the elected representatives of the nation. At the same time, however, because the existing budget remained in force until amended, no amount of dissatisfaction on the part of either or both chambers could prevent the government from collecting existing taxes or continuing its day-to-day activities. In short he proposed a government that would be, in large measure, free from parliamentary control.

For the rest, his Instructions contained the traditional bromides of the royalist platform. Control over education would revert to local government. There would be economy in public finances, order in the administration, independence of the judiciary. A pacifist monarchy would make peace with France's neighbors and put an end to the European arms race. He tactfully said little about the Church except to insist that the clergy would now be respected. Predictably, there were the usual references to "the improvement in the condition . . . of the working populations of cities and countryside." He acknowledged the ascendancy of the middle classes, the "nouvelles couches sociales," insisting that the monarchy offered them at least as much as had the republic. As proof he cited the retention of universal suffrage and the election of mayors in rural communes.

Even as presented, the proposals of the Count of Paris amounted to an authoritarian regime far closer to the Empire (French or German) than to republican France. Privately the pretender preferred a parallel with the American constitution, but the comparison was self-evidently specious.[51] The private constitutional drafts which the Count of Paris thought unsuitable for public consumption reveal just how undemocratic his plans for a monarchy were.[52] Despite his public assurances he clearly intended to modify the principle of universal manhood suffrage. The voting age would be raised to twenty-five years and the residency requirement doubled to one year, thus disenfranchising significant numbers of the transient working class. All those receiving poor relief or otherwise in a state of indigency would be struck off the voters' list. Fathers and widows could vote for sons younger than twenty-five, and widows would retain that right after their sons reached the age of majority. The thrust of these modifications was to strengthen an inherently conservative electorate at the expense of a more radical one.

When he informed the French middle classes that mayors would continue to be elected by municipal councils, he neglected to inform them that these councils would now be chosen in a radically different way. Only in towns of fewer than five thousand inhabitants would all municipal councillors continue to be elected by universal suffrage. In larger towns the percentage of councillors so designated would decrease on a sliding scale, ranging from two thirds in towns below twenty thousand to one quarter in Paris and Lyons. The rest of the councillors would be selected by the top 1 percent of taxpayers through a *collège de capacités* consisting of various categories of notables, and through the chambers of commerce. Faced with the growing militancy of urban France, the Count of Paris retained a certain affection for the *régime censitaire*. Nor was his faith in the political conservatism of small towns absolute either, since even there he intended to deprive mayors of their police powers.

Although most senators would continue to be elected, many would be chosen by a far more exclusive electorate than in the past.[53] Under the restored monarchy formerly purged conservative magistrates would be reinstated, freedom of assembly would be "strictly limited and subject to government control," the press obliged to pay caution money, and a wide range of attacks on King, government, foreign sovereigns, and the Church outlawed. Religious instruction would once again be an integral part of the school curriculum, and while primary education would remain obligatory, it would be free only to those who could not afford to pay. Among the many pages of draft legislation, precisely four lines were devoted to putative social reforms.

The publication of the Instructions created a brief flurry of controversy among conservatives. Legitimists, for whom the monarchy needed no popular legitimation, had predictable doctrinal objections.[54] Some of the purer Orleanists pointedly wondered why they were being offered a warmed-over version of the imperial constitution of 1852.[55] Intransigent Bonapartists claimed, correctly, that the royalists had merely stolen their platform; solutionists like Cassagnac were delighted.[56] Some royalists professed to believe that the plebiscitary flavor of the document had cut the ground from under the Bonapartists and would hasten their reconciliation with the monarchy.[57] The more significant issue raised by the Instructions, the scrapping of parliamentary government, troubled few conservatives, most of whom agreed with Beauvoir that "a system of government that worked well enough in the 1830s . . . can no longer function, given the development of the press, the suffrage, and the prevailing climate of the present time."[58] If anything, the Count of Paris did not go far enough for royalists like the deputy from the Nord, Charles Plichon, who caviled over the retention of universal suffrage.[59] Beyond providing ammunition for Radical editorialists, the latest utterances of an exiled prince were of little interest or concern to republicans who, along with the rest of France, were soon preoccupied by the far more gripping Wilson scandal.

Although it marked an important step in the pretender's thinking, the project of reconciling authority with universal suffrage was hardly an original contribution to political theory and established little beyond the fact that he did not intend to restore "the reign of the seigneurs and the curés." Drafting constitutions was a favorite pastime of exiled pretenders, but it did not get them any closer to power. What was entirely lacking in the Instructions was any indication of how the restoration would be effected. It was reassuring to learn that it could be done peacefully, and it was more or less correct to state that what one assembly had done another could reverse. But it would do so only if filled with royalists. Here was the central point: a "legal" monarchist restoration presupposed that in the next election royalists and their allies be a majority in the Chamber of Deputies. Without that vital precondition, constitutional proposals were merely abstract exercises. Consequently, the principal task facing royalists was to create a political and propaganda machine capable of winning elections. Without it the monarchy could be restored, if at all, only by force.

2

Royalist Political Organization: An Elitist Party in an Age of Mass Politics

The major obstacle to a monarchist restoration was the inescapable fact that both the royalist image and the royalist political organization were outdated. The monarchy was a distant memory: France had lived without it for nearly forty years, and for many Frenchmen monarchist government had either vague or unpleasant connotations. Universal manhood suffrage, expanded literacy, urbanization, and the transportation and communications revolution had all seriously eroded the political influence of the traditional elite of notables. No longer, as in previous generations, would wealth and social prominence automatically translate into political power. Unless they adjusted to the new realities of mass politics, conservatives risked being reduced to impotence. They needed to create an electorally seductive image and, most of all, an effective political organization.

Although it is tempting to agree with the historian who recently awarded French conservatives "the Charles X prize for public relations,"[1] royalists, or at least some of them, were genuinely preoccupied by their self-image. They realized that merely reiterating the shortcomings of the republic and the inherent superiority of monarchical principles and regimes was not likely to win new converts. French royalists would have to cater, in the words of the deputy from the Haute-Garonne, Jacques Piou, to "the modern ideas and democratic aspirations of our times."[2] Too many royalists, Piou argued, believed that unwavering attachment to narrow royalist principles would better bring down the republic than would the dilution of those principles with "modern ideas."

Undiluted royalism had a certain appeal for a few secure western deputies, but in the rest of France it was electorally disastrous. Royalists were going to take the republic not by a frontal assault but by the back door. The only legal way to get rid of the republic was to "begin by entering it," in other words, to elect a majority of royalist deputies. Royalist purity would therefore have to be sacrificed to electoral considerations, since "the country will not make a revolution, even legally, if it knows that it is doing so." There was little to be gained from an exclusively dynastic approach except "the edification of a handful of *hoberaux* from Brittany."[3]

To royalists who were sensitive to the charge of representing the old regime and being out of step with the nineteenth century, the approaching centenary of the French Revolution provided an opportunity to situate royalist ideology in terms of the events of 1789. For Piou it was essential that royalists succeed in persuading France that "the monarchy is the incarnation of all the wise accomplishments of the French Revolution, that it has evolved with the changing nature of a society whose progressive aspirations it shares, and that it recognizes not only the force but also the legitimacy of the new social order created in the last hundred years."[4] As the centenary approached, French royalists insisted that 1789 belonged to them as much as to the current regime, because the first year of the revolution had been a royalist achievement, laying the groundwork for a liberal monarchy. Whatever quarrel they had with the French Revolution was with 1793, not 1789. The Count of Paris insisted, "We were liberals then, we are liberals now, and we will remain liberals." What separated liberal royalists and moderate republicans was not the French Revolution, but the fact that once again royalists were more alert than republican moderates to the Jacobin menace and the impending danger of a new version of 1793.[5]

It was all very well, of course—and a bit unnecessary—for the great-grandson of Philippe Egalité to express his unreserved adherence to the principles of 1789. But it was equally the case, and republicans and royalists knew it, that there were plenty of royalists whose legitimist attachments or Catholic sentiments inclined them to no such reconciliation with the French Revolution. *La Revue de l'Ouest* was still listing the names and occupations of 118 victims of the guillotine during the civil war in the Vendée, while *L'Union monarchique du Finistère* persisted in its attacks on the civil constitution of the clergy.[6] Early in 1888 Baron St. Marc-Giradin expressed his alarm at a group of French Catholics who were already preparing to attack the centenary of the Revolution, choosing as their slogan the provocative name "counterrevolution."

By surrendering 1789 to republicans these misguided Catholics had committed a "serious political error as well as an even greater historical one." As for "counterrevolution," this unhappy choice of name had "deprived them of the means of being practically and effectively antirevolutionary."[7]

In principle, French royalists accepted the legitimacy of universal suffrage, but this adhesion was often formal, reluctant, and highly conditional. Lambert de Sainte-Croix conceded to the Count of Paris that "since we must deal with [universal suffrage] we must formally and clearly adhere to the principle." But at the same time he urged caution on the prince, suggesting that royalists "withhold [their] opinions on the modalities of its application."[8] The point was not lost on the Count of Paris, as his private constitutional drafts so clearly indicated. Entirely typical was the royalist editor who urged his readers to learn to accept democracy while in the same breath admitting, "I have never been very enthusiastic about consulting universal suffrage, that great dupery of the century which rarely says anything intelligent in reply."[9]

Royalists talked often enough about the need to relate to the people but could never quite mask a patronizing stance that bordered on contempt. "The influential, most affluent, and independent voters" were forever being told to "neglect no sacrifice to lead the popular masses, who always yield to those who have the most constant contact with them." There was too much talk of "dissipat[ing] an error or clarify[ing] a doubtful point of view for a worker, peasant, or man of the people; rais[ing] even by one degree the most humble intelligence; insert[ing] the embryo of an idea into the brain of the most obtuse."[10] This tone reflected a belief that the grievances of the lower orders were largely mythical, the product of a generally permissive climate. Low wages were not the cause of the laborers' strike in Paris; their wages seemed low only in comparison to the scandalously high rates paid by a city council callously indifferent to the sacrifices of honest taxpayers. The fact that the strike could continue proved only that "our moronic governments have publicly sided with socialism." If anything, royalists asserted, wages were too high in France, far higher than in Germany, which helped explain the current economic crisis. With too many francs jingling in their pockets, French workers "put luxuries ahead of the necessities of life." Unlike their industrious German counterparts, French workers squandered their money on "coffee, the theater, or days off work."[11] Such diatribes were commonplaces in the royalist press and conveyed much more effectively than the platitudes of the pretender the true sentiments of most monarchists in France.

Ambivalent about the revolutionary legacy, covertly hostile to democracy, French royalists were not much more receptive to the aspirations of the emerging middle classes. Gambetta's famous phrase about the "nouvelles couches sociales," the relatively modest members of the middle classes who would become the governing class of the Third Republic, became an obsession with royalists by the 1880s. Something of a consensus prevailed among royalist thinkers. All agreed that this new class was central to political power and must be addressed. Yet as the more perceptive among them acknowledged, it was precisely the "nouvelles couches sociales" who were most likely to be offended by the aristocratic image of the royalist elite. Dufeuille's correspondence is rife with tales of members of the bourgeoisie whose royalist convictions faltered as a result of real or imagined slights from aristocrats. The persistence of Bonapartism was largely explicable, Dufeuille thought, by the fact that its representatives, like those of the republic, were of more modest social origin than were most royalist leaders. Again he reminded royalists: "Since 1848 new classes have been born to wealth and political activity. Once admitted to the dining rooms and salons of the prefecture, they do not wish to return to the servants' quarters and generally persist in fearing that the monarchy might inflict such a fate on them."[12] The profusion of particled names and noble titles among the royalist leaders might still have impressed the lowest ranks of rural society in many parts of France, but among the ever more influential petite bourgeoisie such aristocratic trappings were likely to prompt a powerful resentment.

Yet while Eugène Dufeuille was privately urging royalists to be more responsive to the sensibilities of the "nouvelles couches," many local royalists were *publicly* expressing their fear of and contempt for the new class. The term *nouvelles couches* itself was generally derogatory; to refer to Boulanger as "le général nouvelles couches" expressed a journalist's scorn for the minister of war. *Le Journal de Lunéville* ranted:

> Nothing is more arrogant, tyrannical, and disagreeable than these parvenus of the "nouvelles couches" who today hold the upper hand without merit having played any role in their rise. Every village has two or three wretched individuals who, never having been able to attain esteem and sympathy, get their revenge by making themselves feared. It is easy for them to do so since they correspond with the local "official" rag and have the ear of the subprefect or even the little dictators who sit in the prefecture. They are the ones who compile dossiers on the gamekeepers, custom officials, police, tavernkeepers, and even the curé.

The "petit bonhomme de maître d'école—'nouvelle couche'—who buys the drinks and urges voters to support the ultra Left" was a standard target of royalist editorial wrath, along with the "cabaret politicians and village tyrants."[13] The world had changed since 1848, but royalists accepted this fact reluctantly.

Programs, platforms, and ideological position papers—no matter how pleasingly or deceptively packaged—did not by themselves win converts or votes. An effective propaganda and electoral organization was also essential. The commission of inquiry into the Paris Commune of 1871 had concluded that France might have escaped the uprising, had there been "a truly strong conservative party . . . active everywhere."[14] Eugène Dufeuille, the best-informed royalist in France, put it succinctly: "We are no longer in 1848 and we will not reestablish the monarchy with the former elite [monde censitaire]. Universal suffrage has displaced and lowered the axis of power, and the critical influences are not where they were forty years ago."[15] Throughout the 1880s, royalists were forever referring to the "régime censitaire," the July Monarchy, with its highly restrictive property franchise, and insisting that the ground rules of that era were inapplicable to an increasingly democratic France. Indeed, throughout the Boulanger affair partisans of the alliance would invoke the need to come to grips with democracy and berate the doubters for not having left the world of the July Monarchy.

The royalist obsession with organization during the 1880s reflected a growing awareness that they could no longer count on their "natural" hegemony to exercise political dominance in most parts of France. As late as the mid-1870s it could be said that the conservative Right "continued to direct all the public services, the army, the police, the navy, the magistracy, the tax collectors, the post office, highway administration, and public education." The army officers, the civil engineers, the rector, and the school inspector were "accustomed to meeting the ladies and gentlemen of high society in clubs, at the hunt, in salons" and remained sensitive to the recommendations of le monde in favor of particular protégés. Before 1877 conservatives were still more reliable intermediaries for those seeking governmental or administrative favors than were republicans.[16] Prominent in the higher echelons of the republican administration were the heads of some of the great royalist families: Viscount Gontaud-Biron, the Duc de La Rochefoucauld-Bisaccia, the Marquis de Bouillé, the Marquis d'Harcourt, the Marquis de Noailles, the Marquis de Beauvoir, Count Melchior de Vogüé.[17] The great majority of the prefectoral corps were conservatives whose administrative career had begun under the Empire.

After the republican victories of 1877, and more pronouncedly still after the resignation of Marshal MacMahon at the beginning of 1879, profound changes took place in the administrative personnel of the state. "La question du personnel" became the central issue among the newly triumphant republicans, who demanded a massive purge of the administration. All but four prefects were replaced, as were the majority of subprefects and senior prefectoral employees. The Council of State, the Bank of France, the diplomatic service, the war ministry, finance ministry, and ministry of cults all saw comparable changes. The magistracy, bastion of conservative sentiment in the 1870s, was an even more important target because only a thoroughly republicanized judiciary could be counted on to apply the anticlerical measures of the early 1880s. Judges whose republican sympathies were not patent were replaced on a massive scale, the results being intensified by the "auto-épuration" of those who resigned rather than apply the decrees concerning unauthorized religious congregations. Between 1877 and 1882, 1,763 magistrates out of 2,148, and 2,536 justices of the peace out of 2,941 were replaced. The "judicial revolution" extended even to the technically irremovable assize court judges. In August 1883, under the guise of rationalizing the judicial system, the government abolished over six hundred posts, thus eliminating an identical number of conservative magistrates. A further three hundred resigned in protest.[18] A lot of old scores were being settled, of course, since administrative purges were hardly a republican innovation. More important, an effective republican partonage network was being established. If the deputy was a republican, so too would be the local tax assessor, and entirely sensitive to the legitimate fiscal difficulties of café owners whose establishments served as centers of republican propaganda. Over time, patronage and the pork barrel, of which the notorious "electoral railroads" were but the most striking example, gave republicans an ever firmer grip on local politics. The *commune-gare* became a "republican bridgehead." The expansion of government meant that many peasants, otherwise unattracted to republican ideals, rallied to the regime, the better to exploit what has been called "the milch-cow state."[19] Although the changes were often less dramatic than conservatives believed and certainly less sweeping than those demanded by the Radicals, both the substance and the appearance of conservative hegemony began to ebb.

An increasingly assertive republican administration sharply diminished the ability of conservatives to translate their superior social and economic position into political power. For royalists it was axiomatic that all government officials, from the prefect to the lowliest forest warden, were republican electoral agents. Subprefects appeared to serve no discernible purpose except that of well-paid ward heelers in the republican political machine. These were predictable charges, but the periodic reports submitted by subprefects with respect to local politics suggest that they were not far wide of the mark. Certainly much of the subprefects' time was spent sounding out the politics of their arrondissement commune by commune, assessing the political influence of local notables and coordinating the republican electoral effort. Nor, to judge by the way these reports were received by prefects, were they encouraged to be the least bit casual in the performance of their political duties. Some indication of the hectoring reflexes of subprefects can be glimpsed in the Hérault, where the prefect finally had to request that the subprefect of Saint-Pons cease his incessant demands for the revocation of civil servants. When there was evidence of political disloyalty, the prefect was prepared to "smite them without mercy," but one simply could not dismiss an agent of the Ponts-et-Chaussées merely because he had been seen in a café frequented by reactionaries.[20]

As nefarious as the subprefect was the local schoolmaster, the famous "lay missionary of the republic." Not only did these arrogant young men fill their pupils with republican and anticlerical propaganda, but they were a linchpin of the local republican political machine. Conservatives often depicted the local republican mayor as being "so crassly ignorant that he is obliged to rely on the enlightenment of the schoolmaster, who is only too pleased to show off his superiority and to lord it over the others [like] a little tyrant." In communes all over France the local administration appeared to be "abandoned to the inexperienced hands of a young teacher who was perfectly convinced of his infallibility." Consequently, "clerical tutelage" had been replaced by "pedagogic tutelage," and France was full of mayors who could "find no better way to pass the time than to conspire with the teacher against the priest."[21] Too clever by half, enamored of their newly acquired learning and with plenty of free time for politicking in the cabarets, the *instituteurs* were both a symbol of what was wrong with the republican regime and increasingly an obstacle to its removal. In practice the *instituteur* was often a far more wretched creature than conservatives imagined, and his influence and esteem among the population a fraction of that assigned him by his royalist antagonists.[22] Yet as one student of royalism has noted: "Faced with the growing rivalry of the republican bourgeoisie, the royalist milieux ceased rather abruptly to enjoy a superiority of knowledge and competence."[23] As the Associations Amicales des Anciens Elèves multiplied, an old-boy network of republican notables could encroach on the influence of the more traditional elite. Increasingly when royalists wrote about a "natural political organization," they referred not to traditional conservative social hegemony but to the republican administrative apparatus.

Even the clergy, so often taken as the inseparable and archly effective ally of the royalists, represented a less than assured asset and a depreciating asset at that. Granted, in the profoundly Catholic regions of France, informed contemporaries often assigned the clergy a determining role in elections. Prefects were impressed by "the recommendations and solicitations coming forth endlessly from . . . the pulpits" and put much stock in the efficacity of "objurgations from the confessional and threats of deprivation of sacraments."[24] Yet while government officials everywhere knew that the clergy were unenthusiastic about the current regime and sentimentally attached to the monarchy, they were frequently unable to demonstrate any direct clerical support for royalist candidates. Their reports on the political influence of the clergy abound with words like "occult," "secret," "discreet," "prudent," "subtle," "elusive," and "in the shadows," and often the only real evidence of political interference was the persistent success of conservative candidates.[25]

In fact, from the late 1870s on, the church hierarchy had begun to adopt a cautious role in elections. Outside some regions of the west, clerical electoral influence was minimal, never as effective as governmental administrative pressure and rarely worth provoking the hostility of civil authorities.[26] By 1889 many government officials were admitting that, whatever their private opinions, the clergy had usually adopted an attitude of relative neutrality during the elections. The statistics on priests charged with political interference would seem to bear this out. After the 1885 elections some 999 priests were charged by the prefects; after the 1889 election, only 297.[27] Clerical political activity usually took the form of reminding the faithful that it was a sin to "mal voter," to vote for candidates "who are not resolved to defend the interests of religion and society."[28] Such messages invariably outraged prefects but were unlikely to dissuade anyone otherwise predisposed to vote for a moderate republican. Moreover, while most clergy remained hostile to the republic, their enthusiasm for the monarchy waned. Repeatedly local royalists complained that the clergy were growing "more and more indifferent to royalism." For their part, French Catholics were aware that royalism was an ever more fragile instrument of religious defense. *La Croix,* the powerful national Catholic newspaper, conceded that royalists were still the best friends of the Church. "But," it asked conservative leaders, "where does your appeal make itself heard? Where are the newspapers that shout it in the street? Where are the public places where people listen to you? For the population you remain unknown and misunderstood—unknown because there is almost no contact between you and them; misunderstood because they therefore view you through the optic of revolutionary newspapers."[29]

With their traditional bases of political influence eroding, royalists desperately needed a modern political organization. The problem, as one local royalist acutely noted, was that there existed "no conservative electoral organization that can face up to that formidable organization composed of the government and all the factions of the republican party; they are legion, whereas we have the greatest difficulty bringing together a small group of our friends; they have branches in every commune, whereas we can barely even count on the fidelity of our correspondents; they command, demand, threaten, and promise, while we are reduced to invoking principles and appealing to dedication."[30]

Two things stand out about royalists and political organization: for the most part the royalists neglected political organization and manifested little or no talent for it, but at the same time they talked incessantly about the problem. Each new blow to royalist political fortunes brought forth a spate of editorials in the local press about the need to organize. The state of the royalist organization was an ever present subject in the correspondence of royalist leaders, and their concern about its shortcomings and their desire for reform were clearly genuine. Yet rarely were they translated into effective action. As an angry young royalist remarked in 1897, the party's traditional refrain of "let's organize" reminded him of an opera chorus which frantically cried "let us flee, let us flee" while manifesting every visible intention of remaining right where it was.[31]

The organizational stagnation of the royalists was not, then, for want of concern. Nor did it reflect ignorance in organizational matters. Royalists knew what they wanted, namely, what the republicans had, or at least what they imagined the republicans had. The requisites were clear enough: a coherent network of committees, not just at the departmental level but in all major centers and cantons, with official correspondents in every commune; a permanent organization with activities not limited to the electoral period; regular meetings and a broad "democratic" membership; incessant propaganda activity through public meetings; a popular and inexpensive royalist press; and regular and massive distributions of royalist tracts, portraits, and almanacs on market days and at religious pilgrimages and fairs. All this was designed to counter the influence of government agents, render the monarchy more attractive to the population, and deliver the votes at elections. The whole enterprise was to be coordinated by the Count of Paris and his agents via the monthly reports from paid secretaries in each department. Supervision of local royalist activities was delegated to the *missi dominici,* who worked full time coordinating the activities of the dozen or so departments under their charge. All this looked impressive on paper and some of it even existed. But royalist organizational activities almost never obtained the hoped-for results.

The critical dilemma faced by French royalists, as they themselves recognized, was that by the 1880s in many parts of France their support came primarily from the wealthier classes. If they could still count on the châteaux and, although to a far slighter degree, the business community, their influence among the "nouvelles couches sociales" was minimal. To broaden royalist influence among these classes, the Count of Paris had established an elaborate and expensive network of political agents. In particular, the *missi* were to act, in Dufeuille's words, as "political *commis voyageurs,"* selling the monarchy in the way that Léon Gambetta had once sold the republic. They were to frequent small market towns, stay in commercial hotels, and eat the businessman's lunch.

There were undeniable advantages to that kind of activity, but the *missi* rarely engaged in it. They preferred to limit their visits to the *chefs lieux* and their contacts to the principal notables of the department. Indeed, most preferred to spend as much time as possible in Paris and rely on epistolary activity rather than slogging through provincial backwaters providing the requested information on "judicial, administrative, and journalistic personnel." Nor was this very surprising. A political traveling salesman is still a traveling salesman, whereas the *missi* came from walks of life that predisposed them to higher expectations. With an average annual salary of eight thousand francs plus expenses, they were in a distinctly higher income bracket. Even Dufeuille, while deploring this attitude, could recall some utterly wretched meals in the Orne and insalubrious accommodations in Avranches and appreciate the position of the *missi.* At the same time he could see that, as a result, the knowledge of the departments possessed by many of the *missi* was no better than that of the departmental committees; worse still, they were rarely in a position to control or rectify the information coming from those committees.[32]

But if the social status of the *missi* was such that the thought of hanging around the Hôtel du Commerce was unappealing, it was far too modest to carry any weight at all with the principal notables of the royalist party. Consequently the effort of the *missi* to coordinate electoral strategy was often no more effective than their mission of expanding the base of the party. A squabble over a senatorial election in the Loire-Atlantique provides a characteristic example. In the summer of 1886 the departmental royalist committee was torn between the claims of two would-be candidates: a legitimist who had been particularly active in the royalist cause over the years, and a former Orleanist whose service to the party was less impressive but who had a serious chance of winning. The Count of Paris was known to favor the latter candidate, but when pressured by a supporter of the legitimist, the belligerent Baron de Lareinty, he characteristically waffled and implied that he was neutral. He was not, of course, and dispatched the *missus* Porteu to ensure the nomination of the more promising candidate. At the meeting of the royalist committee of the department, Lareinty, fresh from defending royal honor in his celebrated duel with Boulanger, made much of the Count of Paris's neutrality. Supporters of the rival nominee, aware of the pretender's true sentiments, protested. After a prolonged and entirely byzantine debate about the real sentiments of the Count of Paris, someone finally noted that the one individual authorized to speak officially for the pretender, Porteu, was waiting in an adjacent room. That Porteu had not been allowed to be present during the extended deliberations was singular enough, but the suggestion that he be called on to resolve the impasse met with a storm of indignation. He was after all an outsider to the department and the committee, as well as a man of distinctly inferior social class. As Lareinty haughtily observed, the royalist committee of the Loire-Atlantique did not "take instructions from a former subprefect."[33] This department was singularly refractory but not unique in its resistance to the coordinating efforts of the *missi*. The royalist committee of the Gironde also pointedly requested that the *missus* assigned to that department stay out of its affairs.[34]

The departmental royalist secretaries also illustrated the limits of royalist organization. In principle every department was to have a secretary, appointed and paid for by the royalist headquarters in Paris; in practice only about 55 of the 83 departments possessed one. Their main task was to furnish detailed information about the political situation in each department in the form of monthly reports. The explicit intention of royalists was to have from their secretaries the kind of information provided to the minister of the interior by the prefects. The secretaries did faithfully submit monthly reports furnishing extensive information about local politics, the regional perception of national events, and the state of the departmental royalist fortunes. Periodically they requested guidance as to the best way to handle recent political developments and occasionally suggested alternative strategies for royalist organization and propaganda. The reports, submitted initially to Dufeuille and Lambert de Sainte-Croix, were forwarded to the Count of Paris, who, to judge by his marginalia, faithfully read them all and dictated a formal, albeit usually perfunctory, reply.

The secretaries, even more pronouncedly than their prefectoral counterparts, developed an acute sensitivity for what their superiors wanted to hear, and their reports were often overly optimistic. The parsimonious Bocher had serious reservations about their value, and even their staunch defender Dufeuille acknowledged that their assessment of local royalist strength was often unrealistic.[35] A more serious deficiency was that they could be little more than sources of information. Unlike prefects, they could report on their side's activity but not direct it. Their impact upon the local royalist elite was minimal; rarely did they exercise any independent authority. Unlike the notables, the secretaries were all from relatively modest social circumstances. Whereas the great majority of local royalist committee members were described as *propriétaires* or (more rarely) *industriels,* secretaries almost never were. Typically a secretary was the editor of a local royalist newspaper or a former functionary, the victim of the republican purges of the late 1870s. Being a royalist secretary was the job for a former magistrate, a *receveur de l'enregistrement,* or a *conseilleur de préfecture.*[36] As the spokesman for the royalists in the Gironde noted, such secretaries, whatever their value as conduits for information, could "fulfill none of the social or political prerequisites necessary to direct political activity in a department." That role required "an individual of importance."[37] Consequently when, as in 1888, unpopular tactics had to be urged on reluctant local royalists, secretaries would be ineffective. When, after 1890, the royalist organization began to disintegrate, secretaries proved capable of little more than recording the fact.

The need for a coherent system of active committees was a favorite theme of royalist commentators. They were mesmerized by the committee network of their republican opponents. Although royalists usually assigned a far higher degree of organizational coherence and effectiveness to republican committees than they ever possessed, there was no doubt that the republican political organization was far superior to their own.[38]

Nearly every department possessed some sort of royalist committee. Beyond that, there was no common organizational pattern. In some departments the central committee was in fact a committee of "conservative union" including Bonapartists as well as royalists. In approximately half of the departments committees also existed at the level of the arrondissement, although more often than not only some of the arrondissements were so organized and, as a rule, such committees met only during election periods. Cantonal committees sometimes existed, although never were more than a fraction of the cantons in a department organized. There was periodic reference to communal delegates. Many committees were ephemeral and the overall committee structure (if there can be said to have been one) was always in a state of flux.[39]

How were these royalist committees constituted and whom did they represent? There were in fact no consistent principles behind the creation of local committees and many were, in essence, little more than self-coopting oligarchies. In some departments (the Indre, Cher, Ardennes, Savoie, Tarn, Charente-Maritime, and Loir-et-Cher, for example), the departmental royalist committee consisted of either the board of directors of the leading royalist newspaper or its principal stockholders. In other departments (the Vienne, Pas-de-Calais, Haute-Marne, Ain, Haute-Savoie, and Somme, for example), the central committee was composed of elected representatives from each canton or in some cases from each arrondissement. Still others formed the central committee from various royalist deputies, senators, and members of the general council and the council of the arrondissement. This system prevailed in the Gironde, Tarn-et-Garonne, Loire, and Basses-Pyrénées. Departments with even this degree of clarity in royalist organization were the exception rather than the rule. Most did not and probably could not explain how a man became a member of a royalist committee, beyond the general premise that such members were ardent royalists with some wealth and political and social influence in the department.

Rather less than half of the departmental organizations collected formal dues. These were modest, never in excess of 100 francs and more typically 50, 25, or even less. Since membership in departmental committees rarely exceeded a few score, the *caisse électorale* of those departments that actually had them was small, so that electoral expenses were covered by wealthy candidates, local donations, or the personal wealth of the Count of Paris. The modest treasuries of royalist committees did not, of course, reflect their potential resources. The royalist committee of the Gironde relied upon the 25-franc annual dues of its 143 members for its 3,575-franc annual income. Yet for the 1889 election it was able to collect 108,000 francs from 304 wealthy donors. Yet despite its obvious affluence the committee of the Gironde was not able, in an ordinary year, to cover its very modest expenses. The cost of running an office, paying a secretary, and carrying on what must have been a very limited propaganda effort was 2,600 francs, but because rather more than half the members of the committee neglected to pay their dues, receipts in 1889 were only 1,725 francs, and 1,525 the next year. These were trivial sums among a group like the royalists of the Gironde, 35 of whom had contributed 1,000 francs apiece to fight the 1889 elections. But the fact that most royalists in the department could not be bothered to pay their nominal dues, and that at annual meetings a disproportionate amount of time was spent discussing "arrears," reveal the cavalier disregard of even relatively dedicated royalists for the day-to-day operation of their party.[40]

The state of local royalist organization rarely reflected the degree of royalist strength. The Calvados and the Eure, for example, were predominantly royalist in sentiment and electoral representation. Yet neither had a royalist organization of any significance; in the Eure the royalist committee existed "on the condition that it would not have to meet." Such organizational apathy might have reflected the relative security of the royalist forces, but in the southeast, absolutely barren territory for royalists, departments like the Isère and the Haute-Savoie also had a purely token royalist organization. In the Isère a royalist committee existed, but the local secretary was unable to say with any certainty who belonged to it. In the Haute-Savoie the royalist committee met a couple of times a year "to affirm its existence rather than to do anything." By contrast in the Corrèze, a department too poor to be anything but *gouvernemental,* there existed for a few years an elaborate committee system replete with an imposing (albeit inherently meaningless) set of statutes.

More interesting than what royalist committees looked like was what they actually did. One of the things they did not do was have much impact outside a narrow circle of the older social and economic elite. As royalist commentators ruefully admitted, their composition was socially exclusive, giving the committees the appearance of a closed social club rather than a political organization. In the Ardennes the royalist committee consisted of the nine-person board of directors of *Le Courrier des Ardennes.* Three were barons, two were counts, and all, with the significant exception of the editor, had particled names. The aristocratic character of the committee did not escape local attention; as one royalist complained, the industrialists of Sedan, the merchant class in Charleville, and the affluent peasant proprietors were acutely aware of the class differences between themselves and "the committee of barons."[41] In the Meurthe-et-Moselle the secretary bemoaned the fact that local royalists catered to the (former) "ruling class" and not to the "business class." When subordinate classes appeared among the ranks of local royalist leadership, they were likely to be revoked magistrates rather than the politically more significant merchants and shopkeepers.[42] In the Hautes-

Pyrénées, the local secretary unhappily acknowledged, the royalist committee represented "the château owners, the particled names, the titles." The classes with growing political clout—"the local doctors . . . the veterinarians, the small notaries and business brokers, the businessmen, the process servers, retailers, and café owners"—were absent.[43] Dufeuille summed it up when he observed that "in general our committees are not democratic enough," rarely in touch with "the middle class and the little people."[44]

The wealth and status of local royalist leaders not only separated them from much of the electorate; it also kept them out of their departments for much of the year. Throughout the 1880s royalists complained incessantly that the leading elements in the party spent too much time in Paris. The Aisne was typical in that the great majority of the members of the royalist committee actually lived in Paris throughout the winter months—a convenient pretext for not holding meetings. Indeed one of the reasons why members of the committee of the Eure sought dispensation from actually meeting was the fact that most of them lived in Paris. In this respect committee members emulated royalist deputies. The secretary of the Nord indicated that one of the reasons for the erosion of royalist support in that department was the fact that its deputies, unlike republicans, spent little time in the department, showing up only for major holidays and the opening of the hunt. Similarly the royalist châtelains of the Mayenne spent more and more time away from their estates, either in Paris or at fashionable spas.[45]

All these deficiencies in royalist organization were the subject of endless discussions in the 1880s, and the unfavorable comparison with republican organization was a constant theme. The problem with the royalist committee of the Marne, the secretary complained, was that it was "formed by too few individuals. It needs to be enlarged, rejuvenated, and no longer limited to the old bourgeoisie of Châlons." By point of comparison he noted that "the republican committee in Châlons does not limit its composition to a dozen members. Nailed to the wall of the tax bureau in town there is, for anyone to see, a large poster entitled 'Members of the Republican Committee of Châlons' with fifty or sixty names." Reforms, of course, were easy to propose but difficult to implement. Why not, one royalist in the Saône-et-Loire asked, emulate republicans and issue a membership card, collect regular dues, and hold meetings at regular intervals established by formal statutes? The proposal met with massive indifference on the part of the principal local leaders. A similar fate awaited the suggestion by a member of the committee of the Loir-et-Cher who proposed sending a mail ballot to royalist representatives in every commune in order to select candidates for election. The royalist committee of the Basses-Pyrénées designed a complex questionnaire in order to obtain detailed electoral information. Of the 150 "correspondents" to whom the questionnaires were sent, only 25 troubled to reply. Even then they rarely bothered to complete the questionnaire and limited themselves to penning a few lines of impressions about their corner of the department.[46]

The elitist premises of the royalist party also affected the nature of its propaganda efforts. The leading royalist spokesmen—Pasquier, Broglie, Bocher, Hervé, Haussonville, Duval, Buffet, Keller, and Calla—did not fail to tour the country, making frequent and eloquent speeches explaining the clear superiority of the monarchy over the current corrupt regime. Yet the effect of their addresses was invariably only to reaffirm the conviction of committed royalists, never to raise doubts among the ranks of republicans. Royalist spokesmen shunned popular or uncommitted audiences. Albert de Mun warned royalists in 1881 that "public meetings should only be attempted in very small centers where we can be assured of facing no active hostility." In a revealing note Pierre Calla, charged by the Count of Paris with organizing speaking tours, indicated that the leading figures in the party would restrict themselves to "elite" gatherings in order to be spared "the hazards of more mixed audiences."[47] Royalist addresses were usually pronounced "a major success," but as a royalist newspaper in Nancy wearily remarked, "one is always a big success when one addresses one's friends."[48] Republican administrators confidently predicted that the impact of a major royalist rally in Toulouse would be "absolutely nil," because the speakers "addressed themselves only to a carefully selected audience whose mind was already made up."[49] During the 1889 elections in the Charente-Maritime, the royalist candidate held an election rally open only to those who had received an invitation. This prompted a major commotion outside the meeting hall by a number of working-class constituents who pointedly asked why, as voters, they were excluded.[50]

Royalists in the Charente-Maritime were notorious for their insensitivity to public opinion, but the distaste for open, popular confrontations was widespread among royalists and often distinguished their campaigns from the far more vigorous campaigns of their republican opponents. The Deux-Sèvres, a department where the quality of the campaign could make a decisive difference, provides an example. Although republicans conquered the Deux-Sèvres in 1877, the two forces were nearly equal, and only 1,100 votes separated the conservative list from the victorious republican one in 1885. Vigorous campaigning might have been expected to redress the balance, yet in an 1886 by-election the veteran royalist candidate Paul Taudière held only eight election rallies, compared to twenty-five for his republican opponent. A September 1887 by-election confronted the republican Léopold Goirand and the royalist Jean Aymé de La Chevrelière. The royalist ought to have enjoyed an advantage, since his family was one of the oldest and most prominent in the department; his father and uncle had both previously been deputies. Goirand, by contrast, came from an obscure family and had lived in Paris most of his life. Consequently he addressed thirty election meetings in less than three weeks, whereas Aymé de La Chevrelière addressed precisely two. He, like Taudière before him, lost by a narrow margin.[51]

The major vehicle of royalist propaganda was the press. The last third of the nineteenth century was in many respects the golden age of local newspapers. Increased literacy, technological advances, and the spread of advertising permitted limited-circulation, low-cost newspapers to flourish. It was not unusual for even small departments to have a score of daily and weekly newspapers representing the entire range of political opinion. Even departments bereft of any visible royalist organization would have three or four royalist newspapers.[52]

Yet while royalists controlled an impressive number of newspapers, both quantitatively and qualitatively they lagged behind the republicans, and the gap was widening. In 1874 *Le Figaro* estimated that there were 336 conservative newspapers in France (255 royalist and 81 Bonapartist), compared to 226 republican ones. Although the circulation of individual republican newspapers was generally greater, the average daily circulation of the conservative press was 316,000 as opposed to 269,000 for republicans.[53] A different calculation (with a different bias) in 1873 identified 124 principal republican newspapers and 127 conservative ones.[54] By 1889 the relative strengths had changed profoundly. In that year the *Annuaire de la Presse* listed just under 500 provincial conservative newspapers, from the big regional dailies to the *feuilles d'arrondissement;* republicans, by contrast, now controlled over 900.

These figures, moreover, understated the republican predominance. The Pas-de-Calais had 14 conservative newspapers compared to 12 republican ones, but the total circulation of the latter was 25 percent higher. The best of the royalist regional dailies were dwarfed by their republican counterparts. Although *L'Eclair* in Montpellier was the most influential royalist newspaper in the Midi, with a circulation of 12,000, it was easily outdistanced by the republican *Le Petit Méridional,* which sold 70,000 newspapers daily. *Le Nouvelliste de Bordeaux* was the most widely read royalist newspaper in the southwest, but its republican competitor, *La*

Petite Gironde, enjoyed a circulation five times greater. The combined circulation of all six major conservative newspapers in the Haute-Garonne was well below that of the republican *Dépêche de Toulouse* alone. *Le Nouvelliste de Lyon,* with a circulation of 35,000, was, after *La Croix,* the largest Catholic-conservative newspaper in France, but even it could not compete with the cheaper and more attractive *Lyon républicain* and *Le Progrès,* with circulations of 75,000 and 60,000, respectively.[55]

Qualitatively the royalist press also suffered by comparison. An 1885 official inquiry into the provincial press frequently disparaged royalist newspapers: "badly written and edited," "little read," "influence: almost nil"—such were typical judgments.[56] Such assessments were partisan but not unlike those made by contemporary royalists. Reading a few dozen provincial royalist newspapers a century later, the historian can only concur. It is not hard to understand why a confidential report on one of the more wretched royalist journals in Brittany asserted that "no one ever reads it twice."[57] Almost all were heavily dependent on subsidies from the Count of Paris, yet they were still in financial difficulty and faced declining circulation.

The real weakness of royalist newspapers was that they were never as attractive, *as newspapers,* as were their republican counterparts. In the 1870s republican newspapers launched two critical innovations that greatly enhanced their popular appeal. They lowered their prices to the nominal sum of five centimes and invested in telegraphic services, so that even the smallest villages could have Parisian and international news the next morning rather than the day after that. This was the origin, as André Cordier of *Le Nouvelliste de Bordeaux* admitted, of the "true popular, democratic, electoral newspaper," which outsold its conservative competitors less because it was republican than because it was "first with the news." What republicans learned to do in the decade of the 1870s, royalists were only beginning to consider ten years later.[58] There was plenty of royalist correspondence in the late 1880s and early 1890s about five-centime newspapers and telegraphic services, but these were still projects rather than accomplishments.

Le Moniteur de Saintogne, in the Charente-Maritime, was a typical royalist newspaper. In 1887 it had a circulation of about 1,200, of which 400 were subscribers and the rest were "street sales." During the next several years, however, circulation declined by 50 percent even though the newspaper expanded its sales territory. Its price, fifteen centimes, was three times that of other newspapers. It appeared only twice weekly instead of triweekly as did its chief rivals. Whereas the rest of the local press had opted for a larger format, *Le Moniteur* persisted in a cramped, unattractive, old-fashioned smaller version. Finally, because its publisher could not be persuaded to adopt the more efficient steam printing, *Le Moniteur* was distributed two hours after its rivals hit the street. Sales suffered accordingly, and increasingly local royalists read the newspaper only out of loyalty. Not even a change in political orientation would help a newspaper like this. When the somewhat erratic publisher briefly switched his allegiance to the moderate republicans in 1889, his circulation plummeted even faster and he soon scurried back to the royalists.[59]

Royalist newspapers did not form the hub of local political activity, as did those of their republican opponents. It has been justly remarked that conservative newspaper editors were rarely as important within the direction of their party as were their republican counterparts. Whereas the editorial office of a republican newspaper was frequently "the meeting place of the leaders and activists of the party," royalist leaders were more likely to meet in private salons where journalists were seldom invited.[60] The picture can be overdrawn: journalists were certainly prominent in the local royalist organizations, and men like Cordier in Bordeaux were the undisputed workhorses of the party. But royalist newspaper editors were invariably of a distinctly different social status from the other leaders of the party, and their editorials were not free of veiled allusions to the "politics of the salon." Certainly local royalist notables did not welcome journalistic contributions to party policy.[61]

Highly visible, coherent, modern organization was not, of course, the only index of royalist political influence, a point routinely made by government agents. Indeed, the absence of any visible royalist organization could be, and often was, taken as proof not of royalist weakness but deep-rooted strength. The subprefects of the Eure insisted that royalists were so well entrenched in the department that "they do not need committees in the arrondissement or the communes to campaign against us." The wealth and social prominence of royalist notables "render[ed] any committee superfluous."[62] Analyses of this kind might have given comfort to royalist organizers, had they not known better. The prefect of the Seine-Maritime might have believed that, in spite of their apparent lack of organization, the royalists constituted "an important reactionary element," but royalist internal documents continually stress that deplorable organization was dramatically eroding royalist influence in the department.[63] Moreover, even when the prefects' assessment of the power of informal royalist networks was correct, they were describing a traditional mechanism of conservative domination, predicated on a constellation of social forces that was steadily disappearing throughout France. The informal organization that might still be effective in the Eure would be of little use in much of the rest of France and was losing its potency even in the Eure.

Royalist predominance in local social life was paying fewer political dividends as the years went by. Both prefects and royalists emphasized the importance of the latter's continued domination of agricultural societies, racing clubs, and cultural associations. These were "organic" associations and royalist activity came more naturally here than it did in committees. Effective control over such organizations, it was often suggested, could be a viable substitute for more modern forms of political activity. Here too, however, royalists tended to exaggerate the political importance of local societies. Count d'Aymery from the Eure-et-Loir boasted that royalists controlled the Racing Society and hence the major social event in the department, the annual races. The result was "an excellent occasion for conservatives to present themselves, as they really are, to the major influences in the countryside." Had Aymery not, at this point, become engrossed in a mouth-watering description of the gastronomic feasts that followed the races, he might have noted that those in attendance at the races, or as he preferred to put it "this little government," were extremely unrepresentative of the voters in the department.[64]

Moreover, increasingly, social paramountcy in rural society did not translate into effective political domination. In the Saône-et-Loire, royalists had traditionally organized most of the regional festivals—music competitions, agricultural fairs, celebrations of Lamartine's birthday. This was a preponderance they had deliberately sought and which no one had seriously challenged. But as the local secretary dourly acknowledged, no one had repaid these social services with votes; all the royalists had to show for their activity was "a certain respectful toleration." When it came to political power, he concluded, informal royalist organization did not compare to "the almost military organization of our adversaries."[65]

Everybody talked about royalist political organization and nobody achieved very much. An important reason for this was the fact that, in the end, many of the most prominent royalists found the idea of organizational reform unappealing. To say, as royalist journalists repeatedly did, "Look at our enemy and do as they do" made good editorials and probably good sense, but it neglected the fact that devout royalists usually did not want to resemble their republican opponents. Of course it was true that small-town lawyers and veterinarians were becoming major forces in French politics. But that very fact was precisely one of those things royalists found so disagreeable about the republican regime, and therefore not a compelling reason for inviting members of these famous "nouvelles couches" into royalist committees to hobnob with representatives of France's oldest families. Opening up royalist committees to a more "democratic" element, handing out membership cards, holding statutorily obligatory meetings, and mailing out postal ballots might enhance royalist political influence, but it was a crassly plebeian approach and, more important, threatened the prerogatives of a handful of individuals who saw themselves as part of a natural (and small) elite.

The deputy Marquis Julien de La Rochejacquelein was the royalist leader in the Deux-Sèvres. He was also notoriously suspicious of any kind of "democratic" organization which reflected, as Dufeuille perceptively noted, "a personal fear of losing some of his influence, should the departmental committee in Niort attract some new royalist recruits." He was, the subprefect reported, "too old-fashioned ever to accept the control and initiative of committees." Fear of losing power and autonomy to a committee, especially a committee whose composition was uncomfortably "democratic," was a commonplace among conservative politicians during the Third Republic and invariably hampered efforts at political organization.[66]

Even without the damper exercised by notables like La Rochejacquelein, members of royalist committees were unlikely to bring much zeal to their mandate. Royalists in the Eure who consented to sit on the departmental committee only on the condition that "they should not have to meet" were fairly typical in their platonic commitment to political activity. Their attitude was entirely analogous to that of contemporary academics whose theoretical commitment to university government is seriously undermined by the amount of time the process consumes. Membership in royalist committees was usually open only to mature, socially prominent, and economically successful men for whom politics was at best a secondary activity. Regular meetings, incessant propaganda efforts—all those things that royalist editorials invariably demanded—required an inordinate commitment of time from individuals who had little personally to gain from the process. Politics was rarely an avenue of upward mobility—as it might be, say, for a republican veterinarian; instead, it detracted from managing the family business or fortune. The royalist secretary in the Gironde, reflecting on the gradual withdrawal from active politics of many royalists, noted that "most of them, now past middle age and preoccupied by family and business matters, no longer have the necessary time and energy to lead an active opposition campaign."[67]

Similar analyses were common among contemporary royalists, who were dimly aware that the advantage of drawing members from the ranks of the wealthy, prestigious, and influential could be vitiated by the fact that these very people were likely to treat political activity as a distinctly secondary concern. For many royalists a committee was a club where one periodically discussed national and local politics with one's ideologically like-minded peers; it was not an organization for serious political activity. The Vicomte d'Adhémar, leader of the royalists in Toulouse, once remarked in frustration, "Our committees restrict themselves to a consultative role and are not active enough; we pass resolutions but don't do any work." Too often a royalist would consent to preside over a local committee not because of a consuming interest in political activity, but because it would enhance his prestige. As a "representative of Monseigneur" he could legitimately write to the Count of Paris announcing births, deaths, and marriages and then casually allude to the Count's replies at the races or the hunt. The consequent paucity of true "militants" on the political right would also be the source of embittered commentary throughout the life of the republic.[68]

Royalists attempted to compensate for the political lethargy of the elite by creating parallel organizations to mobilize elements of the population who, by reason of age or social status, were unlikely to be at home in the more traditional royalist formations. Sometimes what they had in mind was counterrevolutionary violence. In the mid 1880s Parisian royalists contemplated the formation of a Ligue de la défense sociale. This was to be "an organization of 'street demonstrators' that can be in action on two hours' notice"—"brave gens" assembled for a "contre émeute." Although the Count of Paris endorsed the idea, it was never actively pursued.[69]

The Ligue Populaire Royaliste, founded in 1881, was more typical. Acting independently from the formal monarchist committees, the Ligue focused its attention on the working class and the small shopkeeper, as well as the army rank and file, corporals, and noncommissioned officers. It emphasized social issues and organized meetings at which various questions of political economy were discussed. By the beginning of 1884 the Ligue was reported to have at least 18,000 members and thirty-seven branches outside Paris and to be growing rapidly. Yet the radical rhetoric of the Ligue was ill received by a royalist old guard, to whom the organization appeared to be a group of "anarchists of the Right."

Certainly the Count of Paris never evinced any enthusiasm for the Ligue, nor did he provide it much money. Perhaps he was aware that, for all its "popular" rhetoric, the Ligue's "grande fête" in 1884 cost those who wished to attend the equivalent of a day's wage for a workingman;[70] or that its impact outside Paris was less than the officials of the prefecture seemed to think. At the end of 1883 an ardent royalist in the Vendée wrote a monarchist official in Paris complaining that he had joined the Ligue Populaire Royaliste, which struck him as a welcome exception to the general pattern of royalist inertia, but had heard no word of it since.[71]

In the 1880s and 1890s royalists sponsored a number of youth groups. Official expressions of interest in the Jeunesses Royalistes were always coupled with expressions of concern about unpredictable elements, and warnings that "conservative youth must guard against a natural impetuosity as well as individual ambition."[72] There was some basis for this evident uneasiness about independent youth organizations. The activities of the Jeunesses Royalistes rarely rose above the level of student pranks, and with few exceptions its predominantly aristocratic membership behaved like a rebellious *jeunesse dorée,* justifying its own juvenile antics with veiled criticisms of the excessive caution of party leaders. The political activity of royalist youth was often limited to sending telegrams on royal birthdays and "receiving with joyful unctuousness the banal thanks of the pretender."[73]

Naturally, much was made of the supposed ability of the younger generation to transcend the gulf that separated most royalists from the lower ranks of French society. In fact, such attempts as were made to integrate the working classes into the royalist party were short-lived. Perfectly typical of such ventures was the royalist Comité Ouvrier in the Haute-Vienne, which folded within three months of its creation. The one hundred–odd workers in the group resented the fact that the affluent royalist leaders rarely bothered to attend the meetings, fearing, or so the workers believed, that their presence would compromise them in the eyes of their social peers. Having indignantly noted that royalists showed no apparent concern that workers might similarly be compromised, the group disbanded after auctioning off its few assets, including the library. As it happened, the royalist leaders were equally anxious to see the end of the Comité Ouvrier, having been disillusioned by the small number of workers attracted by the group, most of them unemployed, and irritated by the constant requests for money.[74] In 1888 royalists in the Haute-Garonne created the Comité Monarchique de la Démocratie Toulousaine, claiming 1,200 working-class members. Yet a year later workers who attended a meeting of the Comité Monarchique, in the belief that it was called to discuss the creation of workshops open only to royalist workers, were surprised and outraged to learn that none of the prominent local royalists had seen fit to attend, and that no one in authority seemed very anxious to talk about the proposed workshops.[75]

Some of the listlessness of royalist organization was undoubtedly the result of gradual despair at the prospect of a restoration, a sense that the royalist cause was lost, and a growing willingness to accept a conservative republic as a *pis-aller*. This was certainly true after 1890. But much of the evidence for the foregoing analysis is derived from 1888–89, years of feverish political activity and open possibilities. Boulanger's triumphs in the spring of 1888 could be, and usually were, interpreted as proof of a growing weariness with a corrupt and decadent regime; the Count of Paris was spending money as never before, and some kind of dramatic political change seemed imminent.

By the late 1880s the situation of French royalism was desperate but not beyond hope. Royalism remained the largest, most coherent, and most powerful alternative to the republican regime. While royalists retained the allegiance of only a minority of Frenchmen, the republican hold on the majority was not yet absolute. The sins of the regime had weakened the republican loyalty of a critical segment of the voters, and under the right circumstances an antirepublican majority was conceivable. But disillusionment with the existing regime did not automatically predispose voters toward the monarchy. It was therefore imperative that royalism present itself as a plausible and superior alternative to the republic. To do so necessitated a program attuned to the late rather than the early nineteenth century, and a political apparatus capable of presenting it effectively to the electorate. Royalist leaders, or at least the more politically astute among them, made a serious attempt to attain these prerequisites for political victory. They spoke interminably of the need to shake off the mentality of the *régime censitaire,* come to grips with universal suffrage, become "modern," "open," and above all "democratic."

Their efforts, however, were invariably undermined by the very nature of royalism and its principal adherents. Despite frequent allusions to democracy and modernity, French royalists could not adequately disguise their fundamental contempt for political democracy and its symbols; for them, democracy was not a superior kind of decision-making process but merely a means for coping with mass politics. Nor could they mask their hostility toward the increasingly assertive French middle classes. The same elitist preconceptions rendered ineffective any attempts to create a political machine comparable to that of their opponents. Royalists knew all about the theoretical advantages of continuous grass-roots activity but simply could not bring themselves to engage seriously in it. Their attempts directly to mobilize segments of the poorer classes, desultory enough to begin with, invariably foundered on the obvious insincerity of the project. In short, the direct mobilization of the masses was something that French royalists could not and would not achieve.

To create a significant popular movement whose ultimate trajectory would benefit the royalist project, three vital conditions had to obtain. First, the leaders and symbols of the movement could not evoke images of the old regime, ideologically or socially. Second, the immediate leaders of the movement would have to know how to get their hands dirty and adopt a style of politics suited to mass society. Finally, royalist control of the movement would have to be both secret and in the final instance total. The chance of attaining such conditions were inherently remote, but in 1888 and 1889 it appeared to many that the right combination was about to present itself.

3

Boulanger:
Savior of the Monarchy

By the end of 1887 French royalists desperately needed a savior. They found one in General Boulanger and the Boulangist movement. The discovery that General Boulanger, his past performance notwithstanding, was prepared to be the agent of a monarchist restoration offered the royalists a way out of their stagnation. The prospect of harnessing the dynamic and demagogic general was too tantalizing for the royalist leadership to ignore, but it also posed a host of daunting logical and logistical questions. How sincere and how permanent was Boulanger's "conversion"? How could his radical nationalist following be induced to follow him on his new course? Clearly Boulanger's change of heart had to remain secret, since any open accord with the royalists would deprive him of at least a critical segment of his support. Yet as long as Boulanger posed as a Jacobin, rank-and-file royalists could hardly be expected to aid his cause. Indeed, even if privy to Boulanger's secret intentions, many royalists would have doctrinaire objections to such unprincipled tactics. Others would have a well-founded skepticism about Boulanger's political acumen and his ability to deliver on his promise of a royalist restoration. The whole Boulangist gambit, therefore, depended on persuading both radical republicans and royalists to support Boulanger without either camp drawing some obvious conclusions from each other's deportment. The project was at best a highly problematic one. What is striking is how close the royalists came to pulling it off.

Even during Boulanger's "radical" phase, rumors circulated among conservatives that he was at heart a royalist.[1] The first formal suggestion of Boulanger's interest in the future of the monarchy came on 1 November 1887, when the general's confidant, Count Arthur Dillon, introduced himself to the Count of Paris in London. Dillon was a former army officer who had become a successful, if unorthodox, commercial entrepreneur. He had been a classmate of Boulanger at Saint-Cyr. Although his title was fraudulent, Dillon lived the life of an affluent *rentier,* frequented the aristocratic Jockey Club, and enjoyed intimate connections with powerful royalist families.[2] After expressing his own royalist convictions, Dillon insisted that Boulanger was also a conservative by temperament who felt increasingly ill at ease with his current radical companions. He now deeply regretted his earlier actions, most notably the expulsion of the royal princes. If the Count of Paris could forgive him, Boulanger might be of service to the royalist cause. Just how he would do so was left unspecified, and the Count of Paris limited his response to the platonic observation that "if he contributes in some way to the restoration of the monarchy," past sins would be forgotten. The pretender saw no need to inform his principal councillors of the interview.[3]

The details of the first direct contacts between Boulanger and the royalists are now well known and do not require detailed treatment. The initial alliance was struck in the midst of an exceedingly complex political crisis. In October 1887 Daniel Wilson, son-in-law of the President of the Republic, Jules Grévy, was charged with trafficking in official honors. The affair soon became a major scandal, discrediting Grévy in particular and the republican regime in general. In the face of Grévy's obstinate refusal to resign, the Chamber of Deputies overthrew the government of the day, whereupon all potential premiers refused to form a government until a new President had been chosen. The logical candidate to succeed Grévy was the elder statesman of the Opportunist republic, Jules Ferry. But Ferry was anathema to conservatives owing to his religious and educational policies, no more popular with Radicals because of his pacific foreign policy, and totally unacceptable to the increasingly militant crowds in the streets of Paris. The resulting stalemate opened up possibilities for everyone. Boulanger's gratuitous comments to the press concerning the Wilson scandal had earned him thirty days' confinement to barracks, so he was more eager than ever to replace the current minister of war. His nominal allies, the Radicals, toyed with the idea of supporting the beleaguered Grévy in exchange for the formation of a Radical government. A shabby deal with Grévy would, of course, outrage their electoral clientele, but inclusion of the popular Boulanger in the government might appease much of the wrath. In two celebrated secret meetings Radical leaders explored the possibility, but in the end all putative premiers either distrusted Boulanger or considered themselves promising candidates to succeed Grévy. In principle, any prolonged crisis of the republic was good news for the royalists, but as usual their deputies were badly divided as to how best to take advantage of events. The Count of Paris provided little useful guidance and his representatives floundered in incoherence.

As the political crisis reached its climax late in November, the royalist deputy from the Nord, Edmond de Martimprey,[4] approached one of Boulanger's former classmates at Saint-Cyr, René Félix de Hérissé, deputy from the Ille-et-Vilaine, and asked him about the rumors concerning the general's interest in the royalists. Le Hérissé, a former legitimist but now a Radical, confirmed that Boulanger might find an alliance with royalists useful for his ministerial ambitions. On November 29 Martimprey and the Baron de Mackau, president of the parliamentary Union des Droites, met Boulanger at Le Hérissé's house. Both royalists insisted that the current chaos clearly demonstrated the need for a strong government which only the Count of Paris could provide. Boulanger alone could ensure the necessary restoration. The general promptly agreed and suggested a method. If Freycinet were elected President, he would certainly insist on putting Boulanger back into the Ministry of War. Once in control of the army, Boulanger could quickly become master of France. The growing street demonstrations would be a pretext for a pronunciamento; a few score picked troops could effect it. Once the tarnished regime was overthrown, the monarchy would replace it, and Boulanger would accept the senior post in the new royal army. All he asked was that the plan receive the formal approbation of the pretender, whom he now unctuously referred to as Philippe VII.

In all relevant respects this was a most unlikely scheme. All that could be certain was that Boulanger wanted badly to become minister of war. Beyond that, there were no good reasons for believing anything he said. For all his casual references to December 2, it was obvious that he did not enjoy the same advantages as had Louis Napoleon, nor had he made comparable preparations. The entire enterprise hinged on the election of Freycinet, which Mackau, saddled with the need for secrecy and a fractious royalist caucus, was in no position to ensure. It is therefore a comment on the profound desperation of the royalist leaders that they took the idea at all seriously. Mackau promptly informed the Marquis de Beauvoir, the pretender's private secretary, and the two of them agreed to recommend the strategy to their leader. Each man dispatched a cryptic letter to the Count of Paris, alluding to an impending social and political crisis that could be resolved by a general who would then restore the monarchy. Because each assumed that the other had given more ample details, the letters were vague, and neither one actually mentioned Boulanger. The Count of Paris initially saw no obvious connection between the two letters and his earlier conversation with Dillon and assumed that the general in question was either Galliffet or Billot. He telegraphed Mackau, giving his approval, and only afterward realized that the providential general might be Boulanger and again telegraphed Mackau, demanding more information. Boulanger was shown the first telegram but not the second.

Worried by the apparent irresolution of the Count of Paris, his advisers attempted to inspire more confidence. Beauvoir and the Duc de Chartres both insisted that the risks involved were minimal and urged the pretender not to "close the door" on Boulanger.[5] The Count of Paris was a good deal less sanguine about an attempted coup and wanted no direct association with one, but obligingly conceded that if Boulanger wished on his own initiative to restore the monarchy, he would not quibble about his methods and would reward him with the post he sought.

Assuming a successful coup, it remained to be stated just how the monarchy would be restored. Fortunately the Count of Paris always had plenty of thoughts on that subject and quickly drafted a proposal for Boulanger's benefit. Once in power Boulanger would explain to the nation why he had overthrown the republic, inform it that a monarchy was the sole viable alternative, and demand popular sanction for his actions. He would govern in his own name for a brief transitional period while a new monarchist constitution was drafted. The constitution would be submitted to a plebiscite, after which the Count of Paris would be invited to become Philippe VII of France.

When Mackau and Martimprey presented the document to him on December 26, Boulanger of course accepted it, but not without reminding the royalists that he was not yet minister of war. Indeed, while the Count of Paris sorted out his generals, the political crisis had evaporated. On December 1 Grévy had at last resigned, and two days later the assembled deputies and senators had chosen a successor who was not Freycinet but the relative outsider Sadi Carnot, who had no interest in Boulanger. As even royalists privately acknowledged, Carnot soon proved to be an unexpectedly energetic and respectable head of state and the republican regime emerged the stronger. Royalists gradually lost interest in the quixotic scheme of the previous year.[6]

By the end of February 1888, however, Boulanger was again the center of national attention. His name appeared on the ballots in seven by-elections in widely scattered departments. Because of his active military status he was ineligible as a candidate, but he nonetheless attracted a total of 55,000 votes. Queried by the minister of war, Boulanger denied all knowledge of the attempt to present him before the electorate. Naturally, having taken the precaution of intercepting his mail, the government knew full well that Boulanger had authorized the ambitious Bonapartist journalist Georges Thiébaud to conduct the electoral campaign on his behalf. The appearance of the first "Boulangist" newspaper, *La Cocarde,* in the second week of March only confirmed Boulanger's overt electoral ambitions. He was therefore suspended from active duty for three months on the pretext that he had left his command without permission to visit his mistress. His Radical allies in Paris responded with a Committee of National Protest which sponsored Boulanger's name in the next series of by-elections. Although still ineligible, on March 25 he headed the first ballot in an election in the Aisne. The next day he was dismissed from the army.

It was not at all clear to royalists how, or if, they fitted into Boulanger's plebiscitary campaign. A man who could get elected without even formally standing as a candidate was likely to have second thoughts about settling for the senior post in someone else's army. Their anxieties would have been all the more intense had they known that the same Thiébaud who had orchestrated Boulanger's electoral debut had also introduced him to the Bonapartist pretender in January. Worse, even if Boulanger were faithful to his declared intentions of the previous year, his renewed national prominence made him the object of a major hate campaign on the part of virtually all royalists in France.

The political resurgence of Boulanger was of course a serious embarrassment to the government, but few royalists were thereby comforted and the royalist press began a savage campaign against "le Général Béni Sera Le Jour." Boulanger's dubious past and unsavory personal life fueled the editorial venom. To disguise himself on his illicit and celebrated visits to his Parisian mistress, Boulanger had donned dark glasses and carried a cane. This episode prompted some delightfully sardonic editorial sallies. One newspaper mirthfully warned readers against giving alms to any blind cripples they might come across, lest they offend the general who was singlehandedly about to restore Alsace and Lorraine to France. In the old days, another mused, conspirators typically hid daggers under gray cloaks; thanks to the progress of science and democracy, the rapier and slouch hat had given way to the crutch and dark glasses, and in place of the dashing condottiere there now stood "the more modern and humble pose of the crippled and blind."[7]

In the main, however, Boulanger was a source of anxiety, not mirth. At best he presaged a new version of the 18 Brumaire or December 2 which would destroy the republic without restoring the monarchy. The idea might appeal to Jeromist Bonapartists but hardly the royalists. Moreover, many royalists doubted that he was capable of establishing a plebiscitary dictatorship. He was after all no Napoleon but a crass opportunist with the talents of a passable colonel. With considerable prescience one editorialist insisted that Boulanger "will make no coup d'état, will overthrow no parliament and, on the day when 50,000 hoodlums want to lead him down the Boulevard to the Elysée, he will hide."[8] An aborted coup would lead inevitably to "the hideous despotism of the populace, the bloody tyranny of the street," and the worst days of 1793 or 1871. Given Boulanger's "communard promiscuities" and an entourage consisting of "the worst revolutionaries and enemies of society" the whole enterprise seemed destined to lead to revolution.[9] Even a successful Boulangist coup would have devastating domestic consequences, owing to the bellicose nationalism of "le général Revanche" and his followers. War, royalists insisted, was the handmaiden of revolution, and with Boulanger in power war would be inevitable.[10]

Occasionally royalist newspapers alluded to the possibility that Boulanger might, in the right hands, be of use to the monarchy. Royalists impatient with the passivity of the pretender were particularly susceptible to the dynamics of Boulangism. *L'Echo de la frontière,* in an editorial entitled *"Audaces fortuna juvat,"* contrasted the action of Boulanger with the relative inertia of royalist leadership. An impatient populace now looked to the saber for salvation and no longer cared who was wielding it. By manipulating "the street, popular passion, and publicity," Boulanger had created a potent force which, skillfully used, could become "the instrument of God's will."[11] Such speculation, however, remained atypical. For every editorial suggesting that Boulanger's successes augured well for the monarchy, a score countered that they presaged war and revolution. Yet royalist newspapers felt increasingly obliged to denounce unnamed conservatives who blindly and naively looked to Boulanger as a way to escape from the republic. This uneasiness, widespread among the royalist rank and file by the beginning of April, was the result of two inescapable realities: many Frenchmen who ordinarily voted for conservatives were obviously voting for Boulanger, while the leadership of the royalist party had manifestly not taken a clear and unequivocal position on the new phenomenon.

Royalist voters were not heeding the dire warnings of the local press. The Maine-et-Loire was a disciplined royalist department where all eight royalist candidates had been elected in 1885 with only 3,000 votes separating all members of the list. Yet in a February 1888 by-election, in spite of the efforts of several royalist deputies, large numbers of royalist voters had supported Boulanger. More than 10,000 of his 11,400 votes had come from the rural and conservative cantons; by contrast the three principal towns of Angers, Cholet, and Saumur had, as a local royalist paper bitterly noted, "remained republican with a heroism worthy of a better cause."[12] On April 8 he was elected in the Dordogne with a 24,000-vote majority. The Dordogne was a strongly Bonapartist department, but the republicans had narrowly won there in 1885. His margin of victory was impressive, and so was the fact that he received the overwhelming support not only of Bonapartists but also of royalists.[13]

The royalist leadership was giving little guidance in these matters because it was reassessing its relationship with Boulanger. The general's adoption of a plebiscitary strategy was a source of relief to the Count of Paris, for whom the earlier suggestions of a coup d'état seemed fraught with the dangers of civil war and foreign complications. His advisers were more uneasy. Beauvoir noted that, as a result of his phenomenal electoral success, Boulanger was no longer the same man "who once made so many fine promises to Mackau. He said at that time, 'Just let me become minister of war and one fine day I will deliver power to you on a platter.' But today it is no longer a question of a minister of war making a coup d'état, but rather of a plebiscite with hundreds of thousands of voters designating him for the highest office." A coup d'état had been a risky enough idea, but at least it might be a clean surgical stroke, and Boulanger's sole accomplices would be the army and the royalists. What troubled Beauvoir was that, once Boulanger had effectively launched a plebiscite in his own name, his collaborators would be the traditional political rabble that bedeviled France, "springing up like mushrooms on the *nouvelles couches boulangistes*."[14] With his own solid and enthusiastic electoral base, Boulanger could become relatively independent of his royalist allies. This danger would haunt the royalists for the next eighteen months.

Nonetheless, at the beginning of March the royalists and Boulanger renewed their contacts. Exactly who met whom and when has been hotly contested, and even today some aspects of the negotiations remain obscure, since partners on both sides often had reasons to dissimulate their actions. Of the basic outlines, however, there is no doubt.[15] On March 5 Mackau and Martimprey met General Boulanger at the house of Le Hérissé. Boulanger announced that his earlier plan was outmoded and that he now intended to take advantage of his electoral popularity to seek the presidency of the republic. He would present himself in the forthcoming by-elections in the Aisne, the Dordogne, and the Nord, campaigning on a platform of constitutional revision. He assured Mackau that he was not in league with the Bonapartists (who were voting en masse for him), and that his sentiments with respect to the Count of Paris were what they had been in December. Two weeks later Count Dillon contacted Beauvoir and assured him that Boulanger was a monarchist who had no intention of ruling in his own right but sought only to restore the Count of Paris to the throne. He also requested a campaign subvention of 25,000 francs, which Beauvoir promptly obtained from the wealthy royalist dowager, the Duchesse d'Uzès. Within ten days Dillon was back, this time seeking 100,000 francs for Boulanger's projected campaign in the Nord. Beauvoir sought out Marquis Henri de Breteuil, royalist deputy from the Basses-Pyrénées, who secured the requested sum from his personal friend Baron Maurice de Hirsch.

Not entirely convinced by Dillon's facile promises, Breteuil and Beauvoir wanted direct contact with the general. In addition to Mackau, Beauvoir, Martimprey, and Breteuil, three other conservative leaders were by now aware of the negotiations with Boulanger: Jacques Piou, deputy from the Haute-Garonne, had been told by Mackau in December, while Paul de Cassagnac had been informed by Le Hérissé, and Albert de Mun, deputy from the Morbihan, by Martimprey. The seven met early on April 1 and agreed to act in concert. Four days later Beauvoir and Breteuil met directly with Boulanger. News that the royalists had formed a committee to deal with him greatly troubled Boulanger, as did the realization that a number of leading royalists now knew of the recent financial transactions. It was obvious that the royalists were seeking to manipulate him more effectively, but he could hardly say so. He spent most of the interview protesting his lack of interest in money and complaining that the circle of royalist conspirators was expanding too rapidly. Pressed by Beauvoir for some tangible statement of intentions that might be transmitted to the Count of Paris, Boulanger said nothing beyond vague assurances that he was working for the good of the nation. The royalists left visibly disappointed and the next day informed Dillon that, without a far more explicit statement from Boulanger, no further royalist cooperation could be expected.

Dillon appears to have been impressed because the next time Boulanger met Breteuil, Martimprey, and Mackau, on April 9, he was more forthcoming. This time Boulanger assured the royalists that he shared entirely the attitude of Dillon, who would shortly leave for London to consult the Count of Paris. To disarm royalist skepticism, he invoked the question that had most troubled them: foreign policy. He insisted that his greatest worry at the moment was the fear of war and foreign invasion. Monarchical Europe, unaware that his reputation as a warmonger was, as he blithely noted, completed unfounded, might be tempted to make a preemptive strike once he had attained power. Only the Count of Paris with his international connections could reassure the courts of Europe about Boulanger's pacifistic intentions. Finally, and for the first time, he spoke of the projected division of electoral labor. France could be divided into three regions: conservative ones which he would leave alone; Radical ones which even he could not conquer; and those areas where Boulanger or Boulangists could, if allied with conservatives, defeat governmental republicans. In his rudimentary sketch of electoral strategy, Boulanger spoke a language that the desperate royalists could understand. Doubts about Boulanger persisted, but by now the conspirators were prepared to recommend the general to their leader.

At the very moment when royalists began to convince the Count of Paris that Boulanger could be harnessed to the monarchist cause, the department of the Nord gave them a graphic and dramatic demonstration of Boulanger's political potential. The Nord was an ideal region for royalists to select to invest their 100,000 francs in Boulanger. It had a substantial, if declining, conservative electorate and no conservative candidate to vote for. The population of the Nord was deeply and militantly Catholic. Although the textile, mining, and metallurgical industries of the department had created a substantial industrial working class, these had not yet been attracted to socialism. The Opportunists, the principal alternative to the conservatives in the Nord, were primarily preoccupied with agricultural questions and offered little for the urban workers. Consequently conservatives, some of whom espoused a social Catholicism, retained considerable electoral support even in this milieu. In 1885 the conservative list swept the department, electing all twenty of the deputies including two Bonapartists, seven avowed royalists, and eleven royalists who preferred the vaguer appellation of "conservative." The head of the conservative list received 164,924 votes; his Opportunist counterpart, 123,184. In both cases the spread between the top and bottom of the lists was less than 10,000 votes, and the Radical and socialist vote was negligible.

The results of the 1885 elections were, however, misleading, because the conservative victory was largely attributable to local and temporary considerations. The agricultural crisis of 1883–85, which saw a precipitous drop in wheat and sugar-beet prices, and the poor harvest of 1885 helped conservatives who campaigned on a platform of tariff reform. By 1887, however, new agricultural tariffs had been introduced and conservative fortunes declined accordingly. In three by-elections in

1886 and 1887 republican candidates received between 145,515 and 147,275 votes, whereas conservatives obtained only 121,853 to 124,880. These figures, rather than the electoral anomaly of 1885, give a clear indication of the relative strengths in the department, as well as the ebbing influence of conservatives.[16]

So discouraged were the royalists of the Nord by the by-elections of the previous year that prior to the April election only seven of the seventy members of the local conservative committee wanted to run a candidate. Even they, led by the doyen of deputies from the Nord, Charles Plichon, thought victory impossible and wanted only to show the flag. The conservative committee announced that it was husbanding its resources for the general elections of 1889 and indicated that its supporters should vote for neither Boulanger nor his republican opponent. When pressed, local royalist spokesmen reiterated the official position: "ni l'un ni l'autre"; but in fact, the invective of their local newspapers was directed almost exclusively at Boulanger's opponent. Moreover several of the royalist deputies of the department actively campaigned on behalf of the general.[17]

The election of April 15 was a spectacular success for Boulanger. He obtained 172,853 votes, compared to 75,901 for the Opportunist candidate and 7,648 for the Radical. The first reaction of the Marquis de Breteuil, still in London discussing the Boulangist strategy with the pretender, was that royalists had received good value for their money.[18] And more than money had gone into Boulanger's first dramatic electoral breakthrough—so had a great many royalist votes. In his detailed analysis of the Boulangist elections in the Nord, Jacques Néré focused primarily on working-class and republican support for Boulanger. But even by his account, a majority of Boulanger's vote came from conservatives. To be sure, in areas of conservative strength—Flanders, textile-producing regions, and the rural communes generally—Boulanger did not attain the level of support reached by conservatives in 1885. By contrast, in areas traditionally dominated by republicans—the cities and the mining regions—Boulanger's support significantly exceeded that of conservatives in 1885. The distribution of votes and the high rate of abstentions suggest that many conservatives, without a candidate of their own and distrustful of Boulanger, did not vote. Radical and socialist voters, by comparison, presented with a candidate who appeared to appeal to their interests, voted disproportionately for the general. Nonetheless, in spite of some abstentions on the Right and marginal working-class support, the great majority of Boulanger's votes came from conservatives. Néré, despite his preoccupation with leftist support for

Boulanger, estimates that about 100,000 of his 172,000 votes were cast by conservatives.[19] Some contemporaries thought conservative support for Boulanger to have been substantially higher.[20] What is incontestable is that the bulk of Boulanger's support, the magnitude of the victory, and the victory itself were due to French conservatives.

The special significance of this election was not lost on rank-and-file royalists. The absence of a royalist candidate provoked outrage in much of the royalist press. To some degree the adverse editorial comment was part of a long history of journalistic whining about the insufficiencies of royalist action. But the reaction was uncharacteristically sharp, replete with angry (and well-founded) allusions to "secret deals" and "complicity."[21] The dramatic demonstration of Boulanger's electoral appeal, however, prompted some striking *volte-face*. Newspapers that had long treated readers to the standard war-and-revolution diatribes now discovered that Boulanger sought to maintain the peace. Boulanger's much-emphasized personal bankruptcy suddenly became proof that he would not seize power in his own name but would be content with the honorific post of grand constable in a restored monarchy. Once dismissed as a crony of the Communards, Boulanger was now resurrected as the courageous general who "side by side with conservatives did his duty against the Commune." The crimes of Henri de Rochefort, once a staple of Boulanger stories, were increasingly replaced with accounts of the attacks on "le brav' général" by Louise Michel, the Red Virgin of the Paris Commune. The previous month's warnings about domestic radicalism gave way to references to Boulanger's "useful tasks," a possible "year of deliverance," and the need for conservatives to "maneuver skillfully."[22]

This cautious, and by no means unanimous, acceptance of Boulanger's potential utility nonetheless left some important questions unanswered. It was by no means apparent just how royalists would take advantage of Boulanger's assault on the republic. Given that the effective precondition for Boulanger's electoral triumphs was the effacement of the royalist party, the mechanics of a timely monarchist reassertion were not self-evident. Edouard Hervé, who had dramatically run against Boulanger in Marseilles two months previously, now conceded that Boulanger's seizure of power was inevitable. The task ahead would clearly be to replace a Boulangist dictatorship with a monarchy. But how, he rather belligerently asked the Count of Paris, could this be accomplished, when French royalists were keeping such a low profile and their troops were flocking to the camp of the general? If French royalists were to be moved to action, they would need a heartier diet than the pretender's learned treatises on government. Hervé was clearly thinking of a coup d'état and he was not alone. The Duc de Doudeauville-Rochefoucauld, one of the staunchest western royalists, noted that the Count's measured manifestos were usually ignored and were less useful to the royalist cause than a few thousand men "ready to march." He too believed that "the monarchy will not be restored legally and that a coup d'état must be prepared. We must not let slip the first opportunity that presents itself; otherwise it will be too late." Both men were hostile to Boulanger, not because they suspected him of plotting a coup, but because they feared that royalists were not doing likewise.

For many, the astonishing success of Boulangism highlighted the despair of royalists, who seldom heard from their king. Paul Lebreton, senator from the Mayenne, insisted that the royal silence had let "the most conservative popular masses grow accustomed to considering the circus general as the sole savior capable of rescuing them." Boulanger would obtain the support of "a certain number of impatient royalists who despaired of the restoration of the monarchy because they had waited too long and because their king does not speak." Another noble noted that whereas the Bonapartist presenter, Prince Victor, lived just beyond the frontier in Brussels, the Count of Paris was all too comfortably installed in London, which did not suggest that he expected to return imminently.[23]

Indeed, a major problem for the royalist leadership was persuading the Count of Paris to take a firm stand on Boulanger or anything else. Upon his return from Spain on April 14, Beauvoir and Breteuil recounted in detail the events of the last few weeks. The pretender endorsed their actions but manifested no great enthusiasm for the project, maintaining the indecisive reserve that would characterize his relationship to the Boulanger affair throughout. On April 16, the day after Boulanger's election in the Nord, Breteuil and Beauvoir were joined by Mackau, Martimprey, Bocher, and de Mun in a major strategy session with the pretender. The Count of Paris appeared more reticent than ever, wanting solid evidence of Boulanger's good faith. Jacques Piou and Paul de Cassagnac, neither one present, had indicated the need for a written engagement from Boulanger. Mackau shared their sentiment but, as he had earlier informed the pretender, such a demand was both insulting and quite pointless in the light of Boulanger's past record with respect to written commitments.[24] Yet Mackau, Breteuil, and Martimprey all professed to believe Boulanger's expression of devotion to the monarchist cause, contending that the general was a typical military man, neither liking nor understanding politics and far more attracted by the prospect of a prominent place in the army than by a comparable place in the state.

Still, the Count of Paris countered, even if Boulanger could be trusted, there remained the thorny problem of explaining any radical tactical realignment to French royalists. Since they obviously could not be apprised of the secret negotiations, most would be treated to the demoralizing spectacle of royalist inertia or complicity in the face of an undisciplined and unsavory general whose professed allies were mostly pernicious sectarians. Were Boulanger's popularity to prove ephemeral, was it not as shrewd tactically to ally with conservative republicans against the radical republic in its Boulangist guise? Bocher, only recently informed of the secret negotiations and visibly displeased, argued vigorously for this course.[25]

The others present insisted that the wave of popular anger tapped by Boulanger was irresistible. Royalists, they argued, could not and probably should not oppose the general; by contrast they could and probably ought to join him. It was essential "to find an electoral terrain very close to that of the general, if [royalists] don't want to be swept away by the Boulangist tide." In the face of the continued resistance of the prince and Bocher, Albert de Mun, asking pardon in advance for the bluntness of his language, pointedly reminded the pretender about the current state of the royalist party in France. In a word, he argued, there really wasn't one any longer. Even the clergy had grown increasingly indifferent to the dynastic question. There simply were too few people left in France with any direct experience of the monarchy and consequently with much enthusiasm for it. Royalists were unlikely to regain power by universal suffrage; in the next election Boulangism in all probability would destroy much of what was left of royalist representation. Fortunately, de Mun continued, thanks to a "providential permission," the man responsible for this wave of popular passion had "just offered to serve His Majesty and to turn to the profit of the monarchy the support of the extraordinary forces he has at his disposal." Given the chronic weakness of French royalism, Boulangism represented an unparalleled and probably final opportunity for the monarchy.

The crux of de Mun's case for a Boulangist strategy was the inability of the royalist party defending an unadulterated royalist cause to succeed by electoral politics. It was these assumptions that Bocher chose to contest. The royalist party showed far more vitality than de Mun gave it credit for, he insisted; in eighty departments royalist committees were active and yielding results. In an emotional address he asserted that the real threat to the monarchist cause in France was not its alleged inertia, but the temptation to follow a renegade general in a momentary and inevitably abortive adventure. What impact would such a policy have on the royalist following, and what would posterity have to say about their prince? For the *vieux jeux,* as the anti-Boulangist advisers of the prince would soon be known, Boulangism was both dishonorable and unnecessary. Significantly, Count Othenin d'Haussonville, second only to Bocher among the *vieux jeux,* would write the Count of Paris within ten days, echoing his arguments: "Our internal organization is much stronger and more complete than is generally thought. All we lack is the exterior decor."[26]

The trouble with invoking the inherent strength of the royalist party as an argument against an alliance with Boulanger was that it was singularly uncompelling. For all his impassioned rhetoric on April 16, Bocher had written enough reports in the last two years for the prince to know that de Mun's assessment of royalist strength was nearer the truth. Increasingly (as Haussonville would discover to his dismay, when he replaced Bocher), the royalist party in most parts of France amounted to "très peu de chose."

The Count of Paris raised the logical question of explaining a significant political realignment to the royalist rank and file. The ever abrasive de Mun permitted himself to suggest that the head of the royal house need not explain anything and ought to avail himself of the royal prerogative of demanding obedience from refractory monarchists. Moreover, he suggested, the real nature of the alliance could be disguised, if royalists stayed on the ambiguous terrain of constitutional revision and national consultation. Lest this seem to be (as it in fact was) a direct imitation of Boulanger, royalists could invoke the quasi-plebiscitary instructions issued by the prince in the previous autumn. Once a source of consternation in royalist circles, the now nearly forgotten Instructions would permit embarrassed royalists to insist that "revisionism" had been their tactic all along.

The Count of Paris let himself be persuaded by these arguments. They did after all come from individuals of widely divergent political temperaments and from different regions of France, and who, with the exception of Bocher, were adamant that Boulanger was an irresistible force. Yet he betrayed little enthusiasm and left Martimprey with the distinct impression that he would have been happier had the general not existed. On the question of money, which was self-evidently central to the whole enterprise, the pretender was vague and noncommittal. To the dismay of those present, he spoke at length about a forthcoming royalist manifesto. Since the logic of the entire discussion had presumed the complete futility of any more carefully crafted manifestos, the pretender's commitment to the new enterprise seemed decidedly tepid. He did, however, promise to moderate the anti-Boulangist language of those French newspapers over which he could exercise some control.

Two days later the pretender and Count Dillon discussed the electoral mechanics of their alliance.[27] After winning a series of by-elections on the platform of dissolution and revision, Boulanger would persuade a majority of deputies that there was an irresistible popular current seeking dissolution of the Chamber and new elections. In the elections Boulanger would stay out of those departments where royalists retained a secure hold. In the remaining departments Boulanger would invariably head the electoral slate, but would reserve a generous portion of each list for royalists willing to accept his revisionist stance. Given Boulanger's unprecedented electoral attractiveness, there could be no doubt that the newly elected Chamber would be dominated by Boulangists and royalists, and its first step would be to abolish both the presidency of the republic and the Senate. Now the exclusive source of sovereignty, the Chamber would become in effect a constituent assembly entirely in the hands of the general. Boulanger would then propose to it a new monarchist constitution, drafted in consultation with the Count of Paris. Once the assembly adopted it, the new constitution would be submitted to the population by a carefully worded referendum, and the Count of Paris would be invited to return to the throne of France. Boulanger would then settle for the senior military post in France.

The Count of Paris pointedly wondered if this grandiose scheme was really Boulanger's idea or simply Dillon's. He also asked if Boulanger had the requisite political acumen to carry the plan through its complex stages. Dillon predictably answered both questions in the affirmative. After dropping some suggestive hints about Bonapartist interest in the general, he also made much of Boulanger's ardent desire for peace and the need for the pretender to inform the courts and chancelleries of Europe about the irenical nature of France's latest political sensation. The Count of Paris appears to have been impressed, because he promised to raise the matter with the Prince of Wales, his principal intermediary with the German Emperor. Five days later he spoke with the frankly incredulous English prince, disabused him of his belief in Boulanger's bellicosity and persuaded him to mention Boulanger's unsuspected conservative and peace-loving credentials when next in Berlin.

No further commitments were made. The Count of Paris promised to moderate the tone of some royalist journals, but insisted that he could in no sense endorse the general. Dillon responded that this suited Boulanger's tactics perfectly and warmly applauded the draft of the manifesto which had so distressed the pretender's advisers two days before.

The manifesto, published on April 25, declared that the "recent and striking manifestations of universal suffrage" demonstrated a widespread national disgust with existing political institutions and a desire for fundamental constitutional change. Alluding to his 1887 Instructions, the Count of Paris reminded Frenchmen that royalists had been the first to call for constitutional revision as the only means of national salvation. Avoiding any direct attacks on Boulanger, he nonetheless insisted that only the monarchy and not "a single name" could rescue France. It was a typical product of the Count of Paris: thoughtfully crafted with nicely turned phrases, but admitting of radically different readings.

As the Duc de Broglie argued, the only possible way for a royalist to read the manifesto was as a call to restore the revisionist idea's original royalist connotation and redirect it in "an overtly and exclusively monarchist sense." This was clearly the construction put on the manifesto by the quasi totality of the royalist press. But, as de Broglie lamented, the absence of any explicit criticism of Boulanger permitted some in the royalist camp, and not the least of them, to treat the latest pronouncement as "the authorization to enroll in General Boulanger's electoral campaign." In fact, of course, it was designed to be read both ways: to reassure those who distrusted Boulanger and wanted a more assertive royal profile, as well as to justify those of his followers who were clearly in alliance with the general. In the subtle reasoning of the Count of Paris these two positions were not necessarily incompatible, as long as one separated monarchist principles from electoral tactics. He windily assured Broglie that his interpretation of the manifesto was the correct one, while in the same breath calling for a cessation of personal attacks on Boulanger and suggesting that Broglie's *Moniteur Universel* might tone down its treatment of the pro-Boulangist royalist deputies.[28]

The ambivalent nature of the pretender's declaration and its mixed reception exemplified the difficulties inherent in the proposed Boulangist-royalist alliance. Boulanger and his entourage could be difficult allies—badly organized, lacking in discipline and internal cohesion, and utterly avaricious. Yet the chief obstacle to an effective collaboration was the resistance of many French royalists, not least of all the prince. Although the Count of Paris had given the whole enterprise his qualified endorsement, he was sensitive to the repeated expressions of disapprobation coming from some of his intimate advisers, notably Haussonville and Bocher.[29] He would therefore continue to cavil over fine points of doctrine and insist on scrupulous distinctions which served little purpose save to mitigate his own complicity in the Boulangist affair.

By May it was apparent that Boulangism and the revisionist campaign had a dynamic of their own. For royalists to appear to be leading rather than following the current of revisionism, it was necessary to take some dramatic initiative. Royalist leaders considered a national conservative congress where the dissolution, revision, and national consultation program could be launched, but ultimately rejected the idea, since at any large gathering of royalists dissent and controversy were inevitable.[30] It seemed more practical to persuade the various conservative deputies in the Chamber to launch a campaign in favor of revision. There would be resistance from the legitimist deputies from the west, but this could be overcome by invoking the authority of the Count of Paris. Since the conservative deputies, while in majority royalist, also included Bonapartists, solutionists, and dynastically unaffiliated conservatives, the adoption of a politically ambiguous revisionist stance would less obviously compromise royalist principles. Royalist strategists persuaded Dillon that the initiative for the campaign was to come from the conservative deputies who, on May 25, formally adopted the dissolution, revision, consultation formula. A Committee of Twelve was formed to coordinate these actions, containing four representatives from each of the parliamentary groups.[31]

Shortly thereafter the committee founded the Ligue de la Consultation Nationale, intended to mobilize public opinion behind the revisionist campaign. A further purpose of the league was to instill some vigor into conservative political life and to create an electoral machine comparable to that of the republicans. Significantly, Cassagnac introduced the league to his readers with an article entitled "Faisons comme eux." The secretary general of the league and its effective director was Jules Auffray, an energetic and ambitious young royalist who was simultaneously the secretary of the parliamentary Union des Droites. Auffray immediately organized a series of league meetings throughout France and during the next six months strove to create a united revisionist front.[32]

No sooner had the campaign begun, however, when the Count of Paris began partially to disavow the work of his confidants. There were, he felt, too many Bonapartists on the Committee of Twelve. Moreover the committee had employed the expression "direct consultation," which in the political lexicon of the times had a distinctly Bonapartist connotation. Worse, the Ligue de la Consultation Nationale threatened to encroach on the work of the existing royalist committees and had thereby provoked the ire of the notional head of the royalist organization, Lambert de Sainte-Croix. As a result, royalist intransigents in both the official and semiofficial royalist press decried the whole revisionist venture as a surrender not only to Boulangism but to Bonapartism. The frantic appeals of his lieutenants for direct support were rebuffed by the Count of Paris with some stern lectures on the niceties of political theory.

His nonplussed lieutenants tried in vain to assure him that the league sought neither to rival the royalist organization nor to deprive it of resources. With seven loyal royalists and Cassagnac, the Committee of Twelve was firmly under royalist control, so much so, in fact, that Prince Victor was actively denouncing his own representatives on the committee. The expression "direct consultation" was, as Cassagnac noted, taken directly from the pretender's 1887 Instructions; the word "direct" had, in any case, been quietly dropped by the league. Their negotiations with Boulanger were rendered even more difficult when their authority was openly challenged by a royalist press which the head of the party was making only half-hearted efforts to coordinate. As the Duc de Chartres pointedly reminded his brother, men like Cassagnac and Mackau were of far more practical value than was Lambert de Sainte-Croix and ought not to be treated to veiled disavowals. In the light of the agreement struck in April, the pretender's nitpicking on questions of orthodoxy and royalist organization were highly tendentious; a discouraged and disillusioned group of conspirators threatened to resign.[33]

The intense exasperation of the royalist strategists reflected their basic dilemma: they were attempting a bold and risky gamble under the authority of a weak and irresolute prince. The Count of Paris wanted to effect a radical change in royalist policy without anyone really noticing and without having to suffer the attendant consequences. This was clearly impossible. Passing off the revisionist campaign as but a logical continuation of royalist doctrine was an unpromising ploy. Invoking the Instructions of 1887 would do little to mollify those royalists who, even then, had thought them a careless capitulation to the principles of Bonapartism. To claim, as Breteuil did in a May interview in *Le Matin,* that Boulanger had stolen revisionism from the royalists was both false and unconvincing. While it gave the increasingly uncomfortable royalist editorialists something to grasp at, the charge of Boulangist plagiarism was greeted with derision by anyone who thought about it. As the influential republican Emmanuel Arène mirthfully observed, the contention was reminiscent of the cuckolded husband who tried to minimize his embarrassment by insisting that he had, after all, enjoyed his errant wife before all the others had. The Duc d'Harcourt wryly reminded his prince that when it came to political platforms there was little point in invoking copyright law. Regardless of who held the original patent, revision was now universally seen as a chief tenet of Boulangism, and the royalists appeared merely to be following suit.[34]

Having reconciled the apparent contradictions in his own mind, the Count of Paris discovered that his finely tuned synthesis could not satisfy all the camps in France. The strong endorsement sought by Breteuil, de Mun, and Mackau would only antagonize other equally important lieutenants. Not only were Bocher and Haussonville hostile, but even the ever loyal Defeuille, as yet unapprised of the "secret," tactfully observed that while royalist propaganda and electoral tactics were logically distinct, in practice the latter drove out the former. Lambert de Sainte-Croix, nominally still the head of the royalist party in France, grew increasingly embittered as he watched his influence dwindle and attempted repeatedly to sabotage the new course. Periodic invitations to London and the delicate diplomacy of Beauvoir and Bocher delayed but could not prevent his final rupture with the prince.[35]

Lambert's undersecretary, Edmond Boucher, responsible for the departmental press and for the *Correspondance Nationale,* was equally adamant about Boulanger. The Count of Paris wrote him repeatedly complaining of the "excessive" tone of much of the royalist press, formally requesting that he "soften the expressions referring to General Boulanger" because practical politics dictated "an extreme moderation and almost a sincere effort at courtesy with respect to him." None of this had much effect on Boucher, probably because the pretender's letters were also filled with gratuitous allusions to the dangers of Boulangism. Until his final resignation in September, Boucher persisted in giving Boulanger the kind of editorial coverage that the pretender continued patiently to "regret."[36]

The Duc de Broglie was another problem. Believed by many royalists to be an authoritative spokesman for the Count of Paris, Broglie was in fact entirely independent. He never made any secret of his contempt for Boulangism. Asked why French royalists could not emulate the populist campaign style of Boulanger, he replied that one "might just as well ask an honest woman why, with her physical attractions, she cannot earn as much as another who uses them to obtain a furnished apartment and a well-appointed carriage." Broglie's *Moniteur universel* was a great favorite among a portion of the provincial press which erroneously took its editorials to represent the position of the pretender. His disapprobation was shared by the Duc d'Aumale, who bluntly wondered if the Count of Paris's latest stratagem was "as clever as it is bold." As he later observed, the only person in Boulanger's entourage who impressed him was the the general's mistress. Aumale rarely approved of his nephew's actions, of course, and had little interest in politics, but his moral stature among old-guard royalists was high.[37]

The opposition to Boulanger by prominent Orleanists like Bocher, Haussonville, Broglie, Aumale, and Lambert de Sainte-Croix has led most historians to couch the intraroyalist debate in terms of Orleanism and legitimism, and some have gone so far as to assign exclusive responsibility for the Boulangist gamble to the legitimists and a "legitimized" pretender.[38] There is no doubt that many leading Orleanists were unenthusiastic or openly hostile—a perspective shared by the nominally Orleanist "milieux d'affaires." It is equally true that some legitimists saw Boulanger as the savior of the French monarchy. Albert de Mun is the obvious example, but the dogmatically unrepentant legitimist Baron Tristan Lambert became an equally passionate convert to Boulangism.[39]

Yet in practice the categories of Orleanist and legitimist (rarely invoked by contemporaries) did not have the sharp contours usually assigned them by historians of political thought. The Orleanist credentials of the anti-Boulangist Pierre Calla were impeccable. As he incessantly reminded everyone, his family had served the Orleanists for a century and his grandfather had been charged with the education of the future king, Louis-Philippe. But by the late 1880s his principal constituency was the legitimist west, where he was a favorite speaker. Lambert de Sainte-Croix, another faithful Orleanist, struck Breteuil and Mackau as "a royalist of the old school . . . incapable of mentioning the king without simultaneously mentioning God," a man whose political thought was fundamentally closer to the Count of Chambord's than to the Count of Paris's.[40] Moreover, for every Orleanist who opposed the alliance there were others—Beauvoir, Piou, the Duc de Chartres, Jules Auffray—who were actively committed to it. Although Breteuil had once been associated with Bonapartism (like more than one intransigent Orleanist), his open admiration for British parliamentary institutions placed him well within the Orleanist tradition. An Orleanist *vielle souche* like Dufeuille was, by October 1888, so enthusiastic about the general that even de Mun began to urge that he moderate his pro-Boulangist effusions.[41] As for Bocher, whose reservations are so often cited, he was never very keen on schemes that involved spending large amounts of money. Yet from the summer of 1888 on he was a central participant in the whole Boulangist enterprise and, when it was all over, he assured the Count of Paris that he and the arch-Boulangist Mackau had been "constantly and entirely in agreement on everything."[42] These were not the words of a principled opponent of Boulangism. In fact the doubts expressed by certain Orleanists were mild, when compared with the vocal attacks emanating from the legitimist redoubt in the west.

What divided royalists were not conflicting principles but differing assessments about whether or not Boulangism was necessary or feasible. In the west the relative security of many royalists rendered Boulangism a superfluous gambit. Among the financial and business elite, whose commitment to royalism was increasingly platonic, any extralegal assault on the republic—or even a dramatic political upheaval—seemed dysfunctional. Even the most stubborn partisans of the alliance conceded that the risks were very real. None of the central actors betrayed many illusions about Boulanger's personal integrity or the sincerity of his professions of royalism. Piou conceded that Boulangism "might . . . vanish overnight," and Beauvoir admitted that the proposed strategy was "neither the best way nor the most desirable nor the safest."[43] It was, however, the only strategy royalists had left. Their *relative* confidence in Boulanger reflected their superior knowledge of his private contacts with royalists. Significantly, when Haussonville first learned in October that Breteuil had secretly met Boulanger and extracted some formal commitments, he expressed unmistakable relief.[44] With the dangers as well as the possibilities of the Boulangist alliance so evenly balanced, small differences in temperament, self-interest, or knowledge could determine the position of individual royalists.

Electoral considerations weighed more heavily than ideological ones in the debate on Boulangism. The fact that the revisionist campaign had the quasi-unanimous approbation of royalist deputies suggested to some royalist notables that most of them had scrapped their monarchist principles in their haste to ensure reelection. This was a favorite argument among royalist senators who, with a few exceptions, disapproved of a revisionist campaign that might lead to the abolition of the upper house. Were not the principal promoters of the Boulangist strategy—de Mun, Piou, Breteuil, Mackau, Martimprey, and Cassagnac—all deputies? "The deputies," Haussonville huffed, "don't count; only the monarchist party does. The provincial committees are complaining loudly." Of course, as Piou had earlier noted, the approach of elections would soften many an erstwhile intransigent. The resistance of the self-righteous "chevaux légers" outside the Chamber would continue only "until the day they become candidates."[45] Moreover, and Haussonville notwithstanding, the deputies did "count"; electing more of them was central to the entire royalist strategy. As for the "complaining" committees, for the most part that was all they ever did.

Partisans of the new politics liked to argue that it represented the approach of "the most youthful element in the party" and that the discordant notes were but part of a generation gap. This was the burden of Breteuil's interview in *Le Matin* when, ostentatiously invoking the name of the pretender, he dismissed the critics of the current policy as the *"vieux jeux* who preferred standing pat to taking concerted action, and were afraid to throw themselves into the popular movement to attempt to direct it." There was a lot in the generational argument, but many of the old guard pointedly wondered just why the direction of the party should have fallen to relative neophytes. The newer elements retorted that France was in its current disastrous state because such faithful servants of the monarchy as Broglie and Haussonville had had the inspired idea of voting for the republican constitution of 1875.[46]

The Count of Paris also had to deal with a string of earnest reports from royalist secretaries expressing bewilderment and consternation about the Boulangist phenomenon. His responses were invariably disingenuous. When local representatives insisted that they could not tarnish their royalist principles by a compromise with Boulangism, he congratulated them on their energetic activity on behalf of the monarchy but vaguely suggested that, in departments where royalists were weaker and the circumstances less favorable, different tactics might be called for. Upon receipt of complaints about the rapid growth of local Boulangist sentiment, he retorted that Boulangist inroads were a direct result of the lethargy of provincial royalists and bluntly instructed local committees to display more energy. On the rare occasions when local royalists had the temerity to state the obvious—that the spread of Boulangism and the corresponding confusion among conservatives were a direct function of the manifest lack of clear direction coming from the leader—he angrily declared that the duty of his royalist subjects was perfectly clear and that they did not need a daily bulletin from their prince in order to defend the monarchist cause.[47]

If the Count of Paris was irritated by the obvious reticence of some of his agents, it was because he knew that many of them substituted doctrinal purity for effective political activity. By contrast, more energetic royalists were often enthusiastically pro-Boulangist. Julien Dumas was young, wealthy, eloquent, and dynamic. He waged a constant, albeit unsuccessful, campaign against the "timorous, passive, and self-centered" royalists in the Loiret. Like many Boulangists in 1888–89, he was a "royalist in a hurry," considering the popular general as the last hope for the monarchy. Dumas persuaded the Count of Paris to permit him to run in the Loiret in July as a "candidate of revision and dissolution" with the open support of the Boulangists. His candidacy was explicitly designed as a test of Boulangist good faith and royalist tractability. Under pressure from Beauvoir, de Mun, and Breteuil, Dillon promised that Boulangists would support Dumas without insisting that he make favorable reference to the republic, provided that local royalists did not give Dumas "a monarchist coloration that is too pronounced." The local royalist committee reluctantly accepted this compromise, its habitual intransigence tempered by the formal instructions of the pretender and a campaign contribution of 20,000 francs.[48] Because Dumas's campaign and his eventual defeat coincided with dramatic developments in Boulanger's political fortunes, it attracted little attention, but it did establish the basis for all future electoral alliances between royalists and Boulangists.

A decisive factor in the royalist-Boulanger alliance was of course money. Boulanger's elections (and his personal life style) required vast sums of money which only royalists were in a position to supply. Given the widespread lack of confidence in the general's good intentions, money was a decisive means of control. Here too there were discreet limits to the cooperation of the Count of Paris, whose fortune was substantial but whose desire to preserve it was equally strong. The pretender originally, albeit reluctantly, contributed 500,000 francs in May 1888. De Mun and Beauvoir explained to Dillon that the half million francs were conditional on Boulanger's never running against a conservative candidate, and were to be used exclusively for election campaigns, travel in his home department, and a putative revisionist campaign. This sum did not satisfy Dillon, who continued to ask for more money, putting the needed figure close to three million francs.[49] In order to elicit such sums (far in excess of previous allocations for royalist campaigns), Boulangists were not above hinting that the Bonapartists were capable of comparable generosity. Although, given the state of the Bonapartist treasury, this was highly unlikely, the Count of Paris seriously sought additional funds. Early in May he wrote his two principal *bailleurs de fonds,* the barons Maurice de Hirsch and Alphonse de Rothschild, requesting their presence in London. Although neither knew the other had been approached, both were coy and initially reticent about loaning large sums of money to the pretender. The two barons did visit the Count of Paris, but no financial arrangement was initially forthcoming.[50]

At the end of June, however, the Duchesse d'Uzès, now thoroughly fascinated by General Boulanger and urged on by the Duc de Chartres, offered to put her fortune at his service. She visited the Count of Paris at Coblenz and put three million francs at his disposal, to be repaid upon restoration of the monarchy. Since the political acumen of the duchess notoriously did not match her financial largesse, it was critical that she not directly distribute the money to Boulanger and his allies. The disposition of the money was therefore under the control of a committee consisting of Breteuil, Beauvoir, de Mun, Arthur Meyer, and later La Trémoille, who would direct it toward the Boulangist cause only after the pretender's initial contribution had been consumed. Although the royalist leaders would now have to cope with the thoroughly irritating meddling of "la bienfaitrice," her generosity gave them powerful leverage which they would not hesitate to use.[51]

Developments in June and July nonetheless raised some serious questions about the utility of the alliance with Boulanger. In June Paul Déroulède declared himself a candidate for a vacant seat in the Charente. He had the avowed support of Boulanger, who declared that a vote for Déroulède was a vote for him. The presence of Déroulède, whose radical republicanism and militant nationalism had long made him a target of conservative wrath, deeply angered both Bonapartists and royalists.[52] On the first ballot of June 17 a Bonapartist candidate came first with 31,401 votes, followed by an Opportunist with 23,989 and Déroulède with 20,656; in the run-off ballot on July 1 the respective votes were 37,636; 27,305; and 11,694. An angry royalist press drew three conclusions from this election. First, the general's patronage of Déroulède confirmed their belief that Boulangism really stood for war and revolution. Although the pattern of second-ballot votes suggested that many of Déroulède's first-ballot voters had gone to the Bonapartist on July 1, royalists were quick to note that Déroulède had recommended that they support the Opportunist. Few had done so, of course, but the effect of the recommendation was to emphasize the republican dimension of Boulangism which the Count of Paris so wished to have obscured. Second, the royalist press noted that Boulanger's apparent electoral attraction was manifestly not transferable; if Déroulède could not successfully climb on the general's bandwagon, neither could any conservative candidate. Finally, the Charente election underscored the fact that Boulanger and his surrogates could win only in the absence of a conservative candidate and where they enjoyed the active support or at least the benevolent neutrality of the conservative party. So while there was little doubt about what conservatives could do for Boulanger, the Charente election made it most unclear what Boulanger could do for conservatives.[53]

Boulanger's first parliamentary experience ended disastrously. Boulanger was not very interested in parliamentary discussion and limited himself to several pompous lectures on the need to revise the constitution and dissolve the Chamber. He displayed absolute contempt for his fellow deputies and rarely attended sessions. But he faced an unexpectedly formidable opponent. On April 3 the Tirard government was replaced by that of Charles Floquet. Floquet was a decidedly tepid Radical whose most notable accomplishment dated from 1867, when he provocatively shouted at the visiting Czar, "Vive la Pologne, monsieur!" Conservatives thought him the perfect symbol of a shabby regime. Although a mediocre statesman, Floquet was an eloquent speaker and a master of parliamentary repartee who delighted in deflating the newly elected deputy from the Nord. On June 4 he had convulsed the Chamber by reminding Boulanger that at his age Napoleon was already dead. When Boulanger next appeared in parliament, on July 12, Floquet wondered out loud why the former general considered himself the incarnation of a purer republic, when his personal predilections led him to haunt the antechambers of various princes. Since Floquet's abusive observations were also entirely accurate, a furious Boulanger called him an impudent liar with the manners of an ill-bred schoolboy and abruptly resigned his seat. The two men agreed to a duel the next morning. Neither's swordsmanship gave evidence of much recent practice but Floquet, a portly sexagenarian, managed to inflict a serious wound on the younger man. The outcome delighted republicans, whose July 14 celebrations were thereby greatly enhanced. Boulanger emerged from the episode looking perfectly foolish; after several anxious days his life was out of danger, but the same could not confidently be said for his political future.

Only another resounding electoral triumph could restore Boulanger's image. He therefore declared his candidacy for a by-election on July 22 to replace a deceased conservative deputy in the Ardèche. In theory the Ardèche ought to have been an attractive department for Boulanger, because republicans and conservatives were very evenly balanced. With the exception of a few Protestant cantons, conservatives controlled the rural and mountainous regions in the eastern half of the department; republicans had an equally solid hold in the towns and the Rhône valley. Conservatives had narrowly lost control of the department in 1877 but had won it back by an equally close margin in 1885. By attracting all the conservative votes and a fraction of republican ones, Boulanger could be assured of success.[54] All those involved with Boulanger agreed that success in the Ardèche would require the active collaboration of conservatives, all the more so because the general's wounds prevented him from campaigning in the department. Boulanger, in fact, threatened to withdraw if there was any conservative competition.[55]

Royalists in the Ardèche were badly divided on Boulangism. As early as May some leading representatives had contended that the Count of Paris should take advantage of the Boulangist phenomenon,[56] but others remained convinced that Boulanger was a menace that must be resisted at all costs. At the strenuous insistence of Uzès, de Mun, Beauvoir, and Mackau, the pretender instructed the royalist committee in the department to present no candidate. But Boulanger needed more than royalist money and a free hand in the Ardèche. He also required and expected the discreet but active support of local royalists. The royalist leadership expected that the pretender's vague recommendations would be translated by Dufeuille into explicit instructions to vote for Boulanger. But Dufeuille, not yet fully aware of the agreement with Boulanger, failed to make the appropriate impression on the intransigent royalists in the Ardèche, who chose to ignore the gentle hints from Paris. Instead, they interpreted the prince's recommendation of neutrality in the narrowest sense and insisted that no royalist could vote for Boulanger.[57]

As a result, royalists abstained in record numbers and Boulanger lost badly, getting 27,311 votes as opposed to 43,307 for his Opportunist opponent. Since Boulanger obtained 18,000 fewer votes than conservatives had in the February 1886 by-elections, the absence of conservative support was striking. Royalist purists openly congratulated the royalists of the Ardèche for having ended Boulanger's political career.[58] Boulanger's royalist allies, by contrast, were simply furious and inveighed against the simpleminded obtuseness of their colleagues in the Ardèche, as well as the timorous instructions of the Count of Paris. Having counted on the unequivocal support of royalists, Boulanger felt genuinely betrayed. His devoted admirer, the Duchesse d'Uzès, emboldened by her financial sacrifices, permitted herself bluntly to question both the authority and the good faith of the pretender. Albert de Mun, never entirely able to mask his contempt for the Count of Paris, thundered about the lack of discipline among royalists and unsubtly suggested that in the future the head of the royalist party ensure that his orders be understood and obeyed. The equivocation of the Count of Paris annoyed everyone, since it could mean the end of Boulangism or, worse, might encourage the general to drift into the camp of the Bonapartists, who had far less to offer but whose partisans had fewer ideological qualms and, significantly, had voted en masse for Boulanger.[59]

Yet the crisis provoked by the election in the Ardèche should not obscure the fact that even here Boulanger obtained considerable assistance from the royalists. As the royalist departmental secretary later noted, it was the royalists who, in spite of the abstentions, provided Boulanger with the great majority of his votes. When Georges Thiébaud, Jacques Millevoye, and more than a dozen Boulangist agents descended on the Ardèche, they were prepared to run an energetic campaign, but they clearly needed help; their first stop had been the offices of the royalist paper *Le Patriote de l'Ardèche,* where they pleaded for assistance. The editor was evidently convinced, because he printed 25,000 Boulangist brochures and 4,000 posters, working all night to get them out. Moreover, although the intransigent royalists ultimately carried the day, they did so in the face of strenuous arguments from those who sought actively to support the general. One of them, the former deputy Henri Blachère, made it perfectly clear that he intended to vote for Boulanger and would urge other royalists to follow his example. The problem, of course, was that even partial royalist collaboration was not good enough to ensure the electoral success of the general.[60]

After the debacle in the Ardèche, the related issues of Boulanger's political future and his partnership with royalists became open questions. It was now critically important that Boulanger score a resounding victory and equally essential that royalists cooperate fully with him. The latter was of course a necessary condition for the former since, as previous elections had amply demonstrated, Boulanger's mercurial popularity could be sustained only by vigorous conservative support. Given the uncertainty concerning Boulanger's loyalty, it was also imperative that this point be graphically demonstrated. The death of a Bonapartist deputy in the Charente-Maritime and a royalist one in the Somme, coupled with Boulanger's earlier resignation in the Nord, led to three simultaneous by-elections scheduled for August 27 and an opportunity to revive Boulangism and the royalist-Boulanger alliance.

Of the three elections, royalists all agreed that the one in the Somme was the most critical. The Charente-Maritime was primarily Bonapartist territory and the Nord, temporarily at least, was Boulanger's. Only in the Somme could royalists unambiguously demonstrate their indispensability to the general and undo the damage done in the Ardèche. There was no danger of a monarchist rival in the Somme, since local royalists had long ago abandoned hope of finding a plausible candidate. But

Boulanger also needed direct support, and the pretender's advisers strove to persuade him to do what he had failed to do in the Ardèche—unequivocally tell local royalists to vote for the general. Beauvoir, who considered the Somme to be "our last card," urged his prince to ensure royalist cooperation although, always alert to the pretender's sensibilities, he suggested it might be done "without putting anything on paper." Albert de Mun, still convinced that Boulanger was "the only serious instrument that God has put into our hands," demanded that royalists in the Somme be "formally invited" to vote appropriately. Uzès was predictably adamant on this score, and even Bocher concluded that, since royalists would be financing Boulanger's campaign in the department, they might as well openly endorse him.[61]

None of this had much effect on the Count of Paris, who proceeded to give characteristically irresolute instructions to his emissary in the Somme, the royalist deputy Viscount Raoul Blin de Bourdon. No, he would not give local royalists a direct order to vote for Boulanger, nor would he permit his name to be used to justify any such policy, for he wished to remain uncompromised. All he could say was that the royalists of the Somme would "be neither disavowed nor reprimanded, should they feel called upon to abandon their neutrality and fight the official candidate of the Radical government." As he later explained, "to recommend [Boulanger] to royalist voters, with his gang of charlatans and his past history, which they have no reason to forget, would be to mock them and leave them with a pathetic idea of their leader."[62]

He had a point, although, as his lieutenants in Paris incessantly complained, such circumspection left them open to endless abuse from the defenders of royalist orthodoxy. It was also true, as his more passionate Parisian aides (in their anxiety for Boulanger's future) sometimes forgot, that royalist support was useful to the general only when it was covert. Speaking for the pretender, Blin de Bourdon informed the local royalist committee that it could not endorse Boulanger and must leave its followers free to vote as their conscience dictated, "guided only by their patriotism." Boulanger, mindful of the Ardèche experience, complained that the pretender's instructions could mean almost anything, but the campaign coverage of the royalist *Echo de la Somme* left little doubt that it meant vote for Boulanger.[63] The Boulangist campaign manager certainly knew who his allies were. He approached Ansart, president of the departmental royalist committee, explaining that Boulangists feared governmental electoral corruption and needed the royalist network in the department—far more extensive than their own—to scrutinize the voting. Ansart readily agreed and dispatched a note to all

his correspondents in rural areas requesting their full cooperation. Boulanger won handily with 76,000 votes, more than twice that of his republican opponent. His total, however, was barely 6,000 more than the
conservative list had obtained in 1885, and Ansart proudly boasted that
most of the general's votes came from royalists.[64]

Given Boulanger's dramatic victory there in April, the campaign in
the Nord seemed less problematic. Although royalist newspapers were
relatively circumspect,[65] collaboration between royalists and Boulangists
was intimate beneath the surface. The Boulangist campaign in the department was managed by Georges Laguerre, the Comte du Perrier, a
former Bonapartist, and the Baron de Grilleau, a young man from an
old royalist family whose brother was the royalist leader of the Aisne.
All were on excellent terms with the principal royalist newspapers, *Le
Nouvelliste* and *La Dépêche,* making frequent visits to their offices,
whence poured a voluminous stream of Boulangist propaganda. Distribution of this material was assured by the employees of *Le Nouvelliste,*
whose editor-in-chief made daily stops at Boulangist headquarters, taking
elaborate, if futile, precautions to go unobserved.[66] Royalist support
was so obvious that some republicans, in desperation, actually printed
a phony royalist electoral poster in the hopes of drawing some conservatives away from Boulanger. The mounting evidence of his complicity
with conservatives lost Boulanger a substantial portion of the republican
vote he had received in the spring. He nonetheless won easily with
130,000 votes—33,000 more than his nearest opponent.

The election in the Charente-Maritime was also orchestrated by conservatives, although here they were in majority Bonapartist. The undisputed leader of conservatives in this department was Baron Eugène
Eschasseriaux, a devoted Bonapartist and a consummate political organizer. Despite his incessant activity, however, conservative prospects
seemed relatively bleak in the summer of 1888. One of his principal
agents reported in July that conservatives "no longer have any contact
with the electorate . . . ever since conservative deputies deserted the
countryside. . . . Perhaps some soldiers remain but their officers have
disappeared, following the generals who are no longer present."[67] His
other agents told a similar story, complaining that in spite of periodic
talk about the need "to activate the organization of committees . . . as
of now . . . there is nothing." The royalist organization was little better. The leading royalist, son of the mayor of La Rochelle under the
Empire, was Edouard Beaussant, a man of considerable political ambition. Yet while Beaussant was the effective leader of conservative opinion in the arrondissements of La Rochelle and Marennes, he had never

succeeded in establishing a permanent electoral organization in any of the communes. It was therefore in the context of conservative ineptitude, even in a relatively secure department, that the Boulangist campaign began.[68]

Although the electoral fiasco in the neighboring Charente in June had raised questions about the utility of Boulangism, both Eschasseriaux and Beaussant recognized that, if carefully controlled, Boulanger's popularity could be exploited effectively by conservatives. Although unaware of royalist dealings with Boulanger, Eschasseriaux had heard of the general's contacts with the Bonapartists and believed him to be amenable to the conservative cause. When the Bonapartist deputy Albert Vast-Vimeux died, Eschasseriaux convoked the conservative leaders of the department and argued against presenting a candidate. Instead he called on conservatives to aid Boulanger in every way they could, and "use the general as a battering ram to beat the Opportunist" and a means to reaffirm [conservative] cohesion and preponderance in the department."[69]

Eschasseriaux intended that conservative control over the Boulangist campaign be both total and secret. When Paul Wallet, Boulanger's campaign manager, arrived in the department he went immediately to Eschasseriaux, whereupon the two of them mapped out their strategy in minute detail. In predominantly republican urban centers like La Rochelle and Rochefort, Wallet and his agents would accent the general's republicanism. Conservatives would be discreetly absent from the campaign, leaving to the Boulangists "the responsibility for the *apparent* preparations" (emphasis mine). Similarly in Royan the conservatives would officially ignore Boulanger but would quietly supply the personnel needed to print and distribute his campaign literature. In rural areas, where overt conservative involvement would be an electoral asset, Eschasseriaux would manage the general's campaign directly.[70]

Throughout the campaign Eschasseriaux received regular albeit clandestine reports from Boulanger's agents, and he even dispatched a group of his domestic servants to serve as bodyguards and cheerleaders during Boulanger's appearances in the department. Here as elsewhere, conservative insistence that their support for Boulanger go unnoticed reflected the importance of not compromising him among republican voters; concern that in the event of a defeat the conservative leadership not be discredited; and not incidentally, a strong desire to avoid getting stuck with the bill. The "unofficial" nature of conservative support became an issue when the printers of Boulanger's voluminous campaign material quite naturally came to Eschasseriaux for their money, whereupon the flustered deputy had to insist that, appearances notwithstanding, it had been Boulanger's campaign and not his.[71]

The conservative alliance was, however, disputed by the royalists in the arrondissement of Saintes. There the local royalists, their doctrinal purity honed by years of squabbling with neighboring Bonapartists, were as notorious for their inflexible adherence to monarchist principles as for their lack of contact with the local population. Bonapartist support for Boulanger enhanced rather than diminished their already intense hostility to the general. In conformity with what they took to be official royalist policy, they rather belligerently called for royalist abstention and couched their recommendation in savagely anti-Boulangist terms. The local *Moniteur de la Saintonge* published long dossiers on the "crimes" of the general and reminded readers that "Boulanger means the republic and the worst of republicans."[72] But royalists in Saintes were out of touch with their counterparts in the rest of the department, and *Le Moniteur,* whose editor was a recent arrival from Paris, was particularly so. The outmoded purism of *Le Moniteur* exasperated a number of local royalists and Ossian Pic, the editor of the other principal royalist journal, *L'Echo rochelais,* denounced the high-minded meddling of transplanted Parisian journalists and insisted that "one can vote for General Boulanger without ceasing to be a royalist."[73]

When news of the disruptive stance of the royalists at Saintes reached the Count of Paris, he angrily rebuked them. Stung by the pretender's anger, they docilely retracted their earlier statements and ended the anti-Boulanger campaign of *Le Moniteur.* Such last-minute contrition did not, however, translate into effective support for the general. Whereas in the rest of the department the royalists joined with Bonapartists in ensuring Boulanger's reelection, in Saintes abstentions were high and, as a result, Boulanger's total vote was 5,000 below the conservative list of 1885. In the aftermath the Count of Paris and his lieutenants expressed boundless contempt for the indiscipline and general stupidity of the royalists at Saintes, but their scorn was rather unfair. As several of the Saintes royalists plaintively remarked, they were, despite private reservations, perfectly prepared to obey orders, but it had not been at all clear whose orders were to be followed, and their initial stance had been entirely consistent with the instructions of Lambert de Sainte-Croix.[74]

The triple election of August 1888 was a major step in the development of Boulangism, decisively rescuing its namesake from the threat of oblivion and firmly establishing the new phenomenon as *the* critical issue in French politics. The elections also illustrated three important dimensions of the Boulanger-conservative alliance. The Charente-Maritime, the Somme, and the Nord had a number of critical features in common in 1888. In all three departments conservative electoral strength, seemingly so solid in 1885, appeared to be waning. This was particularly true in the last two departments, where conservatives were wearied, demoralized, and reluctant even to contest by-elections. In all three the great attraction of Boulanger was that he offered an opportunity to galvanize the increasingly dispirited and apathetic conservative voters so as to deal the republic a telling blow.

Everywhere the great majority of those who voted for Boulanger were people who ordinarily voted for royalist or Bonapartist candidates. Owing to the varying rates of abstention, the exact percentage of conservative votes cannot be determined, but by any calculation it was high. In the Nord, Boulanger's vote of 130,000 (40,000 fewer than in the spring) was only a few thousand better than royalist performance in previous by-elections. Since royalist endorsement of and support for Boulanger was far more obvious than it had been in the spring, it is reasonable to assume that he lost republican voters and gained royalist ones. Jacques Néré, who is not disposed to exaggerate Boulanger's conservative support, estimates that in August he received considerably more royalist votes than the 100,000 he received in the spring.[75] In the Somme, Boulanger added only 6,000 votes to the 70,000 obtained by conservatives in 1885, and even the Boulangists in the department were prepared to concede that the general had obtained at least 60,000 conservative votes.[76] In the Charente-Maritime, Boulanger's 57,000 votes were 5,000 fewer than obtained by conservatives in 1885, owing to local royalist abstention. In all cases the nonconservative vote for Boulanger was relatively small.

This last point deserves further elaboration, because most accounts of Boulangism stress its appeal among disgruntled republicans in general and among the working classes in particular.[77] According to this reading, the combined effects of the sustained depression of the 1880s and the notorious indifference of the Opportunists to social issues made the working classes receptive to a new political force with a genuinely progressive image. Since organized socialism was still in its infancy, a radical general, surrounded by men who could at least pass as socialists, offered up the hope of a truly "social" republic. Informed contemporaries did identify the working class as being particularly attracted to early Boulangism, and the phrase "Boulangist workers" appears frequently in conservative correspondence. Members of the prefectoral corps were quick to spot the conservative dimensions of local Boulangism, but they also noted that working-class centers were often hotbeds of Boulangist activity. As examples, the port workers of Lorient, La Rochelle, and Brest, the textile workers of Flers and Fougères, the miners of the Nièvre, and the railway workers in La Roche-sur-Yon and Béziers all evinced an early enthusiasm for Boulanger.[78]

Nonetheless Boulanger's appeal among the working classes was significantly greater in the earlier stages of his political career than it would be later on. The subprefect of Béziers indicated that early in 1888 at least 400 of the 450 workers in the nearby marshaling yards were Boulangists, in part, he thought, because many of them came originally from the Nord. By the end of the year a growing awareness of "Boulanger's relations with the reactionaries" had reduced the number of Boulangists to 200. By May 1889 the subprefect estimated that no more than 50 Boulangists remained among the workers. The same official also observed that increasingly the popular elements present at Boulangist meetings were the bailiffs, valets, or tenants of royalist or Bonapartist landowners. It suited the latter to avoid the embarrassment and the nuisance of attending Boulangist functions; in the absence of the social elite, local Boulangists could "pretend that the [Boulangist] committee is composed of republicans." Similarly, Radicals and socialists who had enthusiastically greeted Boulanger when he visited the Allier in October 1887, adamantly rejected the overtures of the departmental Boulangist committee in 1889, because it consisted exclusively of conservatives.[79]

In Montpellier, Boulangism sparked some initial interest among the socialists, one of whom even discussed the possibility of a Boulangist subsidy for a local socialist newspaper. He was dismayed, however, to discover at the Parisian Boulangist headquarters "the principal leaders of the Orleanist and Bonapartist parties" and was sternly rebuked by his colleagues back home, who pointedly wondered why a socialist would be dealing with someone like Dillon. Significantly, in the neighboring industrial city of Sète, where the socialist movement was more advanced, Boulangism was nonexistent among the working classes. Similarly, one important reason for the feebleness of the Boulangist movement in Lyons was the vigorous opposition to it by all the many socialists in the city, with the exception of the Blanquists.[80]

Boulangism certainly made converts among the working classes, although their conversion was less certain and less durable than that of the conservative electorate. In any event, the argument for the essentially conservative valence of Boulangism is in no way vitiated by evidence of working-class support for the movement. It was precisely Boulanger's presumed ability to influence sociological strata definitively lost to royalists that made him so attractive to them. The logic of the alliance dictated that the quasi totality of conservative votes be delivered to Boulanger while he mobilized a small but significant fraction of republican voters refractory to any conservative candidate. In the three August by-elections the republican supporters of Boulanger were a fraction of the total, but they made a crucial difference to the outcome.

Moreover, local conservatives offered Boulanger more than just votes. Strictly speaking, there was no provincial Boulangist organization in 1888; the general's campaigns were run by a handful of Parisian agents who descended on the departments scant weeks before election day. They came with plenty of (royalist) money and some innovative ideas about electoral politics, but they did not know the departments, had no infrastructure in place, and at best could be effective only in the urban centers. In the rural areas, where Boulanger counted on doing well, Boulangists had to rely on the traditional conservative notables and their electoral agents to deliver the vote, distribute propaganda, and scrutinize the polling places. Moreover, it was the conservative newspapers and printing presses that generated the mountains of paper that would be the trademark of Boulangist elections. Ironically, the later history of *Le Moniteur de la Saintonge* illustrates the central role played by the royalist press in Boulanger's campaigns. The newspaper's printer had observed that a great deal of money was being spread around in the campaign and eagerly expected that his royalist connections would guarantee him some major orders for electoral material. When the obdurate editorial stance of *Le Moniteur* rendered this impossible, he was furious and terminated his contract with the newspaper at his first opportunity.[81]

This dependence on the royalist electoral infrastructure did not escape even the most radical Boulangists, who warned that unless the new party developed an effective and autonomous network of local committees, the growing wave of discontent in France might yet redound to the exclusive advantage of royalism.[82] For the next six months republican Boulangists would attempt to emancipate the movement from the creeping domination of the royalists, but royalists would strive—successfully—to ensure that this did not happen.

4

Royalists and Boulangists:
From Secret Support
to Public Alliance

After Boulanger's resounding victories in August it was clear that Boulangism represented a potent political force, and equally clear that royalists were intimately associated with it. For royalists who enjoyed playing with electoral numbers, the events of 1888 were auspicious. As one journalist noted, in the four departments (Nord, Somme, Charente-Maritime, Dordogne) where Boulanger had been elected, he had obtained 61.6 percent of the vote cast, whereas in 1885 conservatives had obtained only 52.1 percent there. In all the 1888 by-elections Boulanger and conservatives together had obtained 55 percent of the vote as opposed to 45.2 percent nationally in 1885. Calculations of this kind proved relatively little except that royalists were now openly staking the future on Boulanger's popularity. As the Count of Paris acknowledged, what had originally been "secret support" now became a "public alliance."[1]

The "alliance" continued to trouble many royalists. Deputies from the west often remained intractable, as did most senators, the business community, and the bulk of the royalist army officers.[2] But many of those who deplored the flirtations with Boulanger admitted that their sentiments were not shared by their electorate, that most of their fellow royalists were partisans of the general, and that most local Boulangists seemed to come from the ranks of the royalists.[3]

One thing all royalists agreed upon was the intimate connection between the Boulangist phenomenon and royalist weakness. With striking

107

consistency the royalist analyses of Boulangism were set in the context of their own organizational incapacity. In the first place, Boulanger had been elected in 1888 because of the absence of royalist rivals. But even without the collusion between the respective headquarters, royalists probably would have been unable to field candidates. Finding and supporting candidates for a by-election required "a permanent army" capable of "continuous action," not "ten bourgeois meeting for two hours in their salons."[4] As the very capable secretary of the Gironde remarked, royalist committees were full of well-intentioned but lethargic notables who, "instead of producing candidates, draft memos of abstention [permitting the leadership] to declare, after the fashion of Saint Paul, that to run a candidate is not bad, but not to run a candidate is perhaps as good."[5]

Boulangists had introduced a new style of politics: "Gone are the days of peaceful elections. Today, if we wish to avoid a crushing defeat, we must descend into the street, start shaking hands, and display an all-consuming activity." Boulangists were not intimidated by government agents, nor did they whine constantly about official corruption. If the mails could not be trusted, they responded by effectively creating their own postal service: committee rooms filled with envelope stuffers and waiting couriers.[6] Boulanger, one journalist exclaimed, "has shown us bold new methods." Where royalists limited themselves to reasoned and dignified speeches, Boulanger "used all the publicity that civilization and mercantile commerce puts at the disposal of politicians and peddlers: brochures, newspapers, portraits, posters, cheerleaders, vendors, receptions, parades, banquets . . . all manner of means to make contact with the voters."[7] A score of royalist editorials drew similar conclusions.[8]

Although entirely accurate in their unflattering assessment of royalist organization, commentators tended to exaggerate the quality of Boulanger's electoral machine. He certainly had plenty of agents willing to spend his newly acquired money, but he did not as yet have a significant local infrastructure. (Indeed, as royalists were to discover to their cost, even in 1889 the local Boulangist organization was often perfectly inadequate.) In the previous by-elections Boulanger had relied heavily on local conservative resources. Nonetheless there was something distinctively different and superior about the political style of Boulangism. Even where Boulangists were relatively rare, as in the Vendée, they impressed informed observers by their knack for "first-rate advertising of the kind that political parties have heretofore left to retail commerce."[9]

One of the most notable features of Boulangist propaganda was the distribution of tracts and colored portraits. The technique itself was not an innovation; republicans and royalists had used it for years. But Boulanger did so on an unprecedented scale, greatly exceeding similar royalist efforts. By the end of October the *missus* of the southwest was convinced that, unless "the royalist party succeeds in penetrating the rural populations," the peasants would all be won over to Boulanger. Royalists would have to emulate the Boulangists and "noisily" distribute portraits, brochures, and almanacs "every day, at every hour of the day . . . and in every village." Activity of this kind, at which Boulangists excelled, was usually beyond the capabilities of local royalist organizations, which lacked the "very special practical skills" necessary. Most royalist committees limited themselves to slipping colored portraits of the Count of Paris into the Sunday edition of the local royalist newspaper. This kind of "centerfold" approach was doubly inadequate. Not only did it restrict distribution to 3,000 or fewer royalist subscribers in any department, but it was also passive and timid, altogether lacking "the magic quality, the noise and language of the street hawkers of the Midi." The local fairs and markets were full of street vendors boisterously and aggressively displaying Boulangist propaganda. Royalists, if they could afford a newspaper subscription, might at best expect a picture of the Count of Paris to fall out of their Sunday paper. Despairing of any significant improvement in royalist activity, the *missus* could only suggest hiring professional distributors with an accomplished sales pitch and a seasoned indifference to obstruction from police and prefects.[10]

What particularly annoyed the Count of Paris was the fact that most of the complaining about the Boulangist alliance was coming from those whose chronic inactivity had made that alliance necessary in the first place. He dispatched an angry note to his *missi* demanding an improvement in royalist propaganda efforts. Why, he wanted to know, were royalist brochures and portraits piling up in warehouses instead of being widely distributed? And why did royalist conferences continue to take place only in large centers and only before convinced partisans of the monarchy, instead of among the peasants of the rural communes? More energetic activity and less uninformed speculation about the wisdom of his grand strategy were what the royalist party needed in 1888.[11] Especially unnecessary were more editorials insisting that royalists could ally only with "honest men," not "rabble." "In politics," he noted privately, " 'honest men' are those that I can use and the 'rabble' are those who stand in my way."[12]

Unfortunately the Count of Paris's public pronouncements were never as precise as his private observations; they were, in fact, impossibly vague. As a result, some prominent royalists were publicly attempting to subvert the Boulangist alliance, all the while posing as authoritative representatives of the pretender. The discordant notes hit by dissident lieutenants like Pierre Calla and Lambert de Sainte-Croix, as well as western legitimists like General de Charette and the powerful deputy from the Loire-Atlantique, Edouard de Cazenove de Pradine, were widely reported.[13] These were old and respected colleagues and the Count of Paris was not temperamentally suited to forcing them into line, the less so since some of the more extreme royalist supporters of Boulanger were widely regarded as fools.[14]

The task of setting the record straight fell to the Marquis de Breteuil. Breteuil was an effective speaker and known to be a confidant of the prince. But the connection was sufficiently tenuous as to permit, should the need arise, selective disavowals.[15] Breteuil chose a general meeting of royalists in Marseilles to give an address to be couched, as he warned the pretender, in "clearly modern and democratic terms."[16] Heretofore, he argued, royalist policy had vacillated between two options. One was to serve as a loyal opposition to the moderate republicans; the other was to stick to the narrow terrain of monarchist orthodoxy. In the 1870s the Orleanists had advocated the first option and the legitimists the second, but neither had saved France from a headlong rush into radicalism. In 1885, however, the conservative union of royalists and Bonapartists had come close to conquering the republic. In 1889 they could succeed, thanks to a new force: Boulanger. His past was blemished, but his "wounds received on the field of battle" and the confidence he had restored in the army now made him an object of respect. He had sided with "the exploited against the exploiters" and was now unconsciously serving the conservative cause. Royalists need not abandon their political faith to cooperate with the man who would enlarge the "breach" through which they could conquer the republic. Nor, he insisted, was there any evidence that Boulanger sought personal dictatorship or foreign war. By allying with Boulanger, royalists were simply serving as the "avant-garde" of "a greater democratic conservative party." After a speech in which the words "royal" and "democratic" were used frequently and together, he closed by declaring, "An ardent royalist drinks to French democracy." Parliamentary compromise and principled politics were a relic of an earlier era no longer suited to the age of mass politics.

All in all it was an extremely skillful address, one that clearly impressed royalists in Marseilles.[17] Elsewhere, however, it didn't bring much more order into the royalist ranks. Some local committees were simply more confused than before as to which royalist spokesman to believe.[18] Breteuil's atypical frankness, which even arch partisans of the alliance rather regretted,[19] outraged many legitimists who considered him to be, at best, "a new convert" to the monarchy.[20] Much of this was a mossbacked hostility to anything new, especially if proposed by someone new. As Cornelius de Witt wryly observed: "The conservative party is a difficult one to serve. It does not like those who have a past; it likes even less those who have a future."[21]

Still, the truly troublesome question for the royalist leadership in the autumn of 1888 was not dissidents within its own ranks but Boulanger himself. Boulanger had a problem. Despite (and indeed because of) his secret alliance with the royalists, he needed to pose as a republican. In the nature of things, Boulanger's public declarations had to be at variance with his private pronouncements. Royalists, however, tended to subject his every utterance to close scrutiny, looking for evidence that his duplicity was not sincere. Pressed hard by republicans on the parliamentary subcommittee on constitutional revision, Boulanger had conceded that, if revision led to a restoration of the monarchy, "two-thirds of the nation would revolt." Realistically, he could hardly have said anything else, and even then he qualified his remarks in ways calculated to appease his secret allies. Nonetheless the "two-thirds" reference made a lasting and negative impression on virtually all royalists.[22]

They were no happier about his projected divorce, for which his mistress was strenuously lobbying. For most conservatives the legalization of divorce had been one of the most pernicious sins of the republic—a blow against public morality, they would remember, struck by Boulanger's friend Alfred Naquet. A divorce would make selling the general to skeptical royalists nearly impossible and would even lose him the support of some of his heretofore staunch supporters, including de Mun, whose increasingly elastic royalist principles were not matched by any flexibility on religious questions.[23]

Finally, there was his speech at Nevers on 2 December 1888. Learning that the Boulangist Republican National Committee had committed Boulanger to address a republican gathering there, royalists attempted to have the meeting canceled. Boulanger pleaded that it was too late to withdraw, but assured his allies that he would "run with the hare and hunt with the hounds."[24] And so he did. Because the date, the anniversary of Louis Napoleon's coup d'état, was emotionally charged, Boulanger felt it necessary to assure his audience that he was not another Bonaparte. Nor, despite conservative electoral support (which he acknowledged for the first time), had he any intention of restoring "one of the old regimes." Once again his disavowal of conservatives was the minimum one possible before republican audiences. Yet although his references to previous dynasties had been, as the republican press pointedly observed, more complimentary than abusive, the entire address had been far too republican for many royalists. As *Le Figaro* acutely observed, Boulanger's problem was that "if he says nothing, he will be forgotten; if he speaks, he risks annoying someone . . . or everyone."[25]

Among the people Boulanger managed to annoy were the radical Boulangists in the Republican National Committee. His ambiguous pronouncements prompted fears that Boulanger and his movement were captives of the royalists. Since the August elections the republican press had been openly speculating about the nature of the royalist-Boulangist alliance, and *La Cocarde* was forced to devote more and more space to dismissing the (entirely accurate) rumors about a secret accord.[26] At the end of October a republican newspaper in the Puy-de-Dôme gave a detailed and partially accurate account of the royalist-Boulangist negotiations, based on the indiscretions of a highly placed but dissident royalist. The more newsworthy Numa Gilly scandal kept that story off page one, but de Mun and Breteuil were sufficiently alarmed as to decide at the last minute against attending the marriage of Boulanger's daughter.[27] The leading Boulangists were hardly innocent of the common understanding with the royalists, but they did not know the details and feared that Boulanger and Dillon had conceded too much to their allies. While negotiating a royalist subvention for *La Presse* with Bocher, Laguerre was outraged to learn that Dillon had *independently* reached an electoral agreement. By December, Boulanger was having to assure his lieutenants (quite untruthfully) that he was "not nearly as committed to the monarchists as you seem to think."[28]

Their anxieties surfaced over a December by-election in the Ardennes. Despite his avowed royalism, Jules Auffray, secretary general of the Ligue de la Consultation Nationale and "the most Boulangist of all royalists,"[29] was an obvious candidate for Boulangist patronage and received the qualified endorsement in the Boulangist *La Presse* of his childhood friend Georges Laguerre. This was no more than Boulangists had done for Julien Dumas the previous summer, but by now Boulanger's entourage was highly sensitive about any visible manifestations of a royalist connection. As a consequence, even veiled support for Auffray was too much for the National Committee, which adopted a resolution proposed by Paul Déroulède insisting that all Boulangist candidates openly accept the republic.[30] This was a cautious enough position, since

France was full of monarchists prepared to baptize themselves as "republican revisionists" in exchange for Boulangist support. Boulanger did his best to render the National Committee's stance more innocuous still. He conceded to *Le Figaro* that he could support no candidate who was not "clearly a republican or rallied to the republic" and would have to support any genuine republican revisionist who might run against Auffray. But most of his interview was devoted to praising Auffray and stressing that the royalist was so close to him that his electoral statement had been drafted in the general's private office.[31] Not only did Boulanger insist that Auffray was the best candidate in the race, but Boulangists made no effort to find their own republican standardbearer, and *La Presse* urged Boulangists in the Ardennes not to abstain.[32]

Royalists were not thereby mollified. They were more impressed by the fact that, in the temporary absence of the more tractable Laguerre, Alfred Naquet had slipped an editorial into *La Presse* warning of "the Machiavellian plans of the Orleanists" and concluding that, as far as Boulangists were concerned, "l'orléanisme, voilà l'ennemi."[33] Naquet's antiroyalist sally was a departure from the usual tone of *La Presse,* but that such a piece should have appeared at all in a newspaper to which they had just accorded 50,000 francs infuriated royalists.[34] Opponents of Boulanger promptly concluded that the sordid little adventure was, at last, over. "This time it is clear," crowed Cazenove's *L'Espérance du peuple;* "General Boulanger has cut the cable."[35]

Short of publicly declaring himself a royalist, Boulanger could hardly have done more to placate his secret allies.[36] As for the Ardennes, it was a hopeless department and, even with an official Boulangist endorsement, Auffray could not possibly have won.[37] But the royalists had become very demanding. At the beginning of December the Count of Paris threatened to cut off all future financial support. De Mun, Breteuil, and even Uzès were so disillusioned by Boulanger that they were, if possible, even more irritated than the prince. Along with Martimprey, Mackau, and Meyer they met Boulanger and Dillon on December 17 and again the next night, demanding firm proof of his good faith. Boulanger pleaded that his margin for maneuver with his republican followers was narrow enough without royalist jitteriness about every platonic reference to the republic. His intention of restoring the monarchy had not diminished, and he had already renounced his divorce, rejected the electoral guidelines of the National Committee, and was even prepared to dissolve it. This pacified the royalists; by December 26 Beauvoir could write his prince, "Note générale: all smooth."[38]

A major reason for the renewed confidence in Boulanger was the

Boulangist conduct in the next series of by-elections, the critical test of their tractability. As conservative strategists were all too aware, there was nothing very clever about using their troops to ensure the successive elections of Boulanger, unless it could be shown that his triumphs would subsequently help them gain—or at least hold—ground. It was therefore crucial that, when Boulanger resigned his seats in the Charente-Maritime and the Somme, there be no repetition of the Ardennes episode. Yet the earlier problems of delivering conservative votes to Boulanger were in all respects reproduced when it came to ensuring Boulangist votes for conservatives.

In the Charente-Maritime, royalists, with the predictable exception of the contingent in Saintes, agreed to endorse the handpicked candidate of the Bonapartist Eschasseriaux. Adolphe Duport was young, energetic, and wealthy and enjoyed the formal endorsement of Boulanger. Although it pleased Duport to describe himself as a man "without a political past," he came from a prominent Bonapartist family and was entirely the political creation of Eschasseriaux. Recognizing that conservatives would form "the great majority" of his electors, Duport and Eschasseriaux insisted that his Boulangist allies limit themselves to "the most anodyne" references to the republic. When the presence of republican Boulangists continued to irritate local conservatives, they were ordered out of the department. Although Boulangists in Paris gamely insisted that Duport was a republican, the claim fooled no one.[39]

Electing Bonapartists (and disguised ones at that) was not the royalist project. It was therefore imperative that Boulanger's successor in the Somme be a genuine royalist. The Count of Paris saw the January 1889 election there as a crucial litmus test of his overall strategy, as well as of the *bona fides* of his allies. But the Somme was a difficult proving ground. In spite of Boulanger's previous success in the department, royalist influence had been declining since 1885. Amiens was the fiefdom of the powerful republican René Goblet, and the kind of ministerial patronage he could deliver would make a difference in a by-election. Bonapartists were a troublesome factor here, since they harbored grievances concerning royalist avarice in 1885 and felt they were owed a chance at the deputation. Finally, the local royalist committee was as cool as ever about the prospect of mobilizing for a by-election. There was a dearth of willing candidates and the most plausible, General Montaudon, was extremely reluctant to stand. Even worse, he was openly contemptuous of his fellow general, Boulanger.

Nonetheless Beauvoir and Ansart, head of the local royalist committee, met with Dillon on October 23 to discuss the election. As usual

Dillon fulsomely acknowledged the support that royalists had given Boulanger in August and now formally promised to reciprocate. In addition to ensuring Boulangist votes for a royalist, he endeavored to keep the Bonapartists out of the race. Lest the importance of his undertaking be lost on Dillon, two weeks later the Count of Paris assured him that, should the seat in question somehow end up going to either a Boulangist or a Bonapartist, not only would all further financial support be ended, but the pretender would make public all his dealings with Boulanger. Suitably impressed, Dillon prevailed on Boulanger to refuse any dealings with the Bonapartists who were seeking his endorsement for the Somme. Montaudon, thanks to the strenuous pleadings of the Count of Paris as well as a check for 50,000 francs, finally and reluctantly agreed to stand.[40]

All that now stood between the partners and a harmonious electoral quid pro quo was the awkward fact that General Boulanger was being asked to endorse an unabashedly pure royalist who abhorred Boulangism. For this reason Dillon had all along been suggesting that Montaudon slip a brief and innocuous reference to the republic into his electoral declaration. The issue of this one word provoked another major fuss. In the eyes of the Count of Paris, for Montaudon to mention neither the monarchy nor the republic was a reasonable compromise which ought to have satisfied both royalists and Boulangists. For Montaudon, it was a dramatic concession which earned him the scorn of moderate newspapers like *Le Temps,* which accused him of gross hypocrisy and contended that he had run as a Boulangist pure and simple. Boulangists and their royalist allies in Paris, however, fully realized that this was neither a compromise nor a concession. For a royalist to omit reference to the monarchy on the campaign trail was nothing new in most parts of France; what marked them as royalist was the absence of any reference to the republic.

De Mun, Martimprey, Mackau, and Breteuil, while otherwise unhappy with Boulanger, recognized that on this issue he had a genuine problem and thought it imperative "to concede him something, not of substance, but with respect to the phraseology." Accordingly, they drafted a text that was "so tortuous, so vague, whose meaning was so imprecise and ambiguous" that no conservative ought to have had problems with it. In fact, their only concern was "by what tour de force General Boulanger would persuade his committee to accept it." Yet neither Montaudon nor the Count of Paris would countenance any reference to the republic. It had been hard enough to persuade Montaudon to run, and harder still to get him to accept the bland statement proposed by the pretender. In the end, and to the surprise of the Parisian royalists, the Boulangists swallowed Montaudon's statement and gave him support.

The support was more real than apparent, however, since the newspaper that passed for the local Boulangist organ, *Le Mémorialiste d'Amiens,* persistently sniped at Montaudon's candidacy, reminding everyone of the lacuna in his declaration and repeatedly stressing his exclusively Orleanist politics. The ire of conservatives was mitigated, however, by the fact that *Le Mémorialiste* was in fact an independent Bonapartist newspaper which had only recently baptized itself as Boulangist. Its editorials were part of an old Bonapartist grudge match, not Boulangist bad faith. Royalists reported that the position of republican Boulangists in the department, while unenthusiastic, had been "correct," so much so that Beauvoir and the ever parsimonious Bocher agreed to pay them 10,000 francs as a "recompense for their friendly attitude." As for local royalists, they distributed a portrait of Montaudon clothed and posed in a manner that made him virtually indistinguishable from General Boulanger.[41]

Coming as it did a month after the debacle in the Ardennes, Montaudon's election was an encouraging sign. A candidate less attractive to the Boulangists would have been hard to find. That they could be induced, however reluctantly, to support Montaudon suggested that their notional republican scruples were unlikely to be an obstacle to an advantageous electoral arrangement. The Count of Paris busied himself with elaborate plans for the forthcoming general elections. But the January 1889 election in Paris and its aftermath once again upset royalist calculations.

The death of the nondescript Parisian deputy Auguste Hude in the last days of 1888 was the occasion for Boulanger's last decisive electoral success. The by-election in Paris was of major importance to both Boulanger and the royalists. Heretofore, republicans had been able to belittle Boulanger's electoral victories by noting that they had been won exclusively in conservative and rural departments, amid populations that remained hostile to the regime. Paris was the great republican bastion of France; a Boulangist victory there would legitimate Boulangism's republican credentials and strengthen its claim to offer a plausible alternative to the existing regime of corruption. Amid the growing speculation about a royalist-Boulangist alliance, Alfred Naquet insisted that only a dramatic success in Paris could parry the creeping domination of the Orleanists.[42] At a minimum, royalists, having so insistently staked their claim to conservative departments while insisting on Boulangist backing, would have to prove capable of reciprocating in archly republican areas.

No royalist had any chance of being elected in Paris. The monarchist political organization in the capital, the subject of endless anguished reports, was notoriously ineffective.[43] Edouard Hervé had led the royalist list in Paris in 1885 with 100,000 votes and had not been elected. Benevolent neutrality in Paris was, therefore, an easy concession to the Boulangists in exchange for their cooperation in the departments; as part of his negotiations with Dillon in November, the Count of Paris had promised not to present a royalist in any future Parisian by-election. Despite royalist weakness in Paris, royalist support was deemed crucial by Boulanger, who repeatedly sent Arthur Meyer to pester Bocher for assurances that royalists would support him and vote for him. In light of Boulangist behavior in the Somme, the demand was a reasonable one.[44]

Paris, however, was a far more difficult constituency for royalists to control than had been the various departments in 1888. The election there would be the focus of national attention, so that covert support would be much harder to dissimulate. Parisian royalists were notoriously intractable and tended to compensate for their inattention to organization by their doctrinaire rigidity. The royalist press in Paris was largely independent of formal control. A significant element of royalist support in the capital came from the "milieux d'affaires"—the liberal professions and the commercial and financial world—all of whom were singularly uneasy about a candidate who seemed to represent international tensions and domestic upheaval.[45] Consequently, when the royalist city councillors met at the end of December, they initially insisted on presenting a candidate.[46]

On its merits, a royalist candidacy in Paris was a singularly futile idea. At best, royalists could hope to attract enough voters to deny Boulanger his election, thus assuring the triumph of the Radical republican mediocrity André Jacques. At worst, and far more likely, any royalist candidate would attract a derisory number of votes which would accentuate the apparent eclipse of the monarchy. Even the putative royalist candidate, Hervé, admitted that, since royalists had failed to present candidates in conservative constituencies in 1888, it hardly made sense to field one in a hopeless location now.[47] The real reason (and the only good one) for presenting Boulanger with a rival was to disrupt an alliance many Parisian royalists deplored.[48]

The Count of Paris formally demanded that there be no royalist candidate. On January 7 the Parisian committee reluctantly obeyed, but not before voting to issue a declaration of abstention accompanied by a strenuous denunciation of Boulanger.[49] No official statement was given to the press, and there followed a week of acrimonious discussion with the pretender's immediate representatives, who were appalled at the idea. No one expected this sort of declaration to have much impact on conservative voters, of course, but were Boulanger to lose (a possibility that royalists did not discount), he could legitimately claim to have been betrayed. Conversely, were he to win, too marked a royalist dissociation from the victory might lead Boulangists to conclude that they did not need their erstwhile allies. In either case the general and his entourage would become "peu maniable" in the forthcoming elections.[50] In the end, the Parisian royalists agreed to an innocuous text which declared neutrality but did not recommend abstention.[51] Not surprisingly, no one paid much attention to this document. Well before the election Bocher and Beauvoir were confidently predicting that at least three quarters of Parisian royalists would vote for the general.[52]

The election in Paris was sensitive because Boulanger's electoral clientele would no longer consist primarily of disgruntled conservatives. The outcome of the election hinged on the support of the Radical and socialist Left. Republicans did their best to counter Boulanger's apparent appeal to the extreme Left. Their candidate, Jacques, was an inept choice and has usually been portrayed as a particularly drab symbol of the Opportunist regime. Although certainly drab, he was a pale version of Floquet, not Ferry, and his status as a pre-1848 republican and an advocate of municipal autonomy for Paris permitted royalists to dismiss him as a Communard. Even the moderate republican *Le Temps* felt the need to disabuse certain conservative republicans of the notion that Jacques was still a revolutionary. Although many representatives of the Parisian Left sided with Boulanger, just as many did not. Among the candidates for the republican nomination were Auguste Vacquerie, former Communard; Abel Hovelacque, future socialist deputy; Albert Martin, the lone working-class representative in the provisional government of 1848; and the nephew of Alphonse Baudin, whose death on the barricades on 2 December 1851 made him a venerated martyr of the revolutionary Left. While a wing of the Blanquist socialists endorsed Boulanger, one of their prominent leaders, the famous Communard Edouard Vaillant, allowed his name to stand for the socialist nomination. He was defeated by Boulé, a self-proclaimed "standard bearer of the Commune and social revolution." Boulé and his supporters reminded the capital's voters that Boulanger was "the personification of the massacres of the bloody week" and "the assassin of the Parisians who defended the Republic."[53] Whereas Boulangists depicted the contest as a struggle between a reinvigorated republicanism and a corrupt Opportunist regime, the general's opponents portrayed a confrontation between 1848 and the Commune, on the one hand, and 1852 and the Versaillais on the other.

Strictly speaking the latter case was superior, but this did not have much impact on Paris. Jacques possessed none of the electoral charm of Boulanger and enjoyed a less effective political machine. Boulangists had created an extensive network of committees in all quarters of Paris, most notably those of the working class. Boulangist penetration into popular districts was due, in some measure, to their alliance with socialist groups, notably the Blanquists, although the oldest and most important group of socialists in the capital, the Possibilists, remained energetically anti-Boulangist. Far more important were the forces of Paul Déroulède's Ligue des Patriotes. The league—"the general's praetorian guard," as it has been called—had from 20,000 to 25,000 members in Paris; "the structure of the league's committees looked and functioned like small armies with hierarchical leadership cadres of seventy-eight men per arrondissement." By January 1889 the league was solidly implanted in the popular districts of the capital, particularly among the petite bourgeoisie. Its disciplined and concerted campaign for Boulanger impressed all contemporaries, and the correlation between areas of league strength and Boulanger's electoral performance was high. He received a total of 245,326 votes, compared to 162,875 for Jacques and 17,039 for Boulé. Boulanger did very well in certain of the most popular quarters of the city, the fifteenth, nineteenth, and thirteenth arrondissements, and equally well in some of the most wealthy and aristocratic ones, notably the seventh, eighth, and sixteenth.[54]

Although the absence of a royalist candidate had prompted predictable protests from the provincial press,[55] Boulanger's decisive victory and the corresponding dismay of republicans temporarily silenced most of the objurgatory lectures. The spectacle of the republic on the run moved even previously hostile newspapers to vote Boulanger a hearty "thank you."[56] In fact, these words might have been more appropriate in the mouth of the general. By all accounts Parisian conservatives voted massively for Boulanger. The public disapprobation of some prominent Parisian royalists seems not to have influenced voter behavior since, as contemporaries wryly noted, their arrondissements went disproportionately for the general. As the voter turnout was greater than in 1885, there were few reasons for supposing that royalist abstention had been significant. Conservative support greatly enhanced Boulanger's victory; it is probable, although not certain, that it assured the victory itself. Since Boulanger's majority was 82,000 votes, a conservative vote equal to the

100,000 of 1885 or even the 87,000 of the December 1885 by-election would have been decisive. Ultimately there is no telling, since there were marked seasonal variations in the size of the conservative electorate, depending on whether *le monde* and its retinue chose to be in the capital or on various country estates. Significantly, even royalist commentators who were least happy with the results of the election, and who most wished to dissociate conservatives from it, rarely put Boulanger's conservative support below 80,000 votes.[57]

Traditional versions of the Boulanger affair long maintained that the indolent general let slip an opportunity for a successful coup d'état on the night of January 27. More recent scholarly accounts have demonstrated that the Parisian Boulangists were not planning, and their royalist allies were not expecting, any kind of assault on the state.[58] Following a victory of such magnitude, however, Boulanger's *legal* assumption of power seemed likely, a possibility which certainly disquieted royalists. While it was comforting to point to the determining role played by monarchists in the election, it was all too evident that January 27 was entirely unlike the by-elections of 1888, and that conservatives were no longer the great majority of Boulanger's electors. A spectacular triumph in republican Paris would inevitably tempt Boulanger to emancipate himself from royalist tutelage; this had been the express intention of Naquet. By early March the Count of Paris clearly feared that, as a result of the Parisian election, Boulanger had effectively escaped his control. Some have even concluded that the election in Paris convinced the pretender that he would never regain his throne.[59]

A more likely explanation for the Count of Paris's evident dismay was the fact that his doctors had just informed him that he had only a few months to live.[60] In any event, neither the prospect of an early death nor the possibility of Boulanger's relative emancipation diminished the Count of Paris's determination to pursue the Boulangist alliance. After a lengthy discussion with him on March 18, Breteuil concluded that the pretender "regretted nothing" and was "resolved to pursue his campaign forcefully, neglecting nothing in his attempt to ensure a conservative majority." Moreover, his principal advisers repeatedly insisted that the election had not rendered either Boulanger or his entourage significantly less cooperative.[61] Despite its potent symbolic importance, Paris was not the key to electoral France, and Boulangist predominance in the capital did not reduce the movement's dependence on royalists in many departments. Strictly speaking, the January election only reinforced a central assumption in royalist calculations: Boulanger's continued ability to attract a following which remained impervious to the conservatives. Significantly it was at this time that the Count of Paris finally dismissed Lambert de Sainte-Croix, whose persistent opposition to Boulangism made him a liability.[62]

Boulanger's subsequent deportment clearly showed that his dazzling success in Paris had not blinded him to his continued need for royalist support. His next major pronouncement represented a significant olive branch to French Catholics. At the request of Jules Delahaye, an impatient and archly Boulangist royalist, Boulanger delivered a major address at Tours on March 17. As usual he assured his audience that the conservatives supporting him did not in any way expect him to betray the republic or contemplate a restoration. On the contrary, their support proved that he could rally conservatives to the republic. But, he added, "in accepting the republic, they want it to be liberal and tolerant, . . . to end the systematic oppression which hasn't even the greatness of the old struggles of our forebears. The republic . . . must repudiate the Jacobin heritage of the current regime." Jules Delahaye replied with a toast to the "open republic," a gesture for which he had sought the prior approval of the royalist leadership.[63] Naquet responded to the toast, speaking for the first time of a "parallel march" of conservatives and Boulangists. Words like "liberal," "tolerant," and "open" were deliberately ambiguous, but they were significant items in the traditional royalist lexicon. A few skeptical royalists discounted the Tours speech, noting that Jules Ferry could have said as much.[64] The republican press did not think so and announced that "Boulanger curé sac au dos" had become "Boulanger, chef des cléricaux."[65] Many previously suspicious royalists took the "open republic" speech as proof that Boulanger had "repented."[66]

Boulanger may not have been out of control, but some royalists were. As almost all the pretender's advisers noted in the weeks following the Parisian elections, royalist notables were now falling over themselves in their desire to be associated with the irresistible general. Prominent royalists suddenly became very visible at Boulangist banquets and meetings, and most of the Jeunesses Royalistes in Paris deserted en masse to the service of Boulanger. Although the Count of Paris issued instructions in early March forbidding royalists to attend Boulangist rallies, a number of deputies continued to make provocative appearances. Even those who had once been vocal in their execrations of Boulanger could now be found pacing the general's antechambers.[67]

The approach of the general elections was responsible for most of the conversions to Boulangism. Local Boulangist organizations, almost nonexistent in 1888, began cropping up everywhere in the spring of

1889. Many of them, in their initial enthusiasm, were making loud claims on all the constituencies in their department. After Paris anything was possible; local royalist incumbents or aspirants attempted to ward off Boulangist designs on a constituency they coveted by independently offering Boulanger a neighboring one. Royalist leaders in February and March expended considerable energy attempting to foil "the intrigues of our provincial royalists who, in order to ensure their personal success, descend on Paris to strike a deal at [Boulangist headquarters] to the detriment of an old friend in a neighboring arrondissement."[68] The supreme importance which royalists now attached to a rigorously defined division of electoral labor no longer reflected their distrust of Dillon and Boulanger, whom they reported as being perfectly cooperative. Instead, they were increasingly concerned to preempt zealous local royalists who were precipitously inviting the general into their departments.[69]

Money, and in large amounts, was essential to maintaining discipline in the alliance. Here developments were encouraging. After six months of negotiations, Maurice de Hirsch finally agreed to put five million francs at the disposal of royalists for the forthcoming elections. A finance committee headed by La Trémoille was charged with allocating the funds. Like Uzès, although for different reasons, Hirsch would become a nuisance. He distrusted the Boulangists and objected periodically that his money was to be used exclusively for royalists. A hypersensitive individual, he flatly declared that if his archrival, Alphonse de Rothschild, volunteered less than 500,000 francs to the royalist campaign chest, honor dictated that the offer be refused. Anticipating a contribution from Rothschild but knowing that it would be beneath Hirsch's "floor," royalists were both frustrated and embarrassed. For all that, given the speed with which the contribution from Uzès was being devoured, the new fund ensured an effective leverage for the general election.[70]

Ironically it was the republican government that rendered Boulanger an effective captive of the royalists. Throughout the late autumn of 1888 Paris had been rife with rumors of the impending arrest of Boulanger. In December Le Figaro had predicted that the Opportunist Pierre Tirard would return to the premiership early in the new year and strike hard at the general.[71] It was right. When Tirard replaced Floquet as premier on February 22, he appointed Ernest Constans his minister of the interior. Constans lost no time living up to his carefully cultivated reputation for utter ruthlessness.[72] He struck first at Déroulède's Ligue des Patriotes, dissolving it on a legal technicality. Constans then circulated rumors of the impending arrest of Boulanger on a charge of conspiracy against the state. Although almost certainly a bluff, the maneuver had the desired effect on its target. Royalists, who knew their man, suspected from the beginning that he would flee France. Mackau, Breteuil, and Beauvoir argued strenuously against an abrupt departure, but had few illusions about the likely resolve of the general.[73] When Boulanger covertly took a train for Brussels on April 1, the news was greeted with some contempt. "Paris," in Bocher's unkind words, "and much more than Paris, is certainly worth a couple of months in prison, even without women or oranges." How different history might have been, one editorialist sardonically mused, if Louis XVI had been able to catch a midnight train.[74]

As always, many royalists walked a fine line with Boulanger, as unnerved by his reverses as by his triumphs. Still, no one thought the cause irretrievably lost. Were the government to secure a conviction—and with Constans anything was possible—Boulanger was more useful out of the country than languishing in a republican prison. In the event the government proved nothing, which royalists thought more likely, it would end up looking even more foolish than its intended victim. More important, Boulanger was once again under certain royalist control. As Beauvoir noted: "[Because] I wanted to use the general as an electoral instrument and *nothing more,* I had been seriously worried since January 27 that the instrument might become greater and more powerful than was desirable." Now, his evident "loss of panache and prestige" had nicely redressed the balance. In exile Boulanger would become the docile auxiliary the royalists so desired.[75]

Much more worrisome, however, were the potential revelations of the High Court's inquiry. The government was clearly making a serious effort at discovering the source of the lavish campaign funds Boulanger had enjoyed. Indeed, this was the question that everyone had been asking, at least since the elections in Paris. Many openly suspected the royalists, although the Bonapartists seemed a more likely source. Just as popular was the theory that Boulanger, while minister of war, had accumulated large sums of money through graft. Royalists, however, had considerable faith in the government's spy network and ability to tamper with the mails, and rather less faith in the ability of all of their number to remain discreet. Any authoritative exposure of the nature of the royalist-Boulanger alliance would (as it ultimately did in 1890) throw both camps into disarray. The republican convictions or pretenses of Boulanger's associates would be shattered, and even many of the royalists who had acquiesced in the subterfuge of the "parallel march" would be openly indignant. But revelations about the source of Boulanger's funds and open electoral connivance were not the greatest threat. Electoral alliances, even perfectly shabby ones, were still legal and could be justified by necessity. The ultimate goal of the alliance, however, could not be.

The leading royalists in Paris, and most notably Beauvoir, the pretender's personal representative, fully expected to be called before the High Court. With their private papers hidden away (and not for the first time), they held a series of anxious meetings at the home of Uzès, planning how best to deal with the anticipated interrogation. All agreed it was imperative that no information be revealed about the various high-level contacts, most notably those between Count Dillon and the Count of Paris. This point needed reiteration since the Count of Paris, in one of his periodic quixotic passions for frankness, was insisting that members of his party not dissimulate before the High Court. Jacques Piou, speaking for the rest of the pretender's lieutenants, pointedly reminded him that Dillon's initial visit could easily be construed "as material proof of an understanding whose purpose was not an electoral alliance but the overthrow of the government." Apart from guaranteeing Boulanger's conviction, any admission of this event would ensure the expulsion of the remaining members of the royal family and lead to legal proceedings against the royalist leadership.[76]

Royalist fears were without foundation. The dossier of the prosecution contained little incriminating evidence against Boulanger and nothing at all concerning his intimate dealings with the royalists.[77] As the government delayed presenting its insubstantial case before the High Court, royalist anxieties about legal action were replaced by an uneasiness concerning the "political truce" induced by the opening of the 1889 exposition in Paris.[78] As Mackau insisted, Boulanger's temporary eclipse had not destroyed Boulangism and it "would be singularly unwise to let the movement collapse." Conservatives must now energetically present themselves to the public as "the necessary successors" of the Boulangist current. It was not a question of replacing Boulangism altogether; "universal suffrage is not ready for such a leap." Royalists still needed the republican Boulangists, but with the general in exile, the political center of gravity of Boulangism could be shifted to the right.[79] A Boulangism without Boulanger would provide French royalists the opportunity for their last concerted assault on the republic.

5

Boulangism Without Boulanger: The Elections of 1889

The elections of 1889 were not, as most accounts suggest, an anticlimactic epilogue to the Boulanger affair. On the contrary, they were its culminating point, the end to which the royalists' assiduous cultivation of Boulangism had always been directed. The general's unheroic departure prompted some temporary recriminations and resignations within the Republican National Committee but did not, in the long run, visibly alter Boulangist determination to challenge the Opportunist republic. Boulanger remained a useful symbol, and his enforced absence minimized the pretentions of his followers, now entirely dependent on royalist support. Royalists had come close in 1885. Infused with the popular dynamism of Boulangism, they now had an opportunity to seize control of the republic.

Even the government's defensive measures seemed to work to the advantage of the royalists. In February the Floquet government had replaced the system of proportional representation by departments (*le scrutin de liste*) with single-member constituencies. Although explicitly directed against Boulanger's plebiscitary campaigns, the new electoral system actually facilitated the royalist-Boulangist alliance. Under the old system, royalists in many parts of France would have had to share places on the departmental slate with Boulangists in order to have any chance of winning. This would inevitably entail some delicate bargaining, and in many areas the prospect of an electoral accord was altogether problematic. The new system, by contrast, dictated an obvious division of electoral labor. In the past, much of the articulate opposition to any collusion with Boulanger had come from deputies in the

125

west, where a conservative slate could win without disreputable allies. Single-member constituencies, however, meant that even in archly conservative departments there would be urban pockets of republicanism where royalists or Bonapartists would be hard-pressed. Even the resolutely anti-Boulangist Cazenove de Pradine now conceded that royalist deputies in the west would need to secure "an agreement with the Boulangist party."[1] In secure constituencies, by contrast, conservatives no longer feared the disruptive meddling of Boulangists because, as a perceptive police agent noted: "the election by single-member constituencies places them in a situation of electoral preponderance because of their connections, wealth, and local influence."[2]

From the very beginning, royalists had a clear idea of how most effectively to exploit Boulangism under the new electoral rules. In those constituencies where conservatives retained a secure hold on the population, candidates could, if they chose, ignore Boulangism altogether. In the far more numerous districts where conservative success was at best problematic, conservative candidates would make such concessions to Boulangism as were necessary to garner the support of a critical percentage of the erstwhile republican voters. Depending on the constituency, such concessions could vary from opaque allusions to revisionism to "Boulangisme à l'outrance." Finally, in those districts where no conservative stood any realistic chance of election, Boulangist candidates would run with conservative support. It was clearly understood that conservative support for Boulangists was predicated on Boulangist support for conservatives elsewhere. The Count of Paris would tell royalists in September: "Where you have candidates, support them energetically. Elsewhere, be inspired by the necessities of the struggle and do not treat as enemies those who are fighting the same adversaries as are we." Both royalists and Boulangists made ample use of that line.

There was much to recommend this strategy. Conservative commentators repeatedly observed that a gain of a mere 400,000 votes over 1885 would yield a majority for conservatives and their allies. This was a comforting but otherwise meaningless figure, of course, since the popular vote was of no political consequence. What mattered were individual constituencies, but here too relatively small shifts in vote could be decisive. In the 1889 elections some 110 conservative candidates either won or lost by a margin of fewer than 1,000 votes (51 won and 59 lost). Even if the Boulangist swing vote represented only a small percentage of the electorate in any constituency, it could make a substantial difference in terms of overall conservative representation.

For the reciprocal alliance to work effectively, the programmatic and ideological affiliations of the respective sets of candidates could not be too pronounced. Boulangist support for intransigent royalists might be hard to deliver; the same was true of conservative support for militantly republican Boulangists. Ideally, Boulangist candidates would be individuals whose republicanism was more apparent than real—apparent enough to win over republican voters, but sufficiently recent or halfhearted as to render them attractive to conservatives and *ralliable* in the event of a revisionist victory. Jules Auffray reported with satisfaction that, "in order to fully reassure conservatives," the Boulangist leaders were searching for candidates "from milieux which would in no way disturb those anxious to ensure that the future regime will be a resolutely conservative one."[3] Since most putative Boulangist candidates were ambitious place-seekers with no political past, or a shady one at best, such assurances were relatively easy. Conservatives, and royalists in particular, tended to be more intractable. Martimprey, charged by the Count of Paris with finding Boulangists for some 200 constituencies, complained that locating cooperative Boulangist candidates was "child's play" compared with persuading conservatives to "understand and practice a bit of practical politics." The "intransigents of the Right" simply had to learn that many constituencies could not be won with "former servants of the monarchy who had played a prominent role in past struggles." What was needed in 1889 were "new men whose pedigree is less pure but who for that very reason are better suited to the necessities of the moment." Unless local royalist committees could recognize that these "candidats à demi-teints" alone could "rally the votes of the masses," the campaign would be lost.[4] Consequently throughout the 1889 campaign conservative strategists consciously sought royalist candidates who (to use the contemporary neologisms) were *boulangisable* and Boulangists who were *royalisable*.

To a large degree, they succeeded. Certainly there were few royalists (and fewer Bonapartists) who felt dynastic references to be either necessary or expedient. This was not a struggle between republican and monarchist principles but between "honest men" and "the regime of corruption," and there was no place in such a noble cause for anything as sordid as individual political preferences. Frequent reference was made to the heinous "laws of exile and proscription," a formula which conveniently appealed equally to Boulangists and royalists. Most conservatives simply labeled themselves "revisionists." Lest the significance of this stance escape inattentive voters, many, like Désiré Desloges in the Calvados, reminded them that this was the very demand that "General Boulanger had inscribed in his program, which was acclaimed by more than a million voters in seven departments."[5] Even royalists who had made a journalistic career out of protesting royalist *effacement* discovered, upon becoming candidates, that their dynastic preferences were "personal opinions" with which the honest electors need not be troubled.[6] Even the euphemism *conservative,* useful enough in 1885, had lost its calculated ambiguity four years later. In thoroughly republican regions conservatives began to try out the designation *liberal,* which sounded reasonably progressive and yet conveyed discontent with the "illiberal" political and religious oppression of the existing regime. Conservative platforms were often indistinguishable from those of pure Boulangists, making Boulangist endorsement relatively painless.

As for the candidates put forward by the Boulangist Republican National Committee, most of them were the "candidats à demi-teints" of whom Martimprey had spoken earlier. Given the inherent ambiguity in the designation *Boulangist* and the complete chaos that prevailed among the Boulangist leadership, the issue of who was or was not an official Boulangist candidate was never entirely clarified. Nonetheless in September the organ of the Republican National Committee, *La Presse,* published a series of lists (entitled "Our Candidates") designating those candidates outside Paris that it was officially endorsing.[7] Of the 239 names, *La Presse* acknowledged that 49 were "our adversaries on several questions but are nonetheless formally committed to demanding revision."[8] This was a backhanded way of saying that these candidates, whom it designated simply as "revisionists," were pure royalists or Bonapartists. As Mermeix noted in *La Cocarde,* the Boulangist party could not be charged with "exclusivism" but was "receptive" to a wide range of political orientations.[9]

Both *La Presse* and *La Cocarde* nonetheless insisted that the "immense majority" of the committee's candidates were genuine republicans. To give this dubious claim a semblance of plausibility, Georges Laguerre had devised two ingenious categories for the nominally republican Boulangist candidates: "rallied republicans" and candidates "of republican origin." What characterized the ninety-two "rallied republicans" was never specified; presumably they were former conservatives who had rallied to Boulanger's version of the open republic. In fact, all that separated the "rallied republicans" from their "revisionist" colleagues was a more nuanced electoral platform and rather less candor. The news that they had recently "rallied" was sometimes greeted with dismay by those so designated; more often the reaction was one of derision.[10] Many of those granted baptismal certificates of republicanism had in fact very clearly stated that their willingness to disguise themselves as Boulangists in no way implied acceptance of the republic.[11]

A number of conservatives could also be found among the ninety-eight candidates deemed by *La Presse* to be "of republican origin." The Baron de Grilleau from the Finistère beautifully illustrated the artificiality of the Boulangist labels. Grilleau was something of a political adventurer who had been an active supporter of Boulanger since early 1888. Nonetheless he came from a deeply royalist family and his brother, a former papal Zouave, was one of the mainstays of royalism in the Aisne. Grilleau privately stressed his attachment to the Count of Paris and the "perfect conformity of ideas" between him and the local royalist committee. He had initially been listed as a "rallied republican" but, feeling that the label did not do justice to his dedication to Boulanger, he subsequently had his status changed to that of a candidate "of republican origin." Count Louis de Béllissen in the Ariège was a devoted royalist, although the republican denomination might have been an asset in his sustained feud with a Bonapartist rival over the conservative nomination. Joseph Dufour, a Bonapartist deputy from the Lot, was also assigned republican status—perhaps because his campaign was otherwise feeble. Ribeyrol in the Dordogne was a man with an ambiguous past, but he was exclusively the creation of a dissident local conservative. Louis Fournier in the Hérault was the son of a devoted royalist who had long headed the local Cercle Catholique. His own history was shadowy, but his conversion to Boulangism dated from a decision by Boulanger to authorize the marriage of his sister to a young officer—something Boulanger's predecessor in the War Ministry had refused. Dr. Félix Debacker in the Nord was "a new man," but also a devout Catholic and former editor of the royalist *Le Monde*.[12]

To be sure, most of the Boulangist candidates "of republican origin" were genuine republicans. As royalists in the Mayenne dyspeptically charged, the candidates "of republican origin" in that department were so republican they were anti-Boulangist.[13] So they were, and not at all happy to find themselves on the Boulangist list. Two of them abruptly denied any Boulangist affiliation whatsoever. A further half dozen candidates "of republican origin" publicly disavowed the patronage of the Boulangist committee, and one quickly designated himself "an anti-Boulangist revisionist." Republican scruples might have been a factor, although at least one continued to accept royalist money. A more probable explanation is that most candidates who so responded were running in the republican bastion of the southwest, where identification with the rebellious general might be an electoral handicap and where even conservatives rejected the Boulangist endorsement.[14]

The odd conservative was distressed to find himself included among the candidates of the Republican National Committee. Jacques Piou, whose inclusion was natural enough, was furious that his name should appear on the same list with a radical Boulangist like Paul de Susini. He demanded, but did not obtain, a rectification in *La Presse* to the effect that his name had appeared as the result of a misprint.[15] Rather more often, however, conservatives clamored to have their names included on the list.[16] As befitted a newspaper wholly dependent on royalist subsidies, *La Presse* catered to these demands whenever possible. When two royalist candidates from the Aisne, Godelle and Desjardins, insisted on the newspaper's support, it promptly added their names under the respective rubrics of rallied republican and revisionist.[17] Even royalists facing an official Boulangist rival could count on a sympathetic treatment. In a tortuous analysis of an election in Boulogne, *La Presse* distinguished between "M. Lefrançois, whom the general honored with a letter of investiture," and his royalist opponent "M. Achille Adam, whose name is known in the entire region." Were they rivals? "Not in the least because with respect to both his program and his declarations M. Achille Adam is one of ours; he is a Boulangist."[18] Such an analysis would have bewildered any honest Boulangist—had there been any by 1889.

The published list of candidates endorsed by the Republican National Committee was an imperfect guide to the Boulangist candidates. It was put together in some haste and much ignorance. Many did not run in the constituencies indicated, and 44 of them did not run at all (4 revisionists, 18 "rallied republicans," and 22 candidates "of republican origin"). In some cases their nomination had been purely frivolous; more often they were bribed or bullied out of the race by conservatives. Replacing them, although usually in different constituencies, were nearly as many candidates who called themselves Boulangists. The committee appears to have considered some of them official candidates; others represented only themselves. As a group they represented roughly the same mix of ideological leanings, personal respectability, and electoral credibility as did those on the official list. Attempting a quantitative statement about the true political valences of Boulangist candidates would, in the light of previous discussion, be a pointless exercise. About all one can say is that, of the candidates formally announced by the committee who ran serious campaigns (i.e., obtained at least 1,000 votes), those designated as being "of republican origin" represented about 35 percent. Eliminating those who were obviously conservatives or who publicly rejected Boulanger's endorsement would reduce that figure still further. Given a certain interpretation of Boulangism, it might be argued that the thinly disguised conservatives given official endorsement were not "true" Boulangists. The fact remains that they were also the great majority of the official Boulangist candidates, and for the royalists that was all that mattered.

Ensuring that a majority of Boulangist candidates were highly tractable did not automatically guarantee a rational division of electoral labor. The logic of limiting Boulangist candidates to constituencies where conservatives stood no chance was more appealing to conservatives than to Boulangists. In theory Boulangists could cater to republican voters, but in practice the great bulk of Boulangist votes in the past had been cast by conservatives. Given that their electorate was likely to be substantially the same as that of conservatives, Boulangists would be strongly tempted to contest conservative constituencies. Correspondingly, constituencies where conservatives stood no chance were likely to be ones where Boulangists could do very little better, especially if their republicanism was suspect. Nonetheless, conservatives had reason to believe that the dangers of overlapping claims could be minimized. Boulanger, now in inglorious exile, was in no position to make extravagant demands, and royalist negotiators reported that his lieutenants were perfectly reasonable in the preliminary discussions over the electoral division of labor. One important reason for this was that royalists had a far better grasp of the intricacies of the 568 constituencies of France than did the Boulangist leadership, whose local infrastructure was often rudimentary or nonexistent. Armed with superior organization and knowledge, royalists felt certain of their ability to ensure a monopoly over promising districts.[19]

Such confidence notwithstanding, rivalries between conservative and Boulangist candidates appeared to be a prominent feature of the 1889 campaign. *La Gazette de France,* guardian of intransigent royalism, spent the entire summer documenting cases of Boulangists challenging royalists; on the eve of the election it listed no fewer than sixty-three examples. Bocher periodically fulminated about the "treachery" of the Boulangists, while Boulanger privately complained of the "imbecilic treason" of the Orleanists.[20] The private papers of Mackau and the Count of Paris are replete with acrimonious exchanges about Boulangist incursions into conservative territory and vice versa. The pretender's dyspeptic conversations with Dillon on this issue have led historians to conclude that the alliance was in disarray.[21]

Some local tensions were inevitable, owing less to any fundamental disagreement between the conservative and Boulangist headquarters than to their inability to control their respective local followers. Internal communications within the royalist leadership were imperfect, and among the Boulangists almost nonexistent. The Boulangist Republican National Committee was always in such a state of confusion that it often had no idea what constituencies had been promised to whom. Throughout the summer a steady stream of unauthorized Boulangist candidates kept popping up, believing, or pretending, that they had the investiture of Boulanger or one of his lieutenants. Some of the more bizarre Boulangists had been cavalierly assigned a provincial constituency for no better reason than to get them out of everyone's way in Paris.[22]

Despite the rantings of *La Gazette de France* (which rarely got its facts straight), what caused local rivalries was not Boulangist bad faith or avarice but incompetence. (Indeed, bad faith and avarice were rather more characteristic of the conservatives.) The elections in the Pas-de-Calais provide a perfect illustration.

The Pas-de-Calais was a department where conservatives had lost much ground since 1885. Although they had taken all seven seats, by 1889 even the most secure conservative felt the need of Boulangist support. In Boulogne the royalist candidate was Achille Adam, scion of a prominent and powerful local banking family. Although the Adam family had a long history of public service in Boulogne and exercised considerable influence, local royalists recognized that he would need the help of the Boulangists to secure election. In exchange for Boulangist support for Adam, they were prepared to mobilize conservatives in Calais behind the Boulangist candidate Charles Georgi. In January Georgi, a wealthy forge master, had vigorously campaigned for Boulanger in the twelfth arrondissement of Paris (where he owned a factory), and he received the official endorsement of the Republican National Committee and Boulanger himself.[23] But while Georgi was a particularly prominent supporter of Boulanger (and for that reason was accepted rather reluctantly by some local royalists), he was fundamentally a conservative who not only belonged to the departmental conservative committee but had run as a conservative in the July cantonal elections. Consequently, local Boulangists treated the Adam-Georgi deal as a shabby attempt by conservatives to claim both major urban centers of the department. Their leader, Lefrançois, loudly demanded at least one of the two seats. This was an impossible demand, since royalists were adamant about Boulogne, and Georgi had long had the public endorsement of Boulanger.

At this point, however, the general's basic ignorance of French electoral geography intervened. In a unique administrative anomaly both Calais and Boulogne were in the same arrondissement, and Boulogne, despite being half the size of Calais, was the administrative seat. Consequently, the electoral district of Calais was technically known as the second constituency of Boulogne. Boulanger, knowing that Adam was in Boulogne no. 1 and Georgi in Calais, blissfully endorsed Lefrançois in Boulogne no. 2, quite unaware that the latter two constituencies were identical. The announcement brought Georgi's true allegiances into sharper focus, for he quickly denounced the Boulangists for having broken their promises to the conservative party. Even Boulanger could not support two candidates in the same district! Since Lefrançois, a resident of Boulogne, had little support in its archrival, Calais, he was eventually assigned a seat in Boulogne—to the consternation of royalists. Throughout the campaign the supporters of Adam adduced evidence to show that their man was the preferred candidate of Boulanger and his headquarters. On the second ballot Boulanger formally requested that Lefrançois withdraw and that Boulangists support Adam. A majority did and he won the seat.[24]

Many of the disruptive rivalries in 1889 had little to do with royalist-Boulangist misunderstandings, but were in fact part of the larger history of intraconservative struggles, usually but not always between royalists and Bonapartists. Royalists considered the Bonapartists to be a leaderless phantom party whose decrepit state ought to render it content with a modest share of safe conservative seats. Bonapartists retorted that royalism was the party of the châteaux, altogether lacking the kind of appeal among the more modest rural classes which the imperial party could claim. Boulangism thus became a useful cover for what were merely feuds about the distribution of seats.

Faced with the difficult task of distinguishing republican Boulangists from conservative ones, most historians have assumed that anyone calling himself a Boulangist and opposing a royalist must fit into the former category. Auguste Engerand, running in the first constituency of Caen, is invariably identified as a "pure" republican Boulangist, presumably because he was challenging the incumbent royalist deputy, Désiré Desloges. In fact he was notoriously a Bonapartist, contributed violent articles to the local Bonapartist newspaper, and was regarded as "the *enfant terrible* of the reactionary party." The Count of Paris was not pleased that Engerand challenged one of his incumbents, but his lieutenants privately acknowledged that he would be a more reliable deputy than his obstreperous legitimist rival. Indeed, although the pretender provided money to bribe Engerand out of the race, royalist headquarters persuaded Desloges instead to withdraw and used the funds to support his rival's second-ballot campaign.[25] Similarly, the unsuccessful Boulangist challenge to Cazenove de Pradine in Nantes was unrelated to Cazenove's articulate opposition to Boulanger. His rival, Gabriel Gaudin, son an an imperial minister, was simply trying to break the royalist political monopoly in the department, a longstanding grievance of the Bonapartists of the Loire-Atlantique.[26]

The election in the fourth district of Bordeaux seemed to pit Paul Princeteau, a wealthy landowner and old-line legitimist, against de Sonneville, a Boulangist with the formal support of the Republican National Committee. Since Princeteau was closely identified with a faction of Girondin royalists who had been outspoken in their hostility to Boulangism, much was made of the ideological tensions in this contest. In fact, little of substance separated the two rivals. Sonneville, in addition to being an old family friend of Princeteau's, was also a former legitimist who had gravitated in the 1880s toward a Jeromist brand of Bonapartism. Princeteau, for his part, was anxious to cater to the Boulangist current, being prepared to "do as much Boulangism as necessary and as can be done without denying his royalist past," and was outraged upon discovering that, notwithstanding his agreement with Georges Laguerre, he was not officially endorsed by the Republican National Committee. Sonneville was left in the contest only because, as even local royalists acknowledged, Princeteau was deemed unlikely to win. Princeteau, significantly, had been prepared to withdraw, if his place were taken by Boulanger himself. In the end Sonneville withdrew after the first ballot and delivered his vote to Princeteau, who lost narrowly.[27]

Bonapartist Boulangists did not restrict themselves to challenging royalists. Bonapartism was a multifaceted phenomenon by 1889, characterized by rifts of every kind. Victorians and Jeromists, former legitimists and crypto-Orleanists, authoritarian republicans, intransigent imperialists, and flexible solutionists all fell under the general label of Bonapartist. Boulangism therefore had a certain appeal for the mutually antagonistic factions. In the Dordogne, a stronghold of Bonapartism in France, Bonapartists were particularly quarrelsome. The appearance of a Boulangist candidate in the arrondissement of Nontron prompted a fresh outbreak of intestine feuding. Nontron was the most Boulangist district in the department but the candidate, Georges Ribeyrol, was entirely the creation of a prominent and dissident local Bonapartist who was deliberately challenging the authority of the local Bonapartist committee. The committee was furious but would have endorsed Ribeyrol, his unsavory past notwithstanding, lest his supporter make good on his threat to sow dissident candidates throughout the department. The nomination, however, was coveted by another intransigent Bonpartist, Albert Sarlande, who also had a history of stirring up dissident candidates. Sarlande, who was given to spending money lavishly during elections, managed in the end to persuade all Bonapartists of the wisdom of giving him the nomination, and a bitterly disillusioned Ribeyrol ultimately withdrew from the race.[28]

Nor were royalists averse to lobbying the local Boulangist committee, if they could thereby dislodge an incumbent Bonapartist.[29] Similarly, given the opportunity to displace an Orleanist rival, even the most intransigent legitimist was prepared to forsake the Count of Chambord for *le brav' général*.[30] To keep nuisance candidates out of their constituencies, even very secure conservatives would adopt the Boulangist mantle. In the Indre, for example, the Bonapartist Paul Benazet was so secure that republicans were reluctant to run against him. But in order to preempt a rumored "Boulangist" challenge, he openly declared his Boulangist sympathies.[31]

Because conservative candidates were almost invariably selected by a small coterie of prominent local notables, Boulangism had an obvious appeal for conservatives who felt that their ambitions would otherwise be thwarted. The characteristics that might make a man unappealing to a conservative nominating committee—youth, a disreputable life style, a questionable past—moved many of them to active participation in local Boulangist organizations. The leader of the tiny Boulangist coterie in La Roche-sur-Yon in the Vendée was the son of a royalist deputy, Paul Bourgeois, who had been a Bonapartist militant during the Empire. Bourgeois had long desired to become a senator in order to yield his seat in the Chamber to his son. In a department where the distinction between royalists and Bonapartists was taken seriously, however, Bourgeois's Bonapartist past was never forgiven him. Under the leadership of the "grand elector" of the Vendée, the bishop of Luçon, local legitimists had always frustrated his senatorial aspirations. The Boulangist activities of his son were part of an effort to shake free of such control so as to realize his political ambitions.[32] In the Aube, the leader of Boulangism in Troyes was the former Bonapartist deputy Argence, who sought the nomination in the face of strong opposition from the local conservative committee.[33] Henri de Maribail was a dedicated royalist in the Haute-Garonne who for years had sought to become a major conservative power broker. Despite his considerable wealth, he never managed to expand his political influence beyond his home canton and was treated by the royalist leadership of the department as a second-rate ward heeler. To enhance his political importance, he became a local Boulangist organizer.[34] William Guynet was a young royalist from the Drôme who preferred the sporting life in Paris to living in Montélimar. For this reason local conservatives looked unfavorably on him and his electoral ambitions. Nonetheless he was the darling of what the subprefect described as the "parti réactionnaire jeune," and he and his youthful friends were the mainstays of Boulangism in Montélimar.[35] Auguste Paille, a royalist and unsuccessful local politician in the Marne, was the leader of the Boulangists in Reims. His repeated requests for money disquieted royalist leaders, who had little confidence in his personal probity, although his childhood friendship with the Duchesse d'Uzès assured him of financial support disproportionate to his limited achievements as a political organizer.[36] Boulangism, like later parties of the "new" Right, had an obvious attraction for conservatives who felt excluded from the mainstream of right-wing politics.[37]

Such bids rarely succeeded. Boulangism might provide ambitious aspirants with a popular power base but, given the transparently reactionary credentials of most of them, support was uncertain. Moreover Boulangism could provide no independent financial leverage. Amédée de Lacrouselle, a twenty-eight-year-old bohemian son of a prominent Bonapartist in the Dordogne, created a Boulangist committee in Périgueux in order to mobilize working-class elements behind his putative candidacy. Unimpressed by his professions of republicanism, the committee refused its support. Failing to persuade any genuine republicans to run, the committee ended up endorsing the wealthy and popular incumbent royalist deputy Alexis Maréchal. Something of the character of Boulangism in Périgueux was revealed when the Boulangist committee sponsored a postelection victory party for Maréchal and then allowed him to pick up the tab.[38] Here, wealth was ultimately more important than ideological nuances. The reason a man of pronounced legitimist sentiments like the Comte de la Panousse could enjoy the support of both Boulanger and the local Boulangists was the fact that he was the richest man in the Dordogne and willing to spend vast sums on his election.[39]

Even the presence of a radical Boulangist running against a conservative did not necessarily represent Boulangist encroachment. Conservatives often sought to split the republican vote and charged their Boulangist allies with the task of creating a "diversion."[40] In cases like this, a genuinely radical Boulangist was more useful than a veiled conservative, a point which at times escaped royalist strategists. In the solidly republican department of the Doubs, the leader of the local royalists, Nicholas Koechlin, had no chance of winning without Boulangist assistance. The Boulangists, of course, were willing to endorse him but, as he patiently explained, such a subterfuge would not seduce a single republican voter, so well known was he for his royalism. What he needed was not Boulangist patronage but a Boulangist rival. Royalist headquarters dredged up a couple of innocuous Boulangists, naively assuring him that they were not "dangerous." A thoroughly exasperated Koechlin retorted that only a radical and therefore "dangerous" Boulangist could make serious inroads on the Opportunist vote and force a second ballot. Credible republican Boulangists were in short supply and usually reserved for more promising circumstances, so Koechlin's urgent pleas were never satisfied.[41]

Some of the more outrageous Boulangist candidates were only in the race because they were all that conservatives could find. The Var, like much of the southwest, was hopeless territory for conservatives. What royalists hoped for was a "conservative in a hurry." What they got was Achille Ballière, a former Communard whom Mackau had pushed out of Paris in exchange for 10,000 francs and the thankless assignment of running against Georges Clemenceau. No one was very pleased by Ballière, and even the usually unflappable Beauvoir thought Mackau was being too clever by half. Ballière was not much of a "conservative in a hurry," but he could equivocate with the best of them and blissfully assured local conservatives that, although a free thinker, he did not believe that "thirty-six million Catholics should . . . be forced to yield to two million Protestants and Jews . . . or bow to the banner of materialists and atheists." This rhetoric must have appealed to some conservatives, since he did well only in those communes dominated by royalists. As the campaign progressed, the royalist newspaper *Le Var* evinced a growing (albeit never very great) enthusiasm for Ballière and incessantly echoed the pretender's recommendation not to "treat as enemies those who are fighting the same adversaries as are we."[42]

Keeping Boulangist candidates out of conservative constituencies often proved easier than persuading them to run in republican ones. In the Nord, local Boulangists and royalists took turns offering one another a free hand in the second district of Avesnes, the fiefdom of the immensely popular Radical deputy Maxime Lecomte. Only at the last minute was an impecunious Parisian Boulangist persuaded to make the attempt.[43] Fortunately for the royalists, many republican Boulangists were pathetic creatures whom they could bully with impunity. Conservatives in the Haute-Marne wanted a Boulangist candidate in the arrondissement of Vassy, which had a substantial working-class electorate and where they believed only a Boulangist could win. The logical choice was the former Radical and incumbent deputy from the department, François Steenackers. Steenackers, like many Boulangists in 1889, felt that his chances were decidedly better in one of the two other arrondissements, Chaumont and Langres, which were far more conservative. Steenackers was stubborn but also notoriously venal, so that 30,000 francs persuaded him to run in Vassy after all. Boulangists also supported conservatives in the other constituencies of the department. Steenackers's obvious collusion with the royalists distressed some of his followers, one of whom slipped a cautiously demurring note into the deputy's local newspaper. Faced with the immediate wrath of the royalists, Steenackers plaintively noted that it was uncommonly difficult for him to retain much credibility as a radical Boulangist, unless he appeared to be ever so slightly critical of conservatives. Royalists, suspecting blackmail, were unimpressed and cut off most of his funding.[44]

The only Boulangists whom conservatives could not easily control were the few incumbent deputies with secure constituencies. Two radical deputies from Nevers, Gaston Laporte and Jean Turigny, had rallied to Boulangism. In the other three predominantly rural constituencies, conservatives faced a close race and noted that the miners and factory workers, among whom Boulangism had made some progress, represented the critical swing vote. They therefore agreed to support Laporte and Turigny in exchange for reciprocal support in their districts. Turigny readily assented, but the electorally more confident Laporte was looking for more than royalist votes. His newspaper, *Le Patriote du Centre,* had an influence that extended into two neighboring departments, the Allier and the Cher. He notified several royalist candidates in the Cher that the price for not being attacked by his newspaper would be 40,000 francs. Since he was already actively attacking a royalist candidate in the Allier, his threat seemed real enough. Royalists were outraged by such impudent blackmail, not least because they were already subsidizing *Le Patriote.* The 10,000 francs designated for his campaign were withdrawn, although, as irritated royalists subsequently discovered, some portion of the money found its way to Laporte by a circuitous route.[45]

That even those royalists who most staunchly defended the Boulangists should have considered Laporte's behavior to be a dramatic example of treason spoke to the degree of submissiveness that they expected from their allies. Although his obstreperous attitude prompted some halfhearted royalist candidacies in Nevers, Laporte was only marginally less cooperative than were most Boulangists in 1889. His "attacks" on the royalist candidate in the Allier consisted of a few snide references in the back pages of his newspaper, coupled with a vague preference for a marginal Bonapartist candidate. Moreover, they were part of a running feud with the Boulangist newspaper in the Allier, which was enthusiastically supporting all royalists. The threatened campaign against royalists in the Cher never materialized, and his newspaper displayed a distinct preference for the conservative candidates over their republican rivals.[46]

Even where they had little to bargain with, royalists demanded firm evidence of Boulangist good faith and could become feisty if they did not obtain it. The department of the Corrèze was poor and devoid of many influential landed proprietors, hence at the mercy of government patronage. Despite periodic efforts at organization, royalists in that department remained in a state of torpor.[47] The growth of Boulangism in the department was therefore welcomed by royalists, who claimed that it "gives them confidence, boosts morale, and appears as a powerful ally," which was another way of saying that they now believed that they could "dispense with all effort, work, or sacrifice."[48] Having long ago given up on the arms-manufacturing city of Tulle, royalists were quite willing to support two radical Boulangists, the incumbent deputies Léonard Vacher and Etienne Borie. But they wanted their support to be acknowledged. Borie did so but Vacher, vice-president of the Republican National Committee, preferred a more discreet posture. Privately he requested 14,000 francs from the royalist campaign fund, but publicly he politely declined to be associated with conservatives. His funding was immediately cut off although, typically, 6,000 francs ultimately filtered down to him. His stance so annoyed local conservatives that they ran a candidate against him and denied him a first-ballot victory.[49] On the second ballot the conservative, whose campaign so resembled that of Vacher that *Le Temps* thought him another Boulangist, gave him full support.[50]

There were, of course, royalist committees which could not forgo the ingrained habit of principled posturing, so that Boulangist candidates were at times treated to gratuitous sniping from the royalist press. The rhetorical froth, however, usually masked a high degree of cooperation.

Count Dillon was assigned the first district of Lorient in the Morbihan, one of the few constituencies in that department where a royalist candidate risked losing.[51] The royalist leadership in the department had been largely refractory to Boulangism; *Le Morbihannais,* run by a notoriously inflexible legitimist, Edmond Fiquet, filled its pages with veiled suggestions that Boulangism represented an elaborate antiroyalist plot. Dillon's name was never mentioned and readers were counseled to submit a blank ballot. For his pains, Fiquet was subject to the savage heckling of his confreres in the republican press, who knew perfectly well that he was in constant contact with local Boulangist leaders, whose influence among port workers he envied. He and everyone else acknowledged that local royalists were paying no attention to *Le Morbihannais* and would vote en masse for Dillon.[52]

Although the point was lost in the subsequent denials and recriminations, the Boulangists served royalists as useful and docile auxiliaries. Neither side was free of erratic individuals, of course, but most of the dysfunctional rivalries involved competing conservatives and were susceptible to second-ballot resolution. The great majority of the troublesome Boulangist candidates had withdrawn by election day, and those that remained usually attracted only a handful of votes. Most Boulangists were little more than veiled conservatives, and those who were not were usually running exactly where conservatives felt they could do them the most good. Even notionally republican Boulangists were prepared to excise the word "republican" from their campaign posters at the behest of royalists, or even let them dictate their electoral declarations.[53] Many, to be sure, were unnatural allies and not a few were complete scoundrels. For all that, they could see the wisdom of appeasing the royalists. Despite the occasional contretemps, royalist insiders usually conceded that the Boulangists had been remarkably conciliatory, and some had gone so far to appease conservatives that they were beginning to sound "almost too monarchist."[54]

Money was decisive in ensuring that kind of tractability. Given the tortuous channels by which money was often delivered, exactly how much the royalists spent on Boulangists during the elections, to say nothing of the exact distribution, cannot be established with certainty. Bocher, Martimprey, and Mackau all had separate funds and were not always anxious to inform one another about their respective accounts. La Trémoille, the treasurer, repeatedly attempted to obtain a precise accounting from Mackau; in turn, he and Bocher had secrets which they jealousy guarded from the others.[55] Boulangists, of course, were even less scrupulous. In September 160,000 francs were allocated to the

Republican National Committee, to be distributed to twenty-seven candidates proposed by Dillon and Auffray and approved by Bocher. By this time Maurice Jollivet, the Boulangist treasurer, had already given or promised money to a host of individuals specifically excluded by Auffray, including candidates like Pendrié in the Ain, for whom 3,000 francs seemed like a steep price for the 33 votes he ultimately attracted, or James in the Sarthe, who obtained 336 votes and was running against a royalist to boot. By trimming the sums formally approved for some candidates and by overspending his budget by 40,000 francs, Jollivet managed to stretch his allocation to cover a total of fifty-two candidates, some of whom were already receiving royalist money by other channels.[56]

Money also passed back and forth between the royalist fund and the nearly depleted treasury of the Duchesse d'Uzès, further obscuring the details. La Trémoille concluded that royalists had spent a total of just over 4.4 million francs on the elections. Subtracting those sums that *appear* to have been exclusively for conservative candidates and propaganda, 1.67 million francs, or roughly 40 percent of the total, was spent on Boulangists.[57] Including the pretender's initial contribution and that of Uzès, royalists in eighteen months spent well over 5 million francs on Boulangism.

While conservative votes could subsequently be forgotten or disavowed, money left more permanent traces. Royalists often extracted guarantees about religious questions and the abrogation of the laws of exile in exchange for opening the purse. Nor were Boulangist candidates permitted any illusions about the source of their funding; they were compelled to sign receipts which unambiguously showed them to be on the royalist payroll. Royalists put considerable store in the subsequent leverage such documentation might give them over successful Boulangist candidates, although the ease with which the ex-Communard Ballière could promise to support royalist religious and educational proposals ought to have prompted some sober reflection. Paul de Susini's gratuitous request that the Count of Paris be reminded of his family's royalist convictions said more about the ex-Radical than it did about his future reliability.[58] In the confusion that prevailed in the last weeks of the campaign, many Boulangists, spotting the receipts for the trap they obviously were, managed to avoid signing them. Flaminius Raiberti, a republican Boulangist running in Nice, dug up his father's imperial connections in order to obtain 4,000 francs from Mackau. Upon being asked for a receipt, he preferred to return the money lest his republican opponents learn of it and "say that I am not sincere because

I am not free." Mackau, probably stunned by such atypical probity, let him keep the money anyway.[59]

Inevitably some republican Boulangists would inadvertently expose their dependence on royalists rather earlier than royalists might have wished. Susini, running against Constans in Toulouse, received 25,000 francs in the form of a check written on La Trémoille's account. He promptly took it to the local branch of the Crédit Lyonnais to have it cashed. Skeptical bank officials considered the association of Susini with La Trémoille unnatural and telegraphed the head office in Paris to confirm the check's authenticity. Since officers of the republican administration notoriously did not consider the confidentiality of the telegraphic service to be an absolute right, and since Susini's opponent was the most ruthless minister of the interior in the Third Republic's history, chance alone seems to have prevented Susini's complete dependence on the royalists from becoming public knowledge.[60]

Despite extensive evidence to the contrary, Boulangism in 1889 continues to be portrayed as a genuinely radical phenomenon having a dynamic quite independent from that of the conservative Right. An important reason for this perception is the fact that in several regions of France Boulangism does not initially seem to fit the patterns heretofore suggested. The elections in Bordeaux and Nancy appear to have pitted genuinely radical Boulangists against intransigent royalists. The Boulangist candidates Maurice Barrès and Alfred Gabriel in Nancy and Albert Chiché, Henri Aimel, and Antoine Jourde in Bordeaux were, or appeared to be, men of the Left with impressive radical or socialist credentials. They won in republican districts with undeniable working-class support and without any apparent aid from the Right. Royalists in these departments had been outspoken in their hostility to Boulangism and in Nancy challenged Boulangist candidates on the first ballot.

Historians of Boulangism in these two regions have cited the 1889 elections as proof of the existence of a genuinely leftist Boulangism devoid of the reactionary tinges that colored the phenomenon in other parts of France. S. Stewart Doty, in a major study of the politics of Maurice Barrès, although correctly noting that the elections in Bordeaux and Nancy were atypical, nonetheless insists that in these two cities "provincial Boulangism buil[t] a movement from scratch on a leftist base and [won] by cutting into Opportunist and conservative strength without allying with either." In an important article on Boulangism in the Gironde, Patrick Hutton has highlighted the importance of Boulangism for the socialist movement there, stressing its active role in the Boulangist campaign as well as the important lessons about mass politics that socialists derived from the experience.[61] Yet a close examination of the 1889 election campaign in both areas reveals a far more intimate alliance between these nominally incompatible groups and demonstrates that here too Boulangists were, and were considered to be, auxiliaries rather than rivals of the conservative Right.

Royalist prospects were not very encouraging in the thoroughly republican Meurthe-et-Moselle. Royalists had trailed the winning republican list in 1885 by 13,000 votes, with the margin particularly great in the city of Nancy. What characterized royalism in the Meurthe-et-Moselle were the latent tensions between legitimists and Orleanists, an elitist social composition, and the sterility of its organization. The landed proprietors, bankers, and industrialists who dominated the party were largely indifferent to organizational questions. The earnest efforts of the local secretary invariably proved abortive, and by the fall of 1888 his succinct conclusion was that "l'organisation ne marche pas."[62]

Throughout 1888 royalists in the department were hostile to Boulanger, their opposition reflected in the vitriolic editorials of their two major newspapers, which routinely excoriated both the general and conservatives who sought an alliance with him.[63] Some royalists changed their minds, however, when in the spring of 1889 the Boulangists for the first time created an effective and powerful local organization. The local secretary commented enviously on the "unbelievable energy" of the Boulangist leaders Maurice Barrès and Alfred Gabriel and on their growing influence among the working classes of Nancy.[64] The royalist *Le Journal de la Meurthe et des Vosges* ceased its attacks on Boulanger and saw its circulation increase as a result.[65] Royalists began to appreciate the possibilities of supporting Boulangists in Nancy in exchange for support in Lunéville, Toul, and Briey, where conservatives at least had some chance of success. As the Count of Paris noted: "It is . . . obvious that a candidate who is too overtly royalist will have no chance in Nancy. Naturally we will have to give the Boulangists a share in order to obtain their support elsewhere."[66]

A major obstacle to such an arrangement, particularly in the light of the continuing reservations of many royalists in Nancy, was the decided radicalism of the leading Boulangists there. By 1889 both Barrès and Gabriel had adopted platforms that could loosely be called socialist. But in the 1880s French socialism was still a vague, nebulous affair, and what passed for socialism was often little more than a general concern for the social question. Alfred Gabriel, who led the Radical list in 1885, called himself a socialist, but his brand of socialism was fuzzy and he often equated socialism with almost any project for social reform. He considered Albert de Mun to be a "convinced socialist" and spoke often about the "socialist ideas" of French conservatives, who "in common with us . . . seek the good of the workers and favor the old age pension." His socialism, although not his anticlericalism, was therefore sufficiently amorphous and ambiguous as to permit him to believe that Boulangists could "make a new revolution with new elements, . . . royalists without a king." Although local royalists never really warmed to him, by the summer of 1889 Mackau's agent could report with satisfaction that Gabriel appeared to have "put water in his wine" and mellowed with age.[67]

Maurice Barrès had rather abruptly converted to socialism under the influence of Gabriel. There has been considerable debate about the authenticity of Barrès's socialism. Stewart Doty has argued that he was, at least by the standards of contemporary French socialism, a genuine socialist, even if his grasp of the ideology was marred by his irrational way of knowing.[68] Yet as Doty admits, Barrès's socialism was always somewhat confused and replete with elements that allowed him to consort with allies unusual for a socialist. The socialism of a man who could praise the German Emperor for having "become socialist," dedicated to improving the conditions of the working poor, was a highly flexible kind of socialism which rendered him sympathetic to local conservatives.[69] Martimprey reported that Barrès was "a very ralliable Boulangist, a monarchist at heart," an assessment shared by Mackau's agent in the department as well as by the president of the royalist committee in Barrès's district.[70] Consequently royalists, or at least some of them, were prepared to cooperate with the radical Boulangist of Nancy.

The leading royalist exponent of such an alliance was Charles Welche, mayor of Nancy during the German occupation, a prefect during Marshal MacMahon's "coup d'état" of 16 May 1877, and one of the directors of *Le Journal de la Meurthe et des Vosges*. Welche was also a perennially unsuccessful candidate. He proposed that Boulangists support his candidacy in the second district of Nancy in exchange for royalist support for Gabriel and Barrès in the first and third districts. Since royalists stood no chance whatsoever in the first and third districts, whereas the second was a reasonably promising one for the Boulangists, the advantages of this proposal for the Boulangists were not obvious. What induced Barrès to accept Welche's strategy was the guarantee of 10,000 francs plus a further 3,000 for Gabriel.[71] Barrès was later to deny any complicity, financial or otherwise, with the royalists, but it is incontestable that he did receive the money and that financial support was intended to implicate him. He received the first installment of 5,000 francs on August 21 and, at the explicit request of the royalist headquarters, acknowledged it with a receipt. A week later he met in Paris with Mackau's secretary, who informed Bocher, "M. Barrès of Nancy can henceforth be considered *comme à nous,* for he is bound by his receipt and by a letter he sent to Auffray."[72] Barrès seems to have realized that the receipt had compromised him, since at the end of September royalist headquarters was still hounding him for a receipt for the second 5,000 francs received on the 18th of the month.[73]

The Welche-Barrès agreement soon came under attack, however, from both Boulangists and royalists. The novelist Paul Adam demanded the Boulangist nomination in the second district, insisting that Welche's royalism and his May 16 associations made him an implausible revisionist and guaranteed his defeat.[74] Local royalists also opposed the arrangement, partly out of distaste for Gabriel but primarily in opposition to Welche himself. Welche's overt endorsement of Boulangism had irritated sensibilities among royalists, who in any case thought his chances of success slim. The president of the local royalist committee insisted that they were not opposed to an electoral accord with the Boulangists; but Welche appeared to them to be as much a Boulangist as a royalist, and his proposed arrangement amounted to the total abdication of the party in the city. Welche managed to dissuade an ambitious local lawyer, René Renard, from running against him as a rival royalist candidate, but was unable (and after Adam entered the race, unwilling) to prevent him from challenging Barrès in the third district. Renard's disruptive presence had little to do with doctrinal purity, since he was a political opportunist who had earlier attempted to strike his own deal with the Boulangists. Even though royalists ultimately opposed the Boulangists in all three urban districts, the local committee explicitly stated that "on the second ballot we can always unite with them against the Opportunists."[75] Royalists came in a distant third in all three races and withdrew in favor of Barrès, Gabriel, and Adam on the second ballot.

In fact, the Count of Paris did make an effort to preserve the second arrondissement of Nancy for Welche, who unlike the other two royalist candidates trailed his Boulangist opponent by only 250 votes. In London, the Count and Beauvoir persuaded Dillon that Paul Adam should retire in favor of Welche, if Barrès and Gabriel wanted second-ballot royalist support. When Beauvoir returned to Paris, however, he learned that Mackau had just dispatched Maurice Barrès back to Nancy with a considerable sum of money intended not to bribe Adam into withdrawing, but to support his second-ballot campaign. In Beauvoir's absence

Bocher, Mackau, and Breteuil had come to an accord with Georges Laguerre on second-ballot withdrawals, and all had agreed that Welche had no chance of winning in a city where he could not even count on royalist support.[76] *Le Journal de la Meurthe et des Vosges* actively supported the Boulangists on the second round. The second-ballot figures suggest that less than half the royalist voters shifted their votes to the Boulangists, enough to elect Barrès and Gabriel but not Adam.

The alignment of forces in Nancy was more ambiguous than in many other regions. A critically disruptive factor was the principled objection of many royalists to an unsavory alliance. Welche repeatedly complained of the machinations of the "ultras" who were "more royalist than the King," preferring defeat in isolation to a victorious alliance.[77] But it is also clear from the responses of a number of local royalists that the prospect of veiled alliance was not unwelcome and that personal antagonisms and ambitions were as important as ideological reservations in obstructing a more fruitful entente. Although royalist support for Boulangists in the second round was only partial, neither Barrès nor Gabriel would have been elected without it, and nothing royalists could have done would have saved Adam. Royalist money and connivance were sufficiently important to bedevil the campaigns of Barrès and Gabriel, obliging them endlessly to explain it away. Ironically, the public hostility of some royalists undoubtedly made their task easier. As the police commissioner observed early in 1889: "Behind Boulangism stands Orleanism. The latter party seems to be repudiating the former, the better to assure its success."[78]

By comparison with the Meurthe-et-Moselle, and indeed most of France, royalism in the Gironde was a cohesive and potent force. Virtually every canton maintained a royalist committee, and the party faithful were wealthy and, at least at election time, generous. There were a half dozen royalist newspapers in the department, the most important of which, the daily *Nouvelliste de Bordeaux,* had a regular circulation of 31,000, rising to 45,000 during the elections. It was also the most influential royalist organ in the dozen departments of the southwest. The political director of *Le Nouvelliste* and secretary general of the royalist committee was André Cordier. Young, energetic, and highly intelligent, Cordier was the workhorse of the royalist party and the key to conservative politics in the department. Reports about Cordier and his fellow royalists submitted by royalist agents in 1889 contrasted strikingly with the often dismal accounts of other departments.[79]

The lavish praise for the Girondin royalists could not, however, disguise the fact that, as a royalist agent soberly admitted, "they have no influence among the masses."[80] Among the agricultural laborers and the small cultivators of the department, royalists commanded none of the popularity that the Bonapartists enjoyed, and were invariably identified as "nobles," "rich bourgeoisie," or "the rich proprietors of the numerous châteaux."[81] As one royalist complained, the party was "almost always inaccessible to the middle classes" because of the preponderance of titled aristocrats in its midst.[82] André Cordier noted with some exasperation that while there were many royalist committees in the department, most were glorified debating societies "which recruit their members not among those who are electorally influential but among those who are socially influential—the two being very different things. Such committees are not and cannot be suited to universal suffrage."[83]

Awareness of their limited popular appeal did not initially render the Girondin royalists receptive to Boulanger or Boulangism. Indeed, their hostility to Boulangism was particularly intense. Throughout 1888 Cordier's trenchant editorials helped galvanize the anti-Boulangist resistance of much of the legitimist west (to the considerable irritation of the royalist leadership in Paris, which felt that his editorial skills exceeded his political acumen). In the autumn Girondin royalists were still trying to force the pretender to abandon the Boulangist alliance. Clearly rebuffed on that issue, Cordier at last admitted that the Boulangists would have to be considered as "part of the conservative army."[84]

Royalists in the Gironde were confronted with two distinct kinds of Boulangism: a radical and socialist Boulangism in Bordeaux and a conservative Bonapartist Boulangism in the rural districts. As the subperfect of the rural arrondissement of Libourne noted, "Boulangists are reactionaries who have changed names."[85] These Bonapartist Boulangists certainly wanted no truck with "revolutionary socialists rallied to Boulangism" and pointedly reminded radical Boulangists with ideas about contesting conservative constituencies that it was impossible for them to win anywhere in the Gironde without the active support of the conservative forces.[86] As elsewhere in France, Bonapartists used Boulangism as a cover for their efforts to dislodge royalists, but the resulting dissident candidacies made no substantial difference to the outcome of the elections.[87]

But if Boulangism outside the city of Bordeaux simply added spice to the perennial intraconservative skirmishes, it was, as André Cordier complained, an inane use of the new political phenomenon. Calling Bonapartists "rallied republicans," he noted, was a pointless exercise, since their politics were too well known for this disguise to fool any republican voters. The whole point of Boulangism was to split the vote of the Left, not the Right; consequently, in his words, the only "useful" Boulangists were the radical ones.[88]

It was, paradoxically, the radical Boulangists in the urban constituencies of Bordeaux who were most appealing to royalists. Here the Boulangists were not the transmuted Bonapartists of the rural constituencies but men with leftist backgrounds, platforms, and clientele. Albert Chiché in the first district and Henri Aimel in the second were Radicals; Antoine Jourde in the third was a socialist. In principle these ought to have been unlikely allies for the royalists, who were the dominant element among the conservatives of Bordeaux, but in practice an alliance was both possible and attractive. Conservatives of whatever hue had no chance of winning in Bordeaux. In 1885 the conservative list had obtained only 9,000 votes, half that of its republican counterpart. Boulangists therefore posed no threat to conservative electoral fortunes. On the other hand, although Boulangists were serious contenders in the city, in all three districts success was unlikely, and in the first and third impossible, without attracting the royalist vote. Moreover, the kind of campaign Boulangists ran was very expensive, and the wealthy Bordeaux royalists alone had the requisite funds. As a further precaution, Cordier insisted that any money emanating from the central conservative coffers in Paris destined for the Boulangists be channeled through him. The need for conservative votes and money gave royalists considerable leverage, and Cordier was shrewd enough to exploit it fully. As he told Mackau's electoral agent, the only Boulangist candidates he was interested in were those who were sufficiently beholden to royalists as to qualify as "transfuges."[89]

Cordier also had one such candidate in mind: Albert Chiché. Although associated with Radical politics, Chiché was the son of a prominent Bonapartist businessman and had rallied to Boulangism out of ambition rather than conviction. Cordier apparently exercised some private control over Chiché, for he insisted that he could "maneuver him at will." Leaving nothing to chance, Cordier obliged Chiché to make a formal written engagement to local royalists before the requisite support and 5,000 francs was guaranteed. Similar arrangements were made with Aimel and Jourde. Jourde's case is interesting because he was an outspoken socialist and one of the founders of the socialist movement in the Gironde. Conservatives nonetheless thought him a mental lightweight and believed that "with a bit of skill we can succeed in demonstrating to him that true socialism can flourish only under the monarchy." Royalists had a similarly low estimate of the radical journalist Henri Aimel, insisting that this "joker" could be entirely controlled by his confrere André Cordier. As a result of conservative manipulation, on the eve of the election Aimel and Jourde could be described as "drawing closer day by day to [the position of] *Le Nouvelliste.*"[90]

For the sake of appearances, royalist support of Chiché, Aimel, and Jourde did not initially extend to officially endorsing them in *Le Nouvelliste,* and Boulangists reciprocated by ignoring royalists running outside the city. Both parties nevertheless waged a common campaign, and their electoral agents distributed the declarations and portraits of both the Count of Paris and Boulanger, "depending on the opinions of the voters," attempting to convince royalist voters that the Count of Paris had endorsed the general, and Boulangist voters that the inverse was true.[91] Just before the election *Le Nouvelliste* recommended that royalist voters support the three Boulangists in Bordeaux, describing them as "very imperfect auxiliaries but auxiliaries nonethless."[92] On the second ballot *Le Nouvelliste* strongly endorsed all three and they were elected. Their electoral margins, however, were relatively narrow—473 for Chiché, 1,135 for Aimel, and 680 for Jourde—so they clearly owed their elections to the several thousand royalist votes that could be delivered in each district.

Nor was this support forgotten by local Boulangists. At a Boulangist victory banquet, toasts were drunk to the conservatives of Bordeaux for having "marched together with honest men against Opportunism." A self-proclaimed socialist congratulated Boulangists "for having extended their hand to the conservatives" and expressed the hope that "the alliance formed against the common enemy would be maintained."[93] In November local Boulangists supported Cordier's bid for a seat on the general council, despite the fact that one of his opponents was a "republican revisionist."[94]

Paris was the one major exception to the nationwide pattern of royalist-Boulangist relations. In the capital Boulangists contested all forty-two seats whether or not royalists wished them to. It was, after all, the one place where most of Boulanger's support had come from erstwhile republican voters and where Boulangism could flourish without careful conservative nourishment. For that reason most of the prominent Boulangists chose to run there, including Lenglé, Naquet, Turquet, Thibaudin, Mermeix, Laisant, Laguerre, and Michelin. Royalists, by comparison, were relatively weak in Paris but did have some possibility of success in the more affluent districts: the first, second, sixth, seventh, eighth, ninth, sixteenth, and seventeenth arrondissements. Yet their chances were certainly no better than those of the Boulangists, whose electoral clientele was far more likely to be in the city in September.[95]

Nonetheless the Count of Paris insisted that royalist candidates be given a free hand in eight districts.[96] Boulangists ignored these demands and presented candidates everywhere, prompting the anger of the pretender as well as periodic threats of financial retaliation. In fact, however, Boulangist leaders really did not have much choice. So many concessions had been made to the royalists elsewhere that only a full slate of Boulangist candidates in Paris would ensure some degree of harmony within their ranks. Since Boulangist candidates in Paris would be primarily dependent on republican voters, even indirect aid to royalists would have compromised them seriously. Moreover, since many of the Parisian royalist candidates had been singularly uncooperative in the January election, Boulangist support was a bit much to expect. Nonetheless Boulangists did what they could for the more sympathetic royalists. *La Cocarde* regretted that, given Edouard Hervé's avowed royalism, it really could not endorse his candidacy. "Nonetheless," it continued, "we cannot forget the noble character and the considerable distinction of M. Hervé . . . whose hand we are proud to shake."[97]

From the royalist perspective the question of its Parisian candidates was never more than symbolic. The president of the Parisian royalist committee conceded that the chances of all except Hervé were slim.[98] Even Bocher tacitly acknowledged that royalist interests would be better served by electing twenty-five to thirty Boulangists in Paris than by obtaining seats for one or two friends.[99] Consequently royalists ultimately funded all Boulangist candidates in Paris, even those running against royalists. To forestall eventual outcries from its own candidates, many of whom were less generously supported than were their Boulangist rivals, the royalist finance committee arranged that Boulangists would receive the money directly from the Duchesse d'Uzès, who in turn would be reimbursed from royalist coffers. By so laundering the money, royalists sought to shift the blame for their own hard-nosed behavior onto the erratic noblewoman.[100] In the end Boulangists outdistanced all but one royalist on the first ballot—at least partially, as the losing royalists would admit, because even on the first ballot many royalists preferred the Boulangist candidate.[101]

What doomed the royalist-Boulangist alliance was not the infidelity of the Boulangists but the contradictions inherent in the alliance itself. Facing an awesome republican electoral machine,[102] royalists needed allies with an independent dynamic and vitality, capable of wooing un-

decided voters. At the same time they needed allies who were ultimately under their control. The two exigencies were difficult to reconcile. Given the radical reflexes of many Boulangist leaders, royalists
were wary of granting them a free hand lest they become dangerous
rather than docile auxiliaries. Yet too much control over the movement
risked reducing Boulangism to little more than the latest in a series of
disingenuous electoral labels used by royalists and Bonapartists. After
Boulanger's decisive victory in republican Paris, royalist leaders had
feared that he or his followers might escape from the conservatives. Until nearly the end of the campaign, the principal preoccupation of royalists had been to tighten control over their allies. Boulanger's exile, the
paucity of local Boulangist electoral organizations, and above all the
royalist monopoly of campaign funds made the allies relatively easy to
domesticate.

Still, a band of Boulangists who did not greatly worry royalists might
not frighten republicans very much either. Endorsing any number of
royalists and Bonapartists was an amiable gesture of good will and had
undeniable electoral utility. But Boulangists were also supposed to be
presenting attractive candidates of their own in the 200 constituencies
lost forever to the conservatives. When the lists of Boulangist candidates began to appear in September, all the royalist leaders were aghast.
What troubled them was not the presence of the odd radical Boulangist
running where he did not belong, but the extreme mediocrity of those
running where they might do some good. With considerable understate-
ment, Cassagnac observed that "the Boulangist party had to take its
members where it could find them, without being too choosy."[103] Only
a handful of genuine Boulangists, royalists correctly noted, had any
plausible prospects of success.

No one ought to have been very surprised, since conservatives had
assigned Boulangists to those very constituencies where republicans were
strong and where Boulangists necessarily faced formidable opposition.
The promise of conservative support in those constituencies would in-
duce few attractive Boulangists to present themselves, since such support was often ineffective. This was why so many Boulangists would
have preferred to run in more conservative constituencies, and why they
failed so often to find promising local candidates in the more republican
ones. All too often the Boulangist banner was carried by an ambitious
outsider, completely unknown in his new district.

Others, although well known, were otherwise electorally unattractive.
Jourdanne was certainly no stranger to Carcassonne, where he had once
been mayor. Unfortunately his term as mayor had abruptly ended with

a conviction and prison sentence for fraud, which was why he amassed exactly 304 votes. Pendrié, the Boulangist candidate in Nantua, made much of his status as a former industrialist and current editor of a financial newsletter. His real notoriety, however, was for persistent economic failure, which explained both his eagerness for royalist financial support and the 33 votes he attracted.[104] The Boulangist candidate in Mâcon, Médéric Roux, had a talent for fraud which had earned him an imposing list of prison terms. So unsavory was he, even by Boulangist standards, that *La Presse* ultimately withdrew its endorsement, although that fact alone probably does not explain the 10 votes he received.[105] Too many local Boulangists were like the self-styled leader in Limoges, Pierre Ferrand, whose criminal record made him an ideal police informer. When not attempting to pry money out of local royalists, he sold copies of his correspondence with Georges Laguerre to the prefecture.[106] Not all Boulangist candidates were so obviously bankrupt, of course. Those who were incumbent deputies were often serious candidates, as were those, like the Boulangists in Nancy and Bordeaux, who could create a genuine popular following. But there were simply too few of them.

The electoral activity of Boulangist agents was often as inept as many of their candidates. Even Jules Auffray, the most accommodating of the royalists, would complain to Dillon that the local activity of the Boulangists was "haphazard, incoherent, a waste of time and money." What was the point of a Boulangist campaign in Lisieux, the absolutely secure fiefdom of the royalist Colbert-Laplace? In principle, organizing a meeting in the second constituency of Abbeville in support of the Bonapartist-Boulangist Jacques Millevoye was a nice idea. But had not Dillon's people rather overlooked the fact that Millevoye was a candidate in the *first* constituency?[107]

Lacking an effective local electoral organization and any personal electoral appeal, most Boulangist candidates were heavily dependent on royalists for the former and on General Boulanger for the latter. But royalist electoral organization was, and always had been, singularly inadequate. Worse, Boulanger's hold on the popular imagination was rapidly slipping. Perhaps Boulanger's coattails had never been long enough to carry most of his nondescript followers; past elections had suggested that Boulangism did not travel well except in conservative containers. But his unheroic departure in the spring had incontestably reduced the electoral force of his name. Exile made him more submissive to the royalists but less attractive to the electorate.

The best indicator of his slumping popularity was the dismal results of the July cantonal elections. Hoping to raise Boulanger's electoral profile by another resounding plebiscitary triumph, Paul Déroulède insisted upon presenting his name in eighty cantons. Royalist leaders, aware that national political issues rarely surfaced in local elections, tried to dissuade him, although plenty of royalists in the departments thought they knew just the canton where the general would be an appropriate candidate. When he was elected in only fourteen of the carefully chosen districts, it was apparent that his name had lost its earlier magic. The elections convinced Bocher that the danger was no longer that Boulangists might be too powerful, but that they would be too weak. The embarrassing results, combined with his conviction by the High Court, both reflected and intensified the waning of the general's popularity. Royalists who with equanimity had watched him leave in April now insisted that only his dramatic return to France could rescue his fortunes and theirs.[108] Since there was no prospect of Boulanger's accepting the role of martyr, by September informed royalists were frankly pessimistic. As that symbol of republican vitality, the Eiffel Tower, neared the 300-meter point, and he surveyed a Boulangist list containing an "almost total absence of viable candidates," Bocher glumly reported, "I fear we shall be more or less reduced to our own [candidates]—in other words to a very inadequate minority." Boulanger alone remained optimistic, predicting on the eve of the elections a conservative and Boulangist total of 310 seats.[109]

In the end even the most dour royalist predictions erred on the side of optimism. Bocher had anticipated the election of between 40 and 45 Boulangists and 200 and 210 conservatives; among the latter, he was confident of 185. When Boulangists and conservatives elected only 130 candidates on the first ballot, even he was disappointed.[110] After the second ballot, conservatives had elected 168 deputies and Boulangists 42. Their combined total was only slightly better than what conservatives alone had obtained in 1885, when at least their ranks did not include so many dubious allies.

In spite of the disappointing results it did not follow, as so many disillusioned royalists were to argue, that the Boulangist alliance had been a tragic error. Given the waning of conservative fortunes after 1885, even 168 deputies was something of an achievement. Royalist strategists had been right to believe that there were a number of constituencies which could be won—or at least denied to the government—by allying with the Boulangists. Where Boulangism had solid roots, as in the Aisne, successful royalists frankly admitted that they owed their election to the support of their allies. Lévis-Mirepoix's cultivation of Boulangism in the Orne yielded the desired results, because he won Alençon by a healthy margin, the first time in twenty-five years that a conservative had obtained a majority there.[111]

There were, however, too few such regions. Mackau's secretary, Croissy, had informed Bocher in August of thirty-two constituencies which looked initially unpromising but which could be won by the right combination of Boulangist-royalist cooperation. Of the candidates he thought appropriate for the task, twelve did not run in the constituencies designated for them, and of the eight who replaced them, only the two Boulangists in Laon were successful. Of the other twenty candidates, only five won. The seven victorious deputies were running in problematic constituencies and were elected because of the royalist-Boulangist alliance. Seven successes out of thirty-two clearly made the exercise worthwhile but hardly presaged a conservative victory.[112]

In the wake of the defeat there was much pious recrimination on the part of local royalists, some of it perfectly disingenuous. *Le Journal de l'Oise* sanctimoniously noted that, unlike other conservatives in the department, Count Robert de l'Aigle had been victorious because he alone was free of the taint of Boulangism. It apparently overlooked the fact that de l'Aigle had been endorsed by Georges Laguerre and had received the active support of local Boulangists.[113] Fondi de Niort, unsuccessful royalist candidate in the Aude, announced that he had lost because royalists hid behind Boulanger instead of flying their own flag. He too evidently forgot that he had proposed Boulanger as a candidate in the July cantonal elections and had privately announced that his platform would have "a more accentuated Boulangist coloration" than that of his conservative colleagues.[114] Even defeated candidates admitted that Boulangist support had helped their campaigns.[115]

Even in their disappointment, royalists believed that they could learn from the Boulangist experience. In the Lot-et-Garonne, despite having catered to Boulangism, all four conservative candidates had been beaten, two by narrow margins. *L'Avenir du Lot-et-Garonne* acknowledged that royalists in the department had derived little benefit from the Boulangist alliance, but insisted that the real reason for their poor showing had been their organization, as feeble in 1889 as in 1885. The Boulangists, by contrast, "succeeded, by their incessant activity, their indefatigable energy, and their unrelenting propaganda, in creating a party that was strong enough to threaten [republicans] and to be taken seriously by all. What those men did, we too can do."[116] The enduring legacy of Boulangism would not be the scandalous qualities of its namesake but a new style of conservative politics.

Royalist leaders made a game effort to cast some encouraging light on the elections. Even Arthur Meyer's celebrated article, "Bonsoir messieurs," usually taken as a definitive termination of the alliance, explicitly left open the possibility of future collaboration with the right wing of the Boulangists.[117] Others believed that the Boulangist adventure had brought royalists into closer contact with "the working masses" and presaged the collapse of barriers of caste and class.[118] Mackau, poring over the electoral statistics in search of evidence of conservative progress, assured the Count of Paris that, without the Boulangist alliance, conservatives might only have elected sixty deputies. So great had been government electoral pressure that the pretender somehow concluded that the election results represented the moral equivalent of a gain of one hundred seats over 1885. Much was also made of the relative decline of the Bonapartists.[119] Boulangism was dead and Bonapartism was dying, but their troops would remain at the service of the monarchy. These were "men of action, not habitués of the salons," who could replace the fading cadres of the royalist party and restore its vigor. Even the radical Boulangists, Barrès and Gabriel, Susini and Lalou, might rally; if not, they would remain as "our more or less acknowledged allies."[120]

None of these comforting pronouncements could hide the fact that the royalist defeat had been decisive and definitive. No longer contemplating a change of regime, royalists struggled desperately to survive under the existing one. The question of electoral invalidations effectively confirmed that both royalists and their republican opponents knew the game was over. The republican administration was remarkably adept at discovering electoral irregularities, especially if committed by conservative voters. Where only a few votes separated candidates, some selective disqualifications could convert a conservative victory into a republican one. The republican majority in the Chamber naturally ratified these procedures.[121] The massive invalidations of 1885 seemed likely to be repeated in 1889.

Even before the second-ballot returns had been counted, Jules Auffray sought to preserve the seats of victorious conservatives by striking a deal with the government. The details are obscure but the discussions certainly involved the promise of healthy sums of money. The Count of Paris rejected the plan, not least because conservatives would thereby be enjoined from denouncing republican electoral corruption. Auffray was not deterred; after the second ballot he concluded an agreement with an authorized representative of Ernest Constans, minister of the interior. Constans was to receive an initial 30,000 francs as proof of royalist good faith. He in turn would address the Chamber of Deputies and speak against any campaign of invalidations. This would earn him a further 50,000 francs. After all conservative deputies and all but three or four disreputable Boulangist ones had been confirmed in their seats, a sum of 100,000 francs would be paid to the patriotic minister. Finally, if tangible evidence could be produced to prove that some ten conservative candidates had lost exclusively because of republican corruption, Constans was prepared to permit them to regain their seats in exchange for 10,000 francs per deputy. Auffray thought this a wonderful arrangement, the more so since the quarter million francs need be paid only after the services had been rendered.[122]

The Count of Paris, moved by some combination of probity, prudence, and parsimony, evidently thought otherwise. In the end it was simpler, and cheaper, for conservative deputies to remain silent about the election scandals and watch impassively while their former Boulangist allies bore the brunt of the invalidations campaign. Constans was the poorer for it, of course, but he derived evident satisfaction from the manifest discomfort of the conservative deputies, who could hardly tell their outraged supporters that their much-remarked passivity during the fall of 1889 was the price they paid to keep their seats.[123]

6

From Boulangism to Anti-Semitic Nationalism: The End of French Royalism

After the crushing defeat of 1889, Boulangists rediscovered their political virtue. Making a virtue of necessity, Boulanger boldly proclaimed that he would no longer "continue the financial alliance that lost us everything" and would henceforth "treat the Orleanists as if they did not exist, whatever it may cost." It would cost a fair bit in fact, as Boulanger was forced repeatedly to remind lieutenants who had grown rather accustomed to a lavish budget.[1]

Worse, Boulangists also lost their greatest single asset: royalist voters. In the May 1890 municipal elections in Paris, previously the great bastion of Boulangism, the Boulangists elected only one candidate, and their 160,000 votes compared unfavorably to the 200,000 obtained by the royalists. Naquet, having forgotten his two years of nagging Boulanger about his complicity with the royalists, admonished his leader: "Your 160,000 votes cannot be extended. You will not attract one republican, nor will you regain any of those conservatives from whom you have separated, a bit too quickly perhaps, since their support is essential for us."[2] Such second-guessing was perfectly petulant but also entirely accurate. Whereas the technically ineligible Dillon had won handily in Lorient in 1889, his chosen Boulangist successor in the January 1890 by-election, now facing a royalist rival, performed miserably. As the prefect observed, "The division between royalists and Boulangists led to the crushing of the latter."[3] Bold professions of advanced republicanism could not conjure away Boulangist dependence on royalists, as even Maurice Barrès, now posing as a socialist, would recognize. Prior to the 1892 municipal elections in Nancy, he approached local royalists for an electoral accord, suggesting a slate composed of equal numbers of royalists and Boulangists. He renewed his bid for royalist support prior to the 1893 legislative elections.[4]

Few royalists were interested in renewing the tactics of 1889; most preferred to forget that their alliance with Boulanger had ever happened. Hopes that the episode would fade from the popular memory were dashed in the fall of 1890, when the details appeared in the Parisian press. After the debacle of 1889 the Boulangist leadership fell into disarray. With Boulanger a permanent and inactive exile, some former Boulangists began to mutter about the "treason" of their leader. One of the most disillusioned, Gabriel Terrail (pen name Mermeix), threatened to desert the party and tell all he knew. At the end of August 1890 he began a series of articles in *Le Figaro* entitled "Les Coulisses du Boulangisme."[5] The series was accurate in most respects and clearly demonstrated that the author's sources included informed royalists. The Count of Paris subjected "Les Coulisses" to detailed scrutiny and could cavil only about trivial details. So well documented was the exposé that the pretender's wrath was reserved for his own confidants, notably the Duchesse d'Uzès, who appeared to be the most likely source.[6]

"Les Coulisses" was an instant sensation. Appearing under a pseudonym, it provoked a rash of speculation as to the authorship: Naquet, Laguerre, Barrès, and even Ernest Constans were suggested. There was also an extended discussion about the possible motives behind "Les Coulisses." Some believed that its appearance was intended to reinvigorate Boulangism; others, less implausibly, saw it as a move by discontented royalists to force the abdication of the Count of Paris. The possibility that Ernest Constans was behind it invited all kinds of ingenious speculation and, inevitably, there were those who thought the series to be the work of the Jews, seeking to sow disharmony in France.[7] "Les Coulisses" also prompted the formation of a minor revelations industry as Parisian journalists sought to expose almost everybody's past behavior. Not to be outdone by its rival, *L'Echo de Paris* printed its own exposé, drawn from stolen royalist correspondence. The best investigative reporting was done by *Le Paris,* which managed to publish a series of informative communications between Mackau's office and Dillon concerning the 1889 elections. In the end everyone got into the act and even *L'Egalité* could not resist dredging up the Boulangist dalliances of socialists like Emile Eudes and Paul Lafargue. A reply from Boulanger was expected at any minute, as was another book rumored, as a skeptical agent in the prefecture wearily noted, to have the whole story on Boulanger's secret negotiations with the Pope.[8]

"Les Coulisses" did not catch royalists unaware, because the editor of *Le Figaro* had kindly offered Beauvoir and Bocher a prepublication glimpse at it. He did so, of course, so that royalists could exercise the option of buying silence. To give them time to weigh the merits of bribing Mermeix, the order of the series was altered so that the first published installment contained relatively innocuous material. After a week of negotiations royalists opted for the safer course of persuading Mermeix to amend his text. In the original version the exclusive source of royalist funding for Boulanger had been the Duchesse d'Uzès's three million francs. Lest the apparent royal parsimony appear unchivalrous, Bocher hastened to apprise Mermeix of the pecuniary sacrifices of the Count of Paris. Since the truth—that the pretender borrowed five million francs from a foreign Jewish baron—was unlikely to be much more palatable to the royalist faithful, Mermeix was given to understand that the Count of Paris had opened a subscription for the 1889 elections, contributed two and a half million francs himself, and obtained a matching amount from individual royalist donors. In his *Figaro* account Mermeix had the pretender opening the subscription in August at the insistence of Beauvoir. Beauvoir subsequently objected that his prince had needed no urging from him. Mermeix obligingly presented a modified (if equally fictitious) account in his published version of "Les Coulisses," dating the subscription from a meeting of the royalist council in London in the spring. All that was true in either "rectification" was the reference to an attempt to raise funds among individual royalists; it had yielded exactly 56,000 francs. The price of Mermeix's cooperation was 6,000 francs.[9]

The publication of "Les Coulisses" caused a brief uproar in royalist circles, and the local press suffered a month of acute embarrassment. Some put on a bold face; some muttered darkly about the need for a "settling of accounts" within the party; others limited themselves to suggesting that the role of the Duchesse d'Uzès proved that women have no place in politics.[10] Still, few royalists could have been very surprised. As the correspondent from the Var plaintively noted, after supporting the ex-Communard Ballière in 1889, local royalists could hardly be shocked by any subsequent revelations. At worst, royalists had to suffer the sarcastic musings of the Bonapartists. In the Charente-Maritime Eschasseriaux, having listened for a decade to lectures on royalist principles, could not resist directing some barbed shafts at his high-minded colleagues.[11] The royalists in the Isère managed to express pious indignation although, as the Count of Paris pointedly reminded them, such doctrinal purity was uniquely appropriate to a department where royalism was little more than a memory.[12] Royalists among the business community of Paris, always suspicious of Boulanger, loudly expressed their reprobation, which, given their increasingly platonic commitment to the monarchy, was both predictable and unimportant.[13]

Most of what could be said about the royalist policy had already been expressed in 1889 by *La Gazette de France* and its followers. The revelations merely provided the occasion for another round of vindictive editorials unsubtly suggesting that the moment had come for the retirement of the current royalist leaders, including the pretender.[14] The Count of Paris issued a frank and succinct statement, taking full responsibility and justifying his actions in terms of political expediency. His unaccustomed candor mollified most royalists. At the very least, the pretender's lieutenants insisted, "Les Coulisses" had reassured skeptical royalists that their prince had indeed wanted to rule France.[15]

The past tense was appropriate. The Count of Paris was dying, as he himself had known since the spring of 1889. Moreover, his doctors repeatedly gave him only a few months more to live. Although he proved them wrong, for the last four years of his life he sought little more than a chance to die in France. Nor did his resignation escape the notice of any but a handful of followers. Anticipating some future debilitating crisis of the republican regime, some royalists, particularly the younger element, began to hope for a more energetic and charismatic standard-bearer. For a while the Duc d'Orléans, eldest son of the pretender, inspired such hopes. In the spring of 1890, on the occasion of his twenty-first birthday, he returned to France and brazenly presented himself for the obligatory military service. His bold defiance of the laws of exile earned him several months' imprisonment, but this welcome display of daring greatly encouraged those royalists who regretted his father's growing inertia. In June a minor Parisian newspaper, *Le Monde,* warned of an attempt to force the Count of Paris to abdicate in favor of his son. A forced abdication would have required more initiative than the Duc d'Orléans could ever muster, but there is no doubt that some royalists actively encouraged the idea, notably that inveterate plotter, Arthur Meyer of *Le Gaulois,* who had been the chief architect of the future pretender's dramatic return. The angry father quickly quashed the rumors, although many contemporaries believed that the indiscretions which produced "Les Coulisses" were part of a further attempt to discredit the current pretender.[16]

The "Dauphin" (as, to the extreme annoyance of his father, the Duc d'Orléans was now being called) certainly represented a radical change. He was everything his father was not, although his qualities hardly helped the cause of French royalism. He remained throughout his life an irresponsible adolescent, the playmate of a handful of bored young aristocrats. In 1889 he had informed his parents of a romantic interest in his cousin, Princess Marguérite, daughter of the Duc de Chartres. Concerned about the question of consanguinity, the royal couple persuaded him to postpone any engagement until after his impending world tour. Upon returning from his travels, the Duc d'Orléans appeared to be as committed as ever to the marriage, so his father relented and the young couple became engaged on 23 May 1890. After his release from prison in June, son and father jointly drafted a public announcement of the betrothal. The timing seemed propitious, since the Duc d'Orléans now enjoyed great popularity, and the fanfare surrounding the announcement was calculated to arrest the growing discouragement within the royalist party. Consequently the Count of Paris was not at all pleased when his son abruptly informed him in August of a newfound concern with the possible genetic consequences of intermarriage and refused to go through with the union. He was even less happy when, shortly thereafter, he learned from the Pope that his son had written him in June, independently seeking an annulment of the engagement on the grounds of consanguinity. Finally, and at the cost of great family embarrassment, the engagement was quietly terminated.[17]

The perils of intermarriage did not, of course, greatly interest the young prince. By contrast, a well-endowed London opera singer, Mrs. Nellie Melba, did. She was inconveniently married, and her husband had responded to her past infidelities by launching well-publicized lawsuits against her illicit partners. None of this deterred the Duc d'Orléans from a very public liaison. Early in 1891, when she went to St. Petersburg to sing, the future pretender followed her. Ignoring protocol, he neglected to inform the Czar of his presence in Russia. The Emperor's first inkling of the unannounced visit came during a performance by Melba, when he spied a boisterous young man in the front row tossing bouquets at the singer in a manner more appropriate to a Parisian music hall than the imperial opera. The Czar's wrath was not significantly appeased upon learning the identity of the miscreant. He nonetheless accorded the young duke a week's stay in St. Petersburg and invited him to an audience. The Duc d'Orléans declined the invitation, overstayed his leave by four days, and then proceeded to create comparable sensations in Warsaw and Vienna. The repeated entreaties of his father had no effect; only a severe case of venereal disease eventually brought him back to London.[18]

The conduct of the future pretender incensed royalists like Bocher and was an important reason behind Bocher's decision to leave the service of the Count of Paris. Nor could the duke's timing have been worse. Such behavior did little to enhance the international standing of French royalism and, having observed the character of the next pretender, the Czar was unlikely to regret his contemplated military alliance with republican France. The impact on Rome was more serious still. The exploits of the Duc d'Orléans coincided with the beginnings of the *ralliement,* the reconciliation of French Catholics with the republic. Agents of the Count of Paris were in Rome strenuously lobbying against papal endorsement of the project. Yet, as they bitterly reported, all the Holy Father wanted to talk about was the ruptured marriage of the Duc d'Orléans and his adventures in St. Petersburg. His demeanor, they lamented, served only "to increase the Pope's skepticism with respect to the future of the monarchist cause in France."[19]

It did not require the public notoriety of the Duc d'Orléans to signal the effective end of royalism. Astute observers had seen it coming for a long time, and the entire Boulangist strategy had been predicated on the assumption that the monarchy could be restored, if at all, only by the back door. Consequently it was the architects of the Boulangist alliance who first drew the inescapable conclusions from its failure. Albert de Mun reminded the Count of Paris that he had recommended the tactics of 1888 because "the monarchist party existed only among the elite, with no roots among the masses." Any attempt now to remain on exclusively monarchist terrain would be futile; temporarily at least, royalists would have to drop all dynastic references and become a party of religious defense and social Catholicism. Both Jacques Piou and Mackau agreed. Some future social or political crisis might again make the restoration a possibility, but in the meantime, outside of a handful of western departments, French royalism was dead.[20]

In March 1890 Piou and fifteen other conservative deputies founded the Droite Constitutionelle as a parliamentary group. In essence it represented a return to Raoul-Duval's abortive proposal of 1886. It was not initially much more successful, because its adherents wanted to abandon dynastic politics without necessarily embracing the republic. The ambiguity of their position satisfied neither republicans nor royalists, and for some months the movement floundered. The active intervention of the Church, however, changed everything. On 12 November

1890 Cardinal Lavigerie, after prior consultation with Pope Leo XIII, drank a toast to the French navy, recommending "adherence without reservation" to the current form of government, the republic. The extended debate about the authority of Lavigerie's pronouncement was ended in February 1892 by the papal encyclical *Au milieu des sollicitudes,* which urged French Catholics to accept the existing regime. Although many Catholics continued to resist the new policy, the encyclical caused a number of royalist leaders to rally to the republic.[21] De Mun was first, in May 1892, followed by Piou in June. Breteuil preferred simply to resign his seat as deputy in August 1892, but not before telling his constituents and the Count of Paris that the monarchy was definitively dead. Mackau, after attempting in vain to persuade the pretender to accept the existing regime, rallied to the republic in October 1892.[22]

The spectacle of men becoming reconciled to a form of government which they had only recently attempted to overthrow was not without its ironies. When republicans expressed satisfaction at the news of Breteuil's desertion, Paul de Cassagnac could not resist reminding them that Breteuil, like de Mun and Piou, had been among the six monarchists who had initiated the Boulanger affair, planning "a revolution which did not hesitate before the eventuality of a coup d'état." He taunted republicans by asserting that while they had been tracking down and convicting the minor actors in 1889, "the true instigators of the affair" had never been touched. Had Floquet been less of a fool, he would have tossed them all into prison; now republicans were welcoming them into their ranks. When Mackau rallied, Cassagnac treated it as a practical joke, intended to expose the ridiculousness of the whole *ralliement*.[23]

Despite Cassagnac's mirth, there was an indisputable logic to the evolution of the former conspirators. The same acute political sense that led them into Boulangism now told them that there was no political future outside the republic. The remaining royalists liked to pretend that the desertion of a feckless few was but a passing reverse. Haussonville, having replaced Bocher as head of the royalist organization in France, insisted that while royalists were experiencing "un mauvais quart d'heure," the local royalist organization remained "fairly well intact."[24] Even Haussonville, whose assessment of the state of royalism in France had always been excessively optimistic, could not possibly have believed any of this. All the reports from royalist secretaries during this period painted an unrelieved picture of gloom. The defeat in 1889, the revelations about Boulangism, and above all the *ralliement* of the clergy deprived local royalism of whatever vitality it might once have possessed.

As the secretary of the Vienne acidly observed, few royalists could appreciate why the tactics advocated by Piou and Lavigerie were less principled than those adopted in 1888–89. "After having accepted an alliance with Boulanger, they do not believe that there is any reason not to fall in behind other men whose personal honor, at least, is incontestable." He had a point, and many of his colleagues noted grimly that there was a logical connection between Boulangism and the *ralliement*.[25]

Haussonville had obviously hoped to change all that and assiduously toured the provinces seeking to reinvigorate party life. But there simply wasn't any. When he called together the forty members of the royalist committee of the Charente, three attended; when he convoked the eighty members in the Lot-et-Garonne, nine appeared. Any attempts to solicit financial contributions from members of royalist committees invariably elicited only letters of resignation. Even he confessed, "The mobilization of the committees is a more difficult task than I had thought."[26] Both he and Dufeuille were shattered when more and more members of the clergy rallied to the republic. The ever optimistic Dufeuille insisted that at least royalists could no longer be denounced as "clericals," but such pronouncements cannot greatly have comforted a pretender who was continually receiving reports complaining that local priests were canceling their subscriptions to royalist newspapers, which they now deemed "anti-Catholic."[27]

The Panama scandal of 1892 briefly revived royalist hopes. In 1888 the Panama Company, already in serious financial difficulty, had obtained parliamentary authorization for a public loan in order to complete work on the Panama canal. The company nonetheless went bankrupt, and in September 1892 reports began to surface indicating that the loan had been approved by parliament only because a number of prominent deputies had been bribed. Since thousands of Frenchmen had lost their modest savings in a venture which, because of parliamentary authorization, had seemed secure, there was massive public outrage against corrupt parliamentarianism.[28] Haussonville and Dufeuille excitedly announced that once again "everything seems possible," that France was "witnessing the revival of the Boulangist state of mind." Dufeuille even allowed himself to reprimand the Count of Paris for his obvious indifference to the new possibilities. Yet their repeated allusions to a "new Boulangism" always acknowledged that one ingredient was missing: a new Boulanger. Without another such providential figure, the Panama scandal provided royalists with little more than an occasion for predictable moralizing about the evils of the republic. When the public uproar subsided, royalists glumly acknowledged that they had made no progress.[29]

Royalists approached the 1893 elections without enthusiasm. For the first time, money was scarce. None of the usual *bailleurs de fonds* were now interested in the monarchy, and the Count of Paris was more reluctant than ever to spend his own fortune. After some prodding from Haussonville, he borrowed 500,000 francs in the United States, allowing barely any money for individual royalist candidates. Of course there were not many of them either. Strictly speaking, the only royalists candidates would be those incumbent deputies who had not rallied to the republic. No new candidates saw any point in identifying themselves with the monarchy. Six months before the elections Haussonville conceded that, outside some departments in the west, few royalists would succeed. Given the dearth of candidates, royalists would have to support the *ralliés,* whose chances of success were very little better. The results were even worse than he feared. Many incumbent royalists declined to run, and eighteen of those who did were defeated. Among the *ralliés* twenty-two incumbents, including Albert de Mun and Jacques Piou, were defeated. Fifty-eight royalists and Bonapartists and thirty-six *ralliés* were elected, reducing the Right to an inconsequential rump in a chamber now dominated by the Opportunists.[30]

Little remained to do except dissolve the remnants of the royalist party. Not willing to send good money after bad, the Count of Paris had drastically reduced his financial support after 1889. Following the 1893 elections, the last of the *missi* and the departmental secretaries were dismissed, and all but a handful of newspaper subventions were withdrawn. By the beginning of 1894 the royalist party in France was effectively dead, preceding the pretender by seven months. All that remained of royalism in France were a few dozen deputies, a handful of isolated local committees, some youth groups, and newspapers like *La Gazette de France,* which stood out as curiosities in the French political scene.[31]

There was still a pretender in the person of the Duc d'Orléans. Hopes that his new responsibilities might tempt him into growing up were soon disappointed. Nothing better illustrates his character than an episode in the spring of 1900 when a French artist, Willette, published some particularly tasteless cartoons of the Queen of England. The pretender, naturally, found them hilarious and told the cartoonist so. Willette, who needed all the endorsements he could get, asked the Duc d'Orléans if he might share his recent letter and, not hearing further from the pretender, did so. When the letter in question found its way into print, neither Queen Victoria nor the British press were amused. The Duc d'Orléans was unceremoniously expelled from all the best London clubs and, since he happened to be abroad at the time, only an abject letter of apology and the vigorous intervention of his embarrassed relatives persuaded Her Majesty's government to let him return to his estates.[32]

Yet, although his behavior scandalized older servants of the monarchy, the Duc d'Orléans was not entirely inappropriate to fin-de-siècle royalism. A dignified pretender adept at drafting learned manifestos had suited an era of electoral politics, but by the late 1890s most French royalists had given up on the ballot box. The republic was electorally unassailable but the decade was replete with scandals, political crises, and a growing threat from the socialist and anarchist Left. Royalists increasingly looked to foreign war, a collapse of civil authority, *l'imprévu,* as the only hope for a restoration. The royalist youth groups, the only royalist element that displayed any vitality, insisted that their place was in the streets and their objective a *coup de main.* By 1893 their impatience with *vieux jeux* like Haussonville and the dying pretender was patent.[33]

With the succession of the Duc d'Orléans, the restless *jeunesses dorées* thought they now had a leader capable of a *coup d'audace.* The new pretender certainly catered to the paramilitary fantasies of his youthful followers. He now corresponded with his agents by means of a series of secret codes so complex that only the prefecture of police could readily decipher them. Where once the counselors of the pretender pored over reports from departmental secretaries, they now drafted detailed plans for smuggling their leader into France. At the disposal of the prince were small-scale military maps, photographs of border crossings, and complex itineraries involving travel by train, boat, bicycle, and foot, all of which said more about the mentality of his entourage than about the likelihood of the indolent duke actually attempting any of their dubious schemes.[34] One can hardly blame him because the overheated imagination of his lieutenants wished him to be forever standing on the Belgian border.

The appeal of a military coup d'état, always latent in French royalism, never died. During the Dreyfus affair royalists conducted a series of fruitless negotiations with sympathetic generals. The generals, probably aware that most royalist correspondence now passed through the hands of the government, limited themselves to saying that they were not adverse to a change in regime, but would take no initiative to bring it about. Moreover, as most royalists secretly admitted, few generals considered an Orleanist monarchy, least of all one headed by the current pretender, to be a plausible alternative to the republic.[35] Indeed, even as they predicted imminent civil war, urged the Duc d'Orléans to keep his bags packed, and whispered in the ears of generals, French royalists knew that their fundamental problem remained. They were a socially exclusive sect in an age of mass politics.

Even if the republican regime collapsed, the monarchy was no longer the obvious successor, because there were now far more popular alternatives. For all their rhetoric and noisy descents into the streets of Paris, the royalist youth lacked both the popular appeal and the popular composition of Déroulède's Ligue des Patriotes. Whereas "the Ligue des Patriotes represented a basically lower-middle-class movement characterized by its internal discipline," royalists, including the royalist youth, were predominantly aristocratic and characterized by no discipline whatsoever.[36] A dissolute young pretender was even less likely to catch the popular imagination than had his erudite father. Just as in 1888, royalists needed to appropriate a popular program. This time it was anti-Semitism.

Until the 1890s political anti-Semitism had been relatively rare among rank-and-file royalists and absent from the party's official program. To be sure, insofar as they were devout Catholics, French royalists shared the Church's traditional prejudices against Jews. As a socially exclusive caste, they regarded the Jew as a symbol of the parvenu, increasingly encroaching on the natural elite. To the degree that Jews endorsed the republic, they earned the scorn of opponents of the regime. Indeed, most anti-Semitic remarks were directed at, and limited to, prominent Jewish *republicans*. When Paul Princeteau ran against David Raynal in Bordeaux in 1889, his supporters did not scruple to refer to him as "le juif Raynal." But they hated Raynal primarily because he was a high-profile Opportunist. Willingness to slander individual Jews was something different from political anti-Semitism. In 1889 Paul de Cassagnac ended a column with the ugly suggestion that the prominent Jewish Opportunist politician Joseph Reinach was an advocate of "free and compulsory circumcision." Yet, the tasteless humor notwithstanding, the article had been an attack on anti-Semitism and had lucidly defended the Jews against most of the charges traditionally directed at them.[37]

The presence of an occasional Jew among the Boulangists provided ammunition for monarchists who deplored the Boulanger-royalist alliance. For some, Boulangism was the work of "la juiverie francmaçonne";

for others, the bellicose general was the tool of Jewish war profiteers.[38]
Incensed by the intimate association between Naquet and royalists exhibited at Tours, disgruntled legitimists in the Vendée described Naquet
as being "crafty as a hunchback, nimble as a monkey, and wily as the
Jew that he is," in an attempt to prove that the father of divorce could
not possibly champion an "open and tolerant republic."[39]

The identification of Jews with disruptive and rapacious capitalism
had a certain appeal among some royalists, notably "social" Catholics
like Denys Cochin and Albert de Mun. When the royalist and Catholic
Union Générale collapsed in 1882, many conservatives preferred to
blame Jewish financiers rather than the bank's demonstrated misman-
agement. A decade later Beauvoir, a chronically unwise investor, admitted that "memories of 1882 ought not to make me tender toward
the Jews." Yet Beauvoir had many close contacts in the Parisian Jewish community, and his remarks were made in the context of his expression of disgust at the pogroms in Russia.[40] The royalist newspaper
Le Var once called for "the exclusion from political and commercial
life of everything tainted by the Semitic race," but this was the sole
reference to Jews in a two-year period.[41] For most royalists, the Jews
were simply not that important. Among the many reasons given for
hating the republic, the role of Jews rarely appeared. Royalist targets
were the instituteurs, the prefects, the "nouvelles couches sociales," and
the Freemasons; the Jews, if mentioned at all, were thrown in as an after-
thought. No one found it incongruous that royalist material was regu-
larly published by the Jewish firm of Calmann-Lévy.

In the 1880s the royalist leadership had been reluctant to embrace
anti-Semitism, because alienating the Jews had seemed politically in-
expedient. The reaction to the publication of Edouard Drumont's La
France juive in 1886 provides a characteristic example. A runaway best
seller, Drumont's book depicted in lurid detail the Jews' supposed grasp
on French society. The two-volume work was a savagely anti-Semitic
document, portraying the cunning mercantile Jew at war with the naive
and high-minded Aryan—an uneven battle resulting in a Jewish stran-
glehold. Royalists too were aware of Jewish influence but drew rather
different conclusions. Shortly before the appearance of La France juive,
Dufeuille reminded the pretender that in recent decades French Jews
had become a major force in French economic, social, cultural, and
administrative life. As a result, he noted, Jews represented an increasingly important constituency that royalists ought carefully to cultivate.
Granting that Jews had heretofore demonstrated a distinct preference
for the republic, Dufeuille attributed this orientation to the "narrowly

clerical" image of French royalists, an image that a "modern" prince
like the Count of Paris could erase. The pretender agreed; two years
later he thought it sound politics for conservatives to protest the government's refusal to fund a Jewish theological seminary.[42] Although the
Catholic press generally gave it good reviews, both Dufeuille and the
Count of Paris considered *La France juive* to be a sensationalistic piece
of trash, a commercial success only because "it responds to a few serious
grievances and a lot of evil passions." The Count of Paris even contemplated writing a rebuttal, but in the end settled for making a contribution of five hundred francs to a fund for Jewish schools. Significantly, Dufeuille argued that the appearance of *La France juive* was
"perhaps not absolutely regrettable from our perspective," but only because, by alerting Jews to the anti-Semitic peril *under the republic,* it
might attract them to the cause of the monarchy.[43]

An important reason for discouraging anti-Semitism among royalists
was the latter's dependence on the financial generosity of two wealthy
Jews: Hirsch and Rothschild. In 1887 Beauvoir complained bitterly that
the social Catholicism of Denys Cochin tempted him to adopt the
rhetoric of Drumont, which made his own financial negotiations with
Hirsch and Rothschild more difficult. Since Hirsch persistently complained that royalist willingness to take his money was not comple-
mented by a similar interest in accepting him into their private circles,
the harebrained anti-Semitism of Cochin was untimely.[44] One reason
why Rothschild ultimately refused to help finance the 1889 campaign
was his unease at the anti-Semitism of some of the Boulangist allies.
Nor was he enthusiastic about de Mun's social Catholicism, which he
took to be the prelude to an anti-Semitic campaign.[45]

For some years the financial consequences of endorsing anti-Semitism
continued to haunt royalists. The first great manifestation of political
anti-Semitism in France was the reelection campaign of the Boulangist Francis Laur in January 1890.[46] Laur, an arch anti-Semite and
friend of Drumont, had as his campaign manager an equally anti-Semitic royalist, the Marquis de Morès. At his campaign rallies could be
seen numerous young aristocrats, among them the intimate friends of
the Duc d'Orléans, "applauding," in the words of a thoroughly disgusted Haussonville, "the socialist and anti-Semitic insanities of citi-
zen Morès." Beauvoir quickly sought out Rothschild to assure him of
the "reprobation" of all royalists at the conduct of a few of their
number.[47]

In 1891 Drumont approached royalists in search of funding for an
anti-Semitic newspaper but was rebuffed by Haussonville, apparently

because of his concern for the sensibilities of Jewish financiers.[48] When Drumont founded *La Libre Parole,* it certainly directed much venom at Haussonville but did not lose interest in a royalist connection. In the spring of 1893 representatives of *La Libre Parole* proposed to Haussonville that, in return for a cessation of its attacks on him (but not on Jews), royalists buy 100,000 francs' worth of shares. Haussonville again refused, but countered with a proposal for a direct royalist subsidy of 20,000 francs, an approach that was both more discreet and considerably cheaper. He also assured the newspaper that, "while regretting some of the attacks of M. Drumont, we admire his talent and recognize the services he has rendered in the Panama affair." Unlike Dufeuille, for whom *La Libre Parole* still represented only "civil and social war," Haussonville could assure the Count of Paris that the 20,000 francs would be money well spent. Because he for some reason did not think Drumont venal, he feared that the offer would be scorned, in which case he thought it imperative that Rothschild be informed of Drumont's *original offer* (but not the counterproposal) and its rejection. Haussonville, like Dufeuille in 1886, believed that anti-Semitism could be best used to attract Jews to the monarchy.[49]

Of particular concern to royalists was the fact that the anti-Semitism of the 1880s seemed especially associated with the extreme Left.[50] After the collapse of the Union Générale, the most outspoken attacks on Alphonse de Rothschild, "le Juif de Francfort," came from Jules Guesde's socialist paper *Le Citoyen;* the Orleanist *Le Soleil,* by contrast, praised Rothschild for helping to minimize the bank's losses.[51] The theoretically muddled socialism of Benoît Malon and his *Revue socialiste* included a persistent antagonism to Jewish finance, and one of the first works of Karl Marx to be translated into French was his essay on the Jewish question, which circulated as an anti-Semitic tract.[52] The first political anti-Semites in France saw themselves as men of the Left, and conservatives often equated socialism and anti-Semitism. Significantly, it was in order to enhance their influence among the working classes that men like Albert de Mun flirted with an anticapitalist and anti-Semitic rhetoric.

Association with a movement emanating from the extreme Left troubled many royalists and most notably those who had deplored the Boulangist adventure. One reason why Haussonville had been so furious at the spectacle of young royalists participating in Laur's 1890 campaign was that he feared lest their actions prefigure a renewal of the Boulangist alliance.[53] Even royalists not troubled by anti-Semitism per

se opposed any formal relationship with men like Drumont. When approached in 1893 by *La Libre Parole* about a renewed version of the
"parallel action," this time with royalists and anti-Semitic "socialists,"
Denys Cochin expressed genuine alarm. His own anti-Semitic views
notwithstanding, he wanted nothing to do with an alliance that was
uncomfortably reminiscent of the Boulangism he had so strenuously
resisted in 1889.[54]

Moreover, anti-Semitism attacked two institutions that royalists cherished: private wealth and religion. Of course it was only Jewish wealth
and the Jewish religion, but in the light of the political origins of so many
anti-Semites, a more generalized assault was a serious danger. This was
something the Count of Paris had to remind some of his remaining
followers who, by the early 1890s, had begun to call for "a break with
the Jews." Disturbed as always by their socially exclusive image and
their inability to relate to the masses, local royalists began to wonder
if a healthy dose of anti-Semitism might overcome the problem. Not
only would it enhance their appeal among rural classes, where anti-
Semitism was making progress, but it would add zest to royalist efforts
"to save a modern society gangrened by the abuses of revolutionary
individualism."[55] The Count of Paris bluntly rejected their suggestions.
Anti-Semitism was certainly popular, but so too were anticlericalism
and socialism. Defenders of religion could not adopt a program that
seemed to attack the Jewish faith. Moreover, if Jews were to be attacked because of their disproportionate economic power, could not the
same arguments be directed against wealthy royalists? While recognizing
the legitimacy "of some of the grievances alleged against the Jews, [he]
consider[ed] the anti-Semitic campaign to be dangerous because it [led]
directly to a war on capital." Convinced that attacks on Jewish capital
"tend gradually to provoke a war on capital in general," he refused to
associate with anti-Semitism "in any fashion whatsoever."[56]

His reasons for opposing anti-Semitism were compelling in their own
right, but it was not accidental that they were given at a moment when
his representatives were still trying to persuade "the two barons" to
fund the 1893 elections. In truth, neither Hirsch nor Rothschild harbored many illusions about royalist prospects. Nonetheless they bluntly
reminded royalists that their enthusiasm for renewing their past generosity was not intensified by the spread of anti-Semitic rhetoric among
certain defenders of the monarchy. They noted, for example, that when
the popular royalist Emile Keller organized a protest rally against the
Panama affair, it quickly degenerated into an anti-Semitic hate cam-

paign.[57] For most royalist leaders (Dufeuille was an exception), tactical and financial considerations were far more important than ethical ones when it came to assessing the merits of anti-Semitism.

Most of these considerations soon disappeared. Hirsch and Rothschild ultimately refused to contribute to royalist coffers in 1893 and were certain to resist all future requests. Since the Duc d'Orléans, to the consternation of his followers, contributed virtually nothing to the party, he had no reason to appease Jewish financiers. Moreover, the next great crisis of the regime, the Dreyfus affair, was one in which anti-Semitism was a central feature.

Royalists did not initially embrace the anti-Dreyfusard cause. Eugène Dufeuille, who remained in the service of the Duc d'Orléans, was convinced from the beginning of the innocence of Dreyfus (allegedly having been so informed by General Galliffet), and he and his close friend the Queen Mother attempted to persuade the pretender to remain noncommittal. For a long time the royalist press remained remarkably cautious about the issue of Dreyfus's culpability.[58] The Duc d'Orléans does not appear to have had any fixed ideas about anti-Semitism or Dreyfus but was alert to the changing sentiments of many of his followers. Upon learning in 1894 that the party faithful who were visiting him in Brussels were also paying respects to the then exiled Drumont, he allegedly replied that, if necessary, he too would become an anti-Semite. By 1898 most of his advisers had become openly anti-Semitic, and the Duke adopted their style. In December 1897 he sent Dufeuille a jovial letter containing some disgusting anti-Semitic asides. Dufeuille, who in any case despised him, resigned on the spot.[59]

During the Dreyfus affair royalists hoped that a military coup would lead to restoration of the monarchy. This outcome presupposed that disaffected elements within the army could be convinced of the future of French royalism, which in turn necessitated evidence of significant popular support. Count Edouard de Lur-Saluces, a retired cavalry officer, leader of royalists in Bordeaux and one of the principal councillors of the pretender, insisted on the need to find the right chemistry for attracting both the army and the masses to the monarchy. Royalists would have "to prepare the most energetic movement possible in the streets of Paris and the other major cities," while simultaneously gaining "the sympathy or at least the neutrality of the army."[60] Since neither the masses nor the army found the Orleanist monarchy the least bit exciting, royalists would have to strike a more appealing programmatic note: systematic anti-Semitism. "One cannot deny," he wrote, "that today anti-Semitism is becoming more and more popular—more so perhaps in the army than among the people." Granted, adopting anti-Semitism would alienate the Jews and their friends, but to a large degree this had already happened. Consequently royalists could now "derive . . . every advantage by diverting to our profit this gigantic movement which grows larger every day." Anti-Semitism had become irresistible because "it is so obvious that [the Jews] represent a national danger. . . . We must exploit this sentiment by frankly and resolutely taking the lead in this preoccupation of the crowd, and no one is better qualified to do so than the King."

With remarkable candor Lur-Saluces admitted:

> I would not have put the same argument to you a few years ago. At that time many people found anti-Semitism to be frightening. If you pillage the Jews, they said, we will end up being pillaged as well. Or they evoked the specter of religious wars. Today such fears no longer exist. There is a sense that it is no longer a question of money and that individual beliefs are not at issue. Everyone has understood that we are struggling *against a race* and defending ourselves against its cosmopolitan power.[61]

Lur-Saluces had acutely recognized that the political exploitation of anti-Semitism had been problematic for royalists only so long as the Jews were perceived as a religious sect or a wealthy elite. Once Jews were identified as a biologically different species, French royalists need no longer fear the social or religious ramifications of anti-Semitism and were free to use it systematically. Royalist appreciation of racial anti-Semitism was governed by political expediency rather than a genuine conversion to the new doctrine, the application of which was highly selective. The royalist secretary-general, André Buffet, was an avowed anti-Semite—but only when it suited him. In 1898 the most promising royalist candidate for the deputation in Amiens was reluctant to run, because his wife was Jewish. Buffet urged him to present himself, insisting that "the royalist party, while maintaining its anti-Semitic note, must not betray an absolute exclusivism."[62]

The logic of his advisers impressed the Duc d'Orléans. Shortly after receiving the letter from Lur-Saluces, he decided to make a major pronouncement on the "Jewish question." In an address given to a group of French royalists at San Remo, the pretender echoed the arguments of Lur-Saluces as well as the doctrines of Drumont and Barrès. "Yes, there is a Jewish question; it would be foolish to deny it. . . . Its causes go back to the time when landed wealth was surpassed by liquid capital." The mission of the monarchy was to protect true Frenchmen "whose passionate attachment to the land is in some respects an extension of their personality, against the menace of anonymous and vagabond wealth." His new stance on the Jews, he repeatedly assured his audience, had nothing in common with "intolerance" or "religious persecution." He sought only to defend native Frenchmen from a people "that does not love the soil and has no attachment to it."[63] The rantings of the Duc d'Orléans no longer interested very many Frenchmen, but at least one individual was impressed. Until 1898 Charles Murras, founder of the virulently anti-Semitic *Action française,* had been a purely sentimental royalist. It was the anti-Semitism that Lur-Saluces had inspired in the pretender that awoke him from his "slumber" and prompted passionate commitment to royalist action.[64]

Royalist accommodation with anti-Semitism was analogous to an earlier rapprochement with Boulangism. Doctrines or passions that move the masses are often inherently dangerous for representatives of a traditional social order. Yet to the degree that defenders of the established order lack popular appeal, such populist movements also exercise a seductive charm, particularly if their political valence is of sufficient ambiguity as to permit a subtle redirection of their initial trajectory. In the right hands, a movement whose original intention had been the radical purification of republican democracy could be directed toward the establishment of a conservative and authoritarian regime. Similarly, by stressing the racist dimension of anti-Semitism, royalists could inoculate themselves againt its latent social radicalism. Although the basic conservative project remained the same, the means varied and the ideological stances that frightened one generation could be embraced by the next.

Royalist adoption of nationalism provides another illustration. This is not the place for a history of late nineteenth-century nationalism.[65] What is striking, however, is the ease with which the war-revolution nexus that preoccupied royalists in the 1880s disappeared in the following decade. Earlier, Jacobin-inspired nationalism seemed to prefigure 1793 or 1871; a peaceful accommodation with Germany was deemed essential to parry domestic upheaval. The Boulanger affair changed all that. If the dashing republican general could be domesticated for conservative purposes, so too by extension could his revanchist nationalism. A nationalism that was shunned when it emanated from those whose revolutionary, or even reformist, convictions were genuine, became more appealing in the hands of a man whose unprincipled opportunism was patent and whose dependence upon conservatives was total. Furthermore, a rabid nationalism that seemed to be the logical extension of radical politics lost its menacing potential if it could be construed as a veritable substitute for radical politics. A working class whose eyes were turned toward Berlin would be less likely to focus on troublesome domestic social issues. Even Gaston Laporte, otherwise such a refractory Boulangist, evinced a willingness to subordinate domestic issues to nationalist preoccupations. When asked about the eight-hour day, Laporte brightly responded that "the only means of attaining that reform is to send a Boulangist majority to the Chamber in order to tear up the Treaty of Frankfort, which binds us to Germany."[66] Ingenious equivocations of this sort, nicely deflecting embarrassing domestic questions into the international arena, were the stuff of which conservative politics were made.

The appeal of nationalism to royalists could only grow in the 1890s as the radical Left gradually separated itself from its Jacobin heritage. As organized socialism grew in strength and ideological rigor, it adopted an internationalist and pacifist stance. The nationalists in its midst, like Barrès, departed and found a more comfortable home on the Right.[67] Shorn of its radical connotations, nationalism was a natural ally of royalism. By 1899 Paul Déroulède's once-despised Ligue des Patriotes was the target of royalist overtures. Rebuffed by Déroulède, royalists sought to use Jules Guérin's Ligue Antisémitique, which they financed and controlled, to infiltrate the Ligue des Patriotes. If and when Déroulède's paramilitary movement overthrew the regime, royalists wanted the Duc d'Orléans to be in the baggage train; royalist money and 30,000 militant *ligueurs* might yet restore the monarchy. It was Boulangism all over again, but this time failure was guaranteed in advance. Déroulède's attempted coup in February 1899 was simply embarrassing. Like Constans a decade earlier, the Waldeck-Rousseau government struck back hard, not only at Déroulède but at the royalist leaders as well.[68] The royalist conspiracy with the Ligue des Patriotes was to Boulangism what the Duc d'Orléans was to the Count of Paris.

Fin-de-siècle nationalism was more than a continuation of Boulangism, but former Boulangists and royalists nonetheless played an important role.[69] Royalists were now far less important, but wherever they retained some influence, in the west and the Midi, they used the nationalist Ligue de la Patrie Française as an electoral auxiliary very much the way they had once used Boulangism.[70] *L'Espérance du peuple* no longer felt, as it had in 1886, that proponents of *revanche* were "criminal charlatans." By 1900 it was actively sponsoring nationalist rallies and boasting that "it was the monarchists who had taken the initiative and had directed the [nationalist] movement and who now lend the anti-Semitic nationalists their disinterested, devoted, and absolute support." "The great nationalist party" was an amalgam of political forces: "The Ligue de la Patrie Française, wih its big battalions, makes up the center, the plebiscitarians of the Ligue des Patriotes . . . , the left flank, and the monarchists—appropriately—the right flank." Of the Ligue des Patriotes, once so cordially detested by royalists of the Loire-Atlantique, *L'Espérance* could only remark that on most issues its program "strangely resembles ours."[71]

Perhaps the best symbol of the evolution of French royalism at the turn of the century is the career of Jules Auffray. A classic Orleanist and a passionate Boulangist, Auffray was by 1900 both an anti-Semite and a nationalist. A member of the Ligue Anti-Juive, he represented the widow of the "martyred" anti-Dreyfusard forger, Major Henry, in her celebrated defamation suit against Dreyfus's distinguished defender, Joseph Reinach. Running as nationalist candidate for the city council of Paris, he informed his future constituents that "France is oppressed by the Jewish influence and by the internationalist party." At his victory celebration he shouted "Vive Déroulède!" Elected as a nationalist deputy in 1902, the only thing he cared to remember about Boulanger was his courageous anti-German stance at the time of the Schnaebelé affair.[72]

Conclusion

"Who was deceiving and who was being deceived during those two years of paradoxical collaboration? The historian who wishes to retrace the period 1888–89 will not find the question easy to unravel."[1] So wrote Charles de Freycinet. In the aftermath of Mermeix's sensational revelations, almost all Boulangists insisted that it was they who had been deceived. By their account Boulanger and, most notoriously, Dillon had kept them completely ignorant of all dealings with royalists.[2] In the light of the available evidence, this defense (accepted implicitly by historians who insist on the radicalism of Boulangism) is singularly implausible. True, the leading republican Boulangists were almost certainly unaware of the details of the accord struck by Boulanger and Dillon. But even the most naive of them could hardly have been innocent of the fact that *some* agreement with the royalists existed. How else to explain the dramatic *volte-face* of the royalists, the subject of endless discussions in the press, both royalist and republican? What other explanation could there have been for the fact that the first stop for Boulangist campaign managers was the office of conservative notables and their newspapers? Why else did Naquet devote so much time, publicly and privately, to agonizing about Boulangist relations with the royalists?

Even the halfhearted attempt to block Auffray's Boulangist candidacy in November 1888 demonstrated a clear awareness that royalists were gradually appropriating the movement. When Boulanger responded so equivocally to their concerns, and when, a month later, Boulangists endorsed a pure royalist like Montaudon, even the most obtuse of the "republican" Boulangists must have recognized the extent of the alliance with monarchist forces. Nor did it require advanced deductive powers to establish the source of Boulanger's funding. The happy coincidence of sudden affluence, a dramatically altered royalist stance, and a series of highly unusual accommodations ought to have provided a clue. Certainly by 1889 the most innocent of the general's followers knew perfectly well where the money was coming from, if only because the royalists took elaborate pains to enlighten Boulangist candidates on that very point. Nor, surely, could Boulangists have believed that pure altruism motivated the royalists. They could not know for sure that Boulanger had promised to restore the monarchy, but they must have wondered what other motive royalists could have for so generously supporting a man they had savaged not a year earlier.

A more plausible hypothesis is that Boulangists were well aware of the covert alliance with monarchists but believed that they were cleverly *using* royalists for their own purposes. In essence, what they believed they were doing was precisely what intransigent royalists feared they might be doing: seducing royalists into a campaign that would bring radical Boulangists (and only them) into power. At least until Boulanger's exile in the spring of 1889, such beliefs had a superficial credibility. But even in the halcyon days of 1888 the notion that Boulangists were somehow manipulating the royalists left a number of critical questions unanswered. Enticing conservative voters to support Boulanger had obvious advantages (including making the general's victories possible in the first place). But these advantages were effectively nullified when conservative votes reverted to royalist and Bonapartist candidates in subsequent by-elections, bringing with them the votes of a number of republican Boulangists. Moreover, that this should happen was an explicit condition of the alliance with the royalists. In the light of the secure position of many royalists, an arrangement whereby royalist votes for Boulangists had to be matched by Boulangist support of royalists could only benefit the latter.

In theory, a massive revisionist victory in 1889 would have opened up interesting possibilities for republican Boulangists, providing always that there were substantial numbers of them in the victorious coalition. Many Bonapartists and a few royalists were soft on the dynastic question; with them, a solid core of radical Boulangists might have worked out a constitution more to the liking of Alfred Naquet than the Count of Paris. But it is hard to see how Boulangists could have believed this to be a very real possibility. It cannot have escaped them (it escaped no one else) that the great majority of the candidates they endorsed were royalists or Bonapartists. Many of the genuinely republican Boulangists were implausible candidates, running in constituencies where the chances of success were virtually nil. Even had they fared much better than they did, republicans would have been a distinct minority among the revisionist deputies.

Even taking their professions of republican radicalism at face value, Boulangists were, from almost the very beginning, the prisoners of an alliance that made even their initial successes hostage to the designs of the royalists. Their dilemma was an unenviable one. With the royalists they might overthrow the detested Opportunist republic, but only to the advantage of conservatives. Without royalists, Boulangism would not have survived the early months of 1888.

Were the Boulangists sincere radical republicans, and their connivance with royalists but a momentary aberration? The question admits of no definitive answer, and the foregoing analysis of the Boulangist episode does not hinge on it. Yet the subsequent evolution of individual Boulangists does suggest that, whatever the depth of their pre-1888 convictions, by the end of the decade their radical days were behind them. Admittedly, once the enterprise had failed and the respective "bonsoir messieurs" had been said, few of the republican Boulangists saw any utility in remaining the political handmaidens of the conservatives. Although defeated Boulangists could still be seen haunting the antechambers of Dufeuille, Breteuil, Beauvoir, and La Trémoille,[3] their parliamentary colleagues distanced themselves from their former allies. In the early 1890s the voting records of Boulangist deputies were closer to the political Left than to the parliamentary Right.[4]

Indeed, many former Boulangists now depicted themselves as socialists. Yet their "socialism" was increasingly out of step with mainstream democratic socialism as it emerged in the last years of the nineteenth century. The peculiar socialism of Maurice Barrès as the best-known example,[5] but that of Paul de Susini provides another. Susini himself made the best case for the ultimate vacuity of his socialism. "I am," he announced, "a socialist in the sense that I would like the slogan 'Liberty, Equality, Fraternity' to be respected, but I am not a collectivist." Still less did he have any use for "revolutionary socialists, the friends of Liebknecht, Bebel, and the other German Jews."[6] So refreshingly free of doctrinaire elements was Susini's socialism that by 1898 he was campaign manager for a Catholic conservative candidate and writing brochures on "National Harmony" for the Assumptionist order.[7]

A few former Boulangists returned to their earlier political homes: Vacher to mainstream Radicalism, Jourde to the Parti Ouvrier Français. But the great majority of those whose careers spanned the decade of the 1890s ended up in the camp of fin-de-siècle nationalism and anti-Semitism. Even Ballière, whose appearance in the Var so dismayed royalists, had by 1899 joined the royalists as a coindicted conspirator in an antigovernment plot, his professions of innocence now published in *La Gazette de France*.[8] The republican Boulangist from the Aisne, Edmond Turquet, a Protestant descendant of a regicide, had by 1896 converted to Catholicism and joined a Franciscan lay order. He ended his career as a Catholic and conservative militant.[9] The suggestion that republican Boulangists were really protosocialists in search of an effective vehicle for political expression is vitiated by the fact that when, in the 1890s, a genuine socialist movement arose, few chose to join it. The highly cynical assessment of Boulangists which Mackau gave at the end of the 1889 campaign does not appear to have been far wide of the mark.

A case has been made that the real victims of the Boulanger affair were the royalists. Disgruntled royalists asserted this at the time, and recently a historian of royalism entitled his book *Boulanger: Fossoyeur de la monarchie*.[10] But this is to imply a causal relationship where none existed. The Boulangist adventure coincided with the definitive eclipse of royalism in France but did not cause it. The causes of the decline of royalism were much more fundamental: monarchist inability to adapt programmatically and organizationally to the rapidly changing social and political world of the Third Republic. It was the decay of royalism that caused its leaders to embrace Boulangism, not the other way around.

A character in Barrès's semifictional *L'Appel au soldat* observes, "We shall meet again in other Boulangisms."[11] And so they would, although the cast of characters and the constellation of forces would be somewhat different. As a serious political force, royalism disappeared. The great royalist families—the Aillières, Andignés, Audiffret-Pasquiers, Desjardins, Duvals, Le Cour Grandmaisons, Juingés, Lasteyries, Des Rotours, Taillandiers, and Taudières—continued to send representatives to parliament, but for the most part they were mute backbenchers in decrepit conservative parties like the Republican Federation. Although the line of descent was not a direct one, these twentieth-century conservatives had much in common with their late nineteenth-century counterparts. Except for dynastic considerations, they displayed the same deficiencies of political organization, the same distaste and ineptitude for mass politics, the same suspicion of democracy, the same anxiety about the social order, and above all the same attraction to dynamic and popular political auxiliaries.

Nor would such auxiliaries be lacking. The Boulangist movement died with its namesake, but individual Boulangists resurfaced in the nationalist leagues of the early twentieth century. Their spiritual descendants founded the antiparliamentary leagues of the interwar years. The Jeunesses Patriotes, for example, the successor to Déroulède's Ligue des Patriotes, was a direct heir. Granted, the Jeunesses Patriotes and the much larger Croix de Feu were not the exact equivalents of Boulangism. To the degree that they were inspired by foreign models, they differed. They adopted an aggressive paramilitary tone that was less prominent in 1888–89. They were ideologically closer to their conservative allies than had been the Boulangists, although this greater affinity reflected primarily the absence of the dynastic stumbling block. By contrast their antiparliamentary language, nationalist vocabulary, and populist militancy were entirely within the Boulangist tradition.

Like the Boulangists, the leagues waged a savage war against a corrupt and decadent parliamentarianism. They too evoked an authoritarian Jacobinism, as in the periodic calls of the Jeunesses Patriotes for a Committee of Public Safety to rescue France. They too put forth their "saviors," men like Pierre Taittinger and Colonel de la Rocque whose demagogic image masked, in the tradition of Boulanger, weak and vacillating personalities. Like the Boulangists, the leagues put forth a vague program of national renovation and insisted that they were above politics. In rhetoric crackling with denunciations of the traditional Right, they insisted, in the words of the Croix de Feu, that they were "ni à droite ni à gauche."

Their denial of any association with the Right is rather reminiscent of similar claims made in *La Cocarde* in 1888—and for the same reason. The leagues were at every level intimately associated with traditional conservatives.[12] The relationship was so close, in fact, that historians who are convinced that fascism must be a leftist phenomenon strenuously deny that the leagues were fascist at all.[13] Yet whatever one calls them, the leagues mobilized unprecedented numbers of Frenchmen on a scale not seen since the Boulanger affair. This is precisely what made them so attractive to conservatives. As the leagues attracted adherents at an unparalleled rate, the conservatives of the 1930s, like royalists before them, watched with a mixture of anxiety and awe. There was something menacing about the new style of politics represented by the leagues, but also something very attractive. Expertise at mass politics—the one thing the elitist parties of the traditional Right so notoriously lacked—was an appealing attribute, especially given the social and political turmoil of the decade. Association with the volatile leagues was not without its dangers (they too saw the parallels with Boulangism), but like conservatives elsewhere, they believed that only an alliance with dynamic and unorthodox allies could stop the erosion of their political influence. The origins of this fundamentally regressive strategy go back to the spring of 1888, when royalists decided to put the future of the monarchy in the hands of General Boulanger.

NOTES

Introduction

1. *Le Journal de l'Oise,* 14 August 1888. Unless otherwise noted, all translations from French sources are my own.

2. Several clarifications of terminology are necessary. Throughout this work reference is repeatedly made to the royalist or conservative "party." Although contemporaries routinely used these terms, there were as yet no French political parties in the modern sense of the word. There were, of course, authorized royalist agents and a loose network of royalist committees, but when contemporaries used the term *party* it denoted a group of individuals who subscribed to a common body of political principles. The terms *royalist* and *monarchist* have usually been used synonymously, although in the parlance of the times the latter term had a broader meaning and could include Bonapartists as well as royalists. The terms *conservative* and *conservatives* also appear frequently in this work. They are employed, as they were by contemporaries, to denote the antirepublican Right: royalists and Bonapartists. The label, which began to appear in the 1870s, had the double advantage of reconciling royalists and Bonapartists and disguising electorally unappealing dynastic affiliations. By the twentieth century the term had all but disappeared from the French political lexicon except as a derisive byword (as in the abusive epithet "conservateur, voilà un mot qui commence bien mal"). That those who sought to overthrow a socially conservative republic should nonetheless call themselves conservatives is entirely appropriate in a nation of euphemistic political labels, where "Left" subsequently meant "Right," "liberal" denoted "conservative," and "moderate" referred to the extreme Right.

3. Mermeix (pseud. Gabriel Terrail), *Les Coulisses du Boulangisme* (Paris: Léopold Cerf, 1890).

4. Adrien Dansette, *Le Boulangisme* (Paris: Fayard, 1946).

5. A significant and important exception is the recent book by Philippe Levillain, *Boulanger: Fossoyeur de la monarchie* (Paris: Flammarion, 1982). Levillain provides by far the most detailed account heretofore of the royalist role, but like Dansette he concentrates almost exclusively on a handful of royalist "conspirators." It is a study in high politics focusing on Paris and the Chamber of Deputies. The royalist rank and file are absent from the book and the local level is largely ignored. Moreover, like Dansette, he treats the royalists as the unwitting dupes of Boulanger, who becomes "the gravedigger of the monarchy." For Levillain the story is effectively over when

Boulanger flees France; the elections of 1889 are dismissed in a few paragraphs.

6. Michael Burns, *Rural Society and French Politics: Boulangism and the Dreyfus Affair, 1886–1900* (Princeton: Princeton University Press, 1984). Admittedly, Burns treats in detail only four departments: the Isère, the Marne, the Gers, and the Orne. Only in the last was either royalism or Boulangism a decisive factor. But in his otherwise valuable analysis of Boulanger's successful electoral campaigns, Burns overlooks the fact that the great majority of peasants who voted for Boulanger had previously voted for conservatives, did not have a conservative candidate to vote for in 1888, and were advised by the local conservative elite to vote for Boulanger. When those conditions did not obtain, Boulanger was not elected.

7. Patrick H. Hutton, *The Cult of the Revolutionary Tradition: The Blanquists in French Politics, 1864–1893* (Berkeley: University of California Press, 1981), 14, 150, 151, 144, 143–44, respectively. The most recent restatement of this position is by Paul Mazgaj, "The Origins of the French Radical Right: A Historiographical Essay," *French Historical Studies* 15, no. 2 (Fall 1987), 287–315.

8. Jacques Néré, "La Crise industrielle de 1882 et le mouvement boulangiste," thèse, doctorat ès lettres, Université de Paris, 1959, 2 vols., and "Les Elections Boulanger dans le département du Nord," thèse complémentaire, Université de Paris, 1959. Neither thesis has been published, but they may be consulted in the Bibliothèque de la Fondation Nationale des Sciences Politiques in Paris, 4° 5776 and 4° 5661.

9. Néré, "La Crise industrielle," 4.

10. Ibid., 300.

11. Ibid., 422.

12. A notable exception is Frederick Seager, *The Boulanger Affair* (Ithaca: Cornell University Press, 1968).

13. Theodore Zeldin, *France, 1848–1945: Politics and Anger* (London: Oxford University Press, 1979), 280.

14. Zeev Sternhell, *La Droite révolutionnaire, 1885–1914: Les Origines françaises du fascisme* (Paris: Seuil, 1978), 75–76, 38–39.

15. Zeev Sternhell, *Maurice Barrès et le nationalisme français* (Paris: Presses de la Fondation Nationale des Sciences Politiques, 1972); C. Stewart Doty, *From Cultural Rebellion to Counterrevolution: The Politics of Maurice Barrès* (Athens: University of Ohio Press, 1976).

16. Pierre Denis, *Le Mémorial de Saint-Brélade* (Paris: Ollendorf, 1984), 107; *La Gazette de France*, 26 August 1980.

17. Jacques Néré, *Le Boulangisme et la presse* (Paris: Armand Colin, 1964), 169.

18. Odile Rudelle, *La République absolue, 1870–89* (Paris: Publications de la Sorbonne, 1982), 260–61. These principles of exclusion are applied less rigorously in practice, because she relies on the designation of *Le Temps* and the electoral declarations of the candidates. Since the first is idiosyncratic

and the second highly (and deliberately) ambiguous, many candidates who were in fact royalists or Bonapartists slip through her net and end up as republican Boulangists.

19. André Siegfried, *Tableau politique de la France de l'ouest sous la IIIᵉ République* (Paris: Armand Colin, 1964), 488.

20. See for example Arno J. Mayer, *Dynamics of Counterrevolution in Europe, 1870–1956* (New York: Harper and Row, 1971); John Weiss, *The Fascist Tradition* (New York: Harper and Row, 1967); Martin Kitchen, *Fascism* (London: Macmillan, 1976).

21. Ernst Nolte, *Three Faces of Fascism* (New York: Mentor, 1969).

22. For the classic statements of this thesis, see Hannah Arendt, *The Origins of Totalitarianism* (New York: Meridian, 1951), and Carl J. Friedrich and Zbigniew K. Brzezinski, *Totalitarian Dictatorship and Autocracy* (New York: Praeger, 1956). For some of the more lucid critiques of the thesis, see Robert Burrows, "Totalitarianism: The Revised Standard Version," *World Politics* 21, no. 2 (January 1969), 272–94, and Mayer, *Dynamics of Counterrevolution.*

23. A. James Gregor, *Italian Fascism and Developmental Dictatorship* (Princeton: Princeton University Press, 1979), xii, 32.

24. Renzo de Felice, *Intervesta Sul Fascismo,* ed. Michael A. Ledeen (Rome: Laterza, 1976), 40–41.

25. Eugen Weber, "Revolution, Counterrevolution, What Revolution?" *Journal of Contemporary History* 9, no. 2 (April 1974), 3–47. This essay has been reprinted in Walter Laqueur's *Fascism: A Reader's Guide* (Berkeley: University of California Press, 1976).

26. Zeev Sternhell, *Ni droite ni gauche: L'Idéologie fasciste en France* (Paris: Seuil, 1983), 11.

27. The expression is from Arthur Schweitzer, *Big Business and the Third Reich* (Bloomington: Indiana University Press, 1964).

28. MacGregor Knox, "Conquest, Foreign and Domestic, in Fascist Italy and Nazi Germany," *Journal of Modern History* 56 (March 1984), 57.

29. Sternhell, *Ni droite ni gauche,* 15.

30. It is argued most notably by Robert Soucy in "The Nature of Fascism in France," *Journal of Contemporary History* 1 (1966), 27–55. Soucy has elaborated on this argument in three subsequent books: *Fascism in France: The Case of Maurice Barrès* (Berkeley: University of California Press, 1972); *Fascist Intellectual: Drieu La Rochelle* (Berkeley: University of California Press, 1979); and *French Fascism: The First Wave, 1924–1933* (New Haven: Yale University Press, 1986).

31. Sternhell, *Ni droite ni gauche,* 10.

32. Ibid., 20.

33. Ibid.

34. Zeev Sternhell, "Barrès et la gauche du boulangisme à la cocarde," *Le Mouvement social* 75 (April–June 1971), 92. The emphasis on the socialist component of fascism by scholars like Sternhell also provides sus-

tenance for a contemporary Right, convinced that "socialism equals fascism." Although Sternhell manifestly argues no such thing, it is significant that in the spring of 1984 he had to contest vigorously exactly this distorted reading of his work by representatives of the extreme Right in France. See *Le Monde,* 7 March 1984.

35. For the comparable crisis of elitist conservative formations in Germany, see Geoff Eley, *Reshaping the German Right: Radical Nationalism and Political Change after Bismarck* (New Haven: Yale University Press, 1980), and D. S. White, *The Splintered Party: National Liberalism in Hessen and the Reich, 1867–1918* (Cambridge: Harvard University Press, 1976).

36. The literature on the new politics of the late nineteenth century is vast. Among the best works are the following: Carl E. Schorske, "Politics in a New Key: An Austrian Triptych," *Journal of Modern History* 39 (1967) 343–86; John W. Boyer, *Political Radicalism in Late Imperial Vienna* (Chicago: University of Chicago Press, 1981); Eley, *Reshaping the German Right;* David Blackbourn and Geoff Eley, *The Peculiarities of German History* (Oxford: Oxford University Press, 1984); David Roberts, "Petty Bourgeois Fascism in Italy: Form and Content," in Stein Larsen et al., eds., *Who Were the Fascists* (Bergen: Universitetsforlaget, 1980), 337–47. The Boulangist/royalist relationship was not identical to that which existed between Carl Lueger and German and Italian radical nationalists, on the one hand, and Viennese liberals, German conservatives, and Giolittian liberals, on the other. The latter group of conservatives was in power, whereas royalists were not. In all cases, however, it was a growing fear of political and social democratization that provided the basis for an eventual accommodation.

37. By the twentieth century the only parliamentary groups in France whose names contained words like *Left, republican, democratic,* and *social* were groups that represented none of those things. Parliamentary conservatives in Italy were divided among groups with names like Democrats, Social Democrats, Democratic Liberals, and Liberal Democrats. The old German Conservative Party became the German National People's Party.

38. Cited in Roberto Vivarelli's *Il dopoguerra in Italia: Dalla fine della guerra all'imprese di Fiume* (Naples: Ricciardi, 1967), 321.

39. The Boulangist deputy was Gaston Laporte. See Commissaire spécial to prefect, 15 September 1889, AD Nièvre, 3M 1126/5 (1889). For Corradini, see Salvatore Saladino, "Italy," in Hans Rogger and Eugen Weber, eds., *The European Right* (Berkeley: University of California Press, 1966), 208–58, and Alexander J. De Grand, *The Italian Nationalist Association and the Rise of Fascism in Italy* (Lincoln: University of Nebraska Press, 1978).

40. Eley (*Reshaping the German Right*) has argued convincingly against the tendency to reduce the radicals of the Right to the passive objects of conservative manipulation. The independent roots and dynamic of the radical Right need to be taken seriously. He nonetheless concedes that conservatives do "appropriate" the radical Right for their own purposes.

41. On the Parti Social Français, see William Irvine, *French Conservatism in Crisis* (Baton Rouge: Louisiana State University Press, 1979); on the Agrarian League, see H.-J. Puhle, *Agrarische Interessenpolitik und preussischer Konservatismus im Wilhelminischen Reich, 1893–1914* (Hannover: Verlag für Literatur und Zeitgeschehen, 1966).

42. Sternhell, *Ni droite ni gauche*, 9, 313. The offending historian, as well as the most articulate dissident from the prevailing consensus about French fascism, is Robert Soucy.

43. Cited in Renzo De Felice's *Mussolini il fascista: La conquista del potere* (Turin: Einaudi, 1966), 226.

Chapter 1

1. Robert R. Locke, *French Legitimists and the Politics of Moral Order in the Early Third Republic* (Princeton: Princeton University Press, 1974), 174–75.

2. On the early elections see Jacques Gouault, *Comment la France est devenue républicaine* (Paris: Armand Colin, 1954).

3. For an example of conservative failure to make progress in 1877 even where they enjoyed massive governmental support, see Georges Dupeux, *Aspects de l'histoire sociale et politique du Loir-et-Cher* (Paris: Mouton, 1962), 479.

4. Rudelle, *La République absolue*, 82–83. In departments seriously contested by conservatives, the results were roughly comparable to those of 1877.

5. For a good account of Bonapartism in the 1870s, see John Rothney, *Bonapartism after Sedan* (Ithaca: Cornell University Press, 1969).

6. Report of Baron d'Orgeval, delegate of the Parisian conservative coordinating committee (the Committee of Twelve), no date but August 1889, and Jules Delafosse to Mackau, 7 August 1889, in Archives Nationales 156 AP 1 (hereafter Mackau papers), carton 108.

7. By far the most comprehensive account of this issue, as well as of the general politics of Bonapartism in the 1880s, is the excellent doctoral dissertation of Karen M. Offen, "The Political Career of Paul de Cassagnac" (Stanford University, 1970). I have relied heavily on this work for the discussion of Bonapartists and their relationship with royalists.

8. On the legitimist organization see Marquis de Dreux-Brézé, *Notes et Souvenirs: Pour servir à l'histoire du partie royaliste, 1872–1873* (Paris: J. Dumoulin, 1902). The Annuaire de la Presse listed 177 legitimist provincial newspapers in 1881, compared to 148 Orleanist ones. See Jeannine Verdès-Leroux, *Scandale financier et anti-sémitisme catholique* (Paris: Editions du Centurion, 1969), 79.

9. See his dossier in the Archives de la Préfecture de Police, Paris (hereafter APP), B/a 1138.

10. See Beauvoir's dossier in APP B/a 956. The exact delimitation of responsibility within the royalist headquarters was often in a state of flux. In 1887, in particular, reorganizational schemes abounded. Bocher, worried as always about money, sought to diminish Dufeuille's operation, which he thought too expensive. Lambert de Sainte-Croix complained endlessly of the superior authority accorded Beauvoir. An outline of nominal responsibilities can be found in the *règlements de service* dated 1 November 1887 in the Archives de la Maison de France (Archives Nationales, 300 AP III), carton 648. (Hereafter this collection is designated AMF.)

11. Dufeuille to Count of Paris, 20 November 1888, in AMF 632.

12. Offen, "Cassagnac," 213–22; Cassagnac to Count of Paris, 29 December 1886, in AMF 611; Beauvoir to Count of Paris, 7 March 1887, in AMF 614. For the most striking example of Cassagnac's comparative treatment of the two pretenders, see *L'Autorité,* 8 July 1888.

13. Dufeuille to Count of Paris, 10 June 1886, and Breteuil to Count of Paris, 12 June 1886, in AMF 605; Calla to Count of Paris, 23 July 1886, in AMF 606. See also APP B/a 1000, 30 August 1886.

14. Dufeuille to Count of Paris, 8 October 1886, in AMF 609. Vicount d'Adhémar, leader of the royalists in Toulouse, to Edmond Boucher, coordinator of the royalist press, 30 April 1884, on the political advantages of a takeover of the Bonapartist *Le Messager de Toulouse;* Oscar Havard, editor of the royalist *Le Monde,* to Boucher, 12 August 1883, on similar reasons for buying out *Le Salut public* of Lyons—both in Archives Nationales 300 AP 3 (Boucher papers). Both newspapers were ultimately acquired by royalists.

15. Pierre de Vallée to Croissy, 17 July 1889, in Mackau papers 109.

16. Albert Verly, *Le Général Boulanger et la conspiration monarchique* (Paris: Ollendorff, 1893), 236.

17. In the 1885 elections each party could submit a slate of candidates in each department. The number of candidates on each slate would be equal to or smaller than the number of seats assigned the department. Each elector had as many votes as there were deputies to be elected in the department, but was not required to cast them all and could distribute them across several lists. To be elected on the first ballot, a candidate had to receive an absolute majority of the votes cast. If the number of candidates elected on the first ballot was fewer than the number of seats, a second ballot was held and the remaining seats were distributed to candidates with the most votes. Since voters did at times vote for candidates on different slates (*voix panachées*), exact calculations of popular vote are difficult.

18. The uncontested departments were the Cantal, the Alpes-Maritimes, the Basses-Alpes, and the Hautes-Alpes. See Louis Teste, *Les Monarchistes sous la IIIᵉ République* (Paris: n.p., 1891), on the role of the Count of Paris in forging the conservative union. Offen, "Cassagnac," 261, n. 106, notes that Teste exaggerates the importance of the pretender's role, arguing

that Cassagnac and Mackau were at least as instrumental in creating the alliance.

19. Rudelle, *La République,* 107–57.

20. For the socially conservative reflexes of early republicans, see Sanford Elwitt, *The Making of the Third Republic* (Baton Rouge: Louisiana State University Press, 1975), chapter 1.

21. Teste, *Monarchistes,* 141.

22. *Le Salut public,* 22 July 1886.

23. Ibid., 13 April 1888. The Catholic royalist newspaper *La Croix* certainly propagated the doctrine of *revanche* in the 1880s, albeit usually on its back pages. Yet its tone became markedly cautious whenever Radical belligerency threatened to drive France to war. See William Francis Ryan, *"La Croix* and the Development of Rightist Nationalism in France, 1883–1889," Ph.D. diss., University of Connecticut, 1970, 162ff., 207–8.

24. *L'Espérance du peuple,* 2 April 1886, 25 May 1887.

25. *Le Soleil du Midi,* 24 April 1887.

26. *Le Messager de Toulouse,* 10 February 1887.

27. *Le Moniteur du Calvados,* 2 February 1888.

28. Irvine, *French Conservatism,* chapter 6.

29. *L'Espérance du peuple,* 25 May 1887.

30. Of the many accounts of the career of General Boulanger, the two best are Dansette, *Le Boulangisme,* and Seager, *The Boulanger Affair.* Fresnette Pisani-Ferry, *Le Général Boulanger* (Paris: Flammarion, 1969), adds little new except a passionate defense of her great-uncle, Jules Ferry. James Harding, *The Astonishing Adventure of General Boulanger* (New York: Scribner's, 1971), is popular history but contains some new material on Boulanger's early years.

31. Beauvoir to Count of Paris, 17 July 1886, in AMF 606.

32. *L'Espérance du peuple,* 2 April 1886; *Le Salut public,* 21 July 1886.

33. De Mun to Count of Paris, 27 January 1887, in AMF 613.

34. Humann to Count of Paris, 29 December 1886, in AMF 611.

35. Beauvoir to Count of Paris, 26 December 1886, in AMF 611.

36. Ibid.; de Mun to Count of Paris, 13, 27 January 1887, in AMF 613.

37. Duc de La Ferronnays to Count of Paris, 20 January 1887, in AMF 613, and 4 June 1887, in AMF 616; La Rochefoucauld to Count of Paris, 13 June 1887, in AMF 616; Beauvoir to Count of Paris, 26 April 1887, in AMF 614.

38. Duc de La Ferronnays to Count of Paris, 4 July 1886, in AMF 606; Dufeuille to Count of Paris, 18 October 1886, in AMF 609; Beauvoir to Count of Paris, 10 December 1886, in AMF 611.

39. Paul de Leusse to Count of Paris, 1 February 1886, in AMF 601. He later elaborated this argument in his book *La Paix par l'union douanière franco-allemande* (Strasbourg: J. Busseniers, 1888).

40. Martimprey to Mackau, 10 February 1888, in Mackau papers 102.

41. Beauvoir to Count of Paris, 18 February 1888, in AMF 624.

42. Beauvoir to Count of Paris, 8 July 1887, in AMF 617.

43. Bocher to Count of Paris, 4 July 1886, and Dufeuille to Count of Paris, 26 July 1886, in AMF 606.

44. See for example Dufeuille to Count of Paris, 25 November 1886, on the defeat of a royalist in a by-election in the Nord, a department swept by conservatives in 1885, in AMF 610; Beauvoir to Count of Paris, 1 March 1887, in AMF 614.

45. François Goguel, *Géographie des élections françaises de 1870 à 1951* (Paris: Armand Colin, 1951), 22. No one has yet satisfactorily accounted for this rigid geographical determinism. A useful survey of the various attempts is given by William Brustein, "Regional Mode of Production Analysis of Political Behavior: The Case of Western and Mediterranean France," *Politics and Society* 10, no. 4 (1981), 355–98. The author's own attempt, while interesting, is not very helpful for the 1880s.

46. Benjamin F. Martin, *Count Albert de Mun: Paladin of the Third Republic* (Chapel Hill: University of North Carolina Press, 1978), 58–61.

47. The best recent account of Raoul-Duval is J. El Gammel, "Un préralliement: Raoul-Duval et la droite républicaine, 1885–1887," *Revue d'histoire moderne et contemporaine* 29 (October–December 1982), 599–621.

48. On the attacks levied against even legitimist deputies, see Duc de La Ferronnays to Count of Paris, 4 June 1887; de Mun to Count of Paris, 19 June 1887; Rochefoucauld to Count of Paris, 13 June 1887—all in AMF 616. Mackau was even afraid to leave Paris to visit the pretender, lest intransigent royalists revolt: Beauvoir to Count of Paris, 14 June 1887, in AMF 616.

49. Dufeuille to Count of Paris, 8 September 1887; Haussonville to Count of Paris, 16 September 1887; Bocher to Count of Paris, 16 September 1887—all in AMF 619. Even today there is some debate as to the reasons for the pretender's inept timing. The most recent account (Levillain, *Boulanger,* 38) argues that the Count of Paris had failed to consult his associates˙and was motivated by Prince Victor's vigorous reassertion of Bonapartist principles the previous month. This cannot be correct, however, since the pretender had been preparing his manifesto since the beginning of the year, and it had been the subject of considerable debate within the party leadership. See for example Dufeuille to Count of Paris, 31 March 1887, and Edouard Hervé to Count of Paris, 4 April 1887, in AMF 614; Dufeuille to Count of Paris, 14 and 21 May 1887, and Bocher to Count of Paris, 19 May 1887, in AMF 615. See also a note from the Count of Paris, no date but April 1887, in AMF 614, referring to changes he had made in response to his lieutenants' suggestions.

50. There was in fact one major procedural difficulty. Article 8 of the Constitution provided for constitutional revision, but it had been amended

in 1884 to exclude the possibility of a regime other than a republican one. Revising article 8 was therefore a precondition for the rest of his proposals.

51. Count of Paris to Edmond Boucher, 23 September 1887, AN 305 AP 2 (Boucher papers).

52. The drafts are in AMF 648.

53. Although under the Third Republic senators had always been chosen by a limited number of electors, the overwhelming majority of them, especially after the electoral reforms of 1884, had been delegates of the municipal councils. The Count of Paris chose to permit these delegates to elect only 120 senators, whereas the far less numerous members of the departmental general councils would elect a further 82. Magistrates, chambers of commerce, and the universities and other institutions of higher learning would select 54 more senators.

54. Cazenove de Pradine to Count of Paris, 18 September 1887, in AMF 619.

55. Haussonville to Count of Paris, 16 September 1887, and Dufeuille to Count of Paris, 17 September 1887, in AMF 619, on the complaints of the Orleanists *milieu d'affaires.*

56. For the reaction of Bonapartists see Offen, "Cassagnac," 305–6.

57. Breteuil to Count of Paris, 11 September 1887; Bocher to Count of Paris, 19 September 1887; de l'Aigle to Count of Paris, 24 September 1887—all in AMF 619.

58. Beauvoir to Count of Paris, 22 September 1887, in AMF 619.

59. Plichon to Count of Paris, 8 January 1888, in AMF 623.

Chapter 2

1. Norman Stone, *Europe Transformed, 1889–1919* (London: Fontana, 1983), 288.

2. Jacques Piou to Count of Paris, 19 January 1887, in AMF 613.

3. Jacques Piou to Count of Paris, 21 February 1887, in AMF 614; Piou to Count of Paris, 22 February 1888, in AMF 624.

4. Piou to Count of Paris, 19 January 1887, in AMF 613.

5. Count of Paris to unidentified, 30 June 1886, in AMF 605.

6. *La Revue de l'Ouest,* 24 January, 3 March 1888; *L'Union monarchique du Finistère,* 18 February 1888.

7. St. Marc-Girardin to Count of Paris, 3 February 1888, in AMF 624.

8. Lambert de Sainte-Croix to Count of Paris, 15 October 1886, in AMF 609.

9. *Le Vrai Dauphiné,* 14 January 1888.

10. *Le Courrier du Var,* 18 August 1889; *Le Nouvelliste de Bordeaux,* 21 January 1888.

11. *L'Avenir du Lot-et-Garonne,* 4 August 1888; *Le Soleil du Midi,* 29 March 1887.

12. Dufeuille to Count of Paris, 3 September 1886, in AMF 608.

13. *Le Journal de Lunéville*, 14 August 1889; *Le Propagateur picard*, 24 June 1888; *L'Electeur des Côtes-du-Nord*, 28 November 1888.

14. J. M. Roberts, "La Commune considérée par la droite, dimension d'une mythologie," *Revue d'histoire moderne et contemporaine* 19 (April–June 1972), 203.

15. Eugène Dufeuille to Count of Paris, 11 October 1886, AMF 609.

16. Charles Seignobos, "L'Evolution de la 3ᵉ République," in E. Lavisse, ed., *Histoire contemporaine de la France,* vol. 8 (Paris: Hachette, 1921), 54–55.

17. Louis Teste, *Anatomie de la république (1870–1910)* (Paris: Librairie du XXᵉ Siècle, 1910), 114–20.

18. On the administrative purges see Jean-Pierre Machelon, *La République contre les libertés* (Paris: Presses de la Fondation Nationale des Sciences Politiques, 1976), 280–99; Jeanne Siwek-Pouydesseau, *Le Corps préfectoral sous la troisième et la quatrième République* (Paris: Armand Colin, 1969), 77; J. P. Royer, R. Martinage, and P. Lecocq, *Juges et notabilités au XIXᵉ siècle* (Paris: Presses Universitaires de France, 1982), 357–88. For an example of the extent of the purges even in a thoroughly republican department, see François Viple, *Sociologie politique de l'Allier* (Paris: R. Richon et R. Durand-Auzias, 1967), 191–92.

19. Machelon, *La République,* 288. For an incisive discussion of the "milch-cow state" and its political impact on conservative peasantry, see P. M. Jones, *Politics and Rural Society: The Southern Massif Central c. 1750–1880* (Cambridge: Cambridge University Press, 1985), 272–304.

20. Prefect to subprefect of Saint-Pons, 26 August 1888, AD Hérault, 39M 277; Jones, *Politics,* 299.

21. *Le Courrier de l'Aude,* 22 February 1888.

22. For a good example see Barnett Bruce Singer, *Village Notables in Nineteenth-Century France: Priests, Mayors, Schoolmasters* (Albany: State University of New York Press, 1982).

23. Michel Denis, *Les Royalistes de la Mayenne et le monde moderne, xixᵉ et xxᵉ siècles* (Paris: Librairie C. Klincksieck, 1977), 460.

24. Prefect to minister of interior, 18 October 1984, AD Loire-Atlantique, 1M 520; prefect to minister of interior, 25 September 1889, AD Côtes-du-Nord, 3M.

25. Procureur général du Cour d'Appel of Poitiers to minister of justice, 11 November 1889, AN F¹⁹ 5618; prefect of the Haute-Garonne to minister of interior, 30 October 1881, AN F¹⁹ 5617; Denis, *Les Royalistes,* 479; Jones, *Politics,* 292.

26. Jacques Gadille, *La Pensée et l'action politique des évêques français au début de la IIIᵉ République,* 2 vols. (Paris: Hachette, 1967), vol. 2, 260.

27. The source for these figures is AN F¹⁹ 5618. There would appear to be no correlation between those regions where priests were frequently

charged with illicit political activity and areas of royalist electoral strength. In 1885 there was a higher than average number of alleged violations in conservative strongholds like the Finistère, Côtes-du-Nord, Loire-Atlantique, Vendée, Orne, Somme, Ardèche, Lozère, Aveyron, Landes, and Basses-Pyrénées. On the other hand, republican strongholds like the Ariège and the Meuse reported an even higher incidence of violations. And in the Morbihan, Nord, Eure, and Maine-et-Loire, where the conservatives swept the elections, no violations were reported whatsoever. Given the highly subjective nature of the charge, it is unlikely that the incidence of reported violations is even a very reliable indicator of the attitude of clergy. The incidence of violations is given in AN F^{19} 5617.

28. From the *Supplément au catéchisme diocésan*, in AD, Ille-et-Vilaine, 1M 142.

29. Reports from secretary of the Savoie, 20 May 1889, and secretary of the Morbihan, 29 December 1889, in AMF 577; *La Croix*, 13 June 1888.

30. Charles Grimblest to Eugène Dufeuille, 24 November 1886, in AMF 610.

31. Anon., *Notes sur l'organisation du parti royalist* (Paris: n.p., 1897), 3–4.

32. Dufeuille to Count of Paris, 14 September 1886, in AMF 608; Dufeuille to Bocher, 21 January 1887, in AMF 613; Dufeuille to Count of Paris, 12 November 1887, in AMF 621; Dufeuille to Count of Paris, 23 February 1889, in AMF 636.

33. See the report on this affair from the Duc de La Ferronnays to the Count of Paris, 6 August 1886, in AMF 607.

34. Reports from Pradelle, 17 and 18 August 1887, in AMF 578.

35. Bocher to Count of Paris, 28 February 1887, in AMF 614. See also the uncharacteristic anger of Dufeuille concerning the wildly inaccurate predictions of the secretary of the Aisne prior to the 1889 by-election: Dufeuille to Count of Paris, 5 June 1889, in AMF 641.

36. A list of the former occupations of a majority of the secretaries can be found in AMF 575. A similar assessment was made in a report to the minister of the interior (26 September 1887, AN F^7 12431) which stressed that departmental secretaries were "chosen in preference from among the former magistrates, subprefects, and prefectoral councillors."

37. André Cordier to Edouard Lur-Saluces, 7 January 1891, in AMF 660.

38. For a discussion of the limitation of Radical organization, see Jean Thomas Nordmann, *Histoire des Radicaux* (Paris: Editions de la Table Ronde, 1974), 296–308; Serge Berstein, *Histoire du parti radical*, 2 vols. (Paris: Presses de la Fondation Nationale des Sciences Politiques, 1980), vol. 1, 33–34.

39. The results of a survey of departmental organization made early in 1888 can be found in AMF 576. Nearly sixty departmental secretaries responded to an elaborate questionnaire concerning their organization. The

nature of their responses does not permit a systematic quantification, which would in any case be meaningless, since in many cases they described an organizational structure that existed only on paper.

40. Report of annual meeting of the Comité Départemental Royaliste de la Gironde, 16 November 1888, and report of executive meeting of the same, 4 July 1889, in AMF 578; report of annual meeting of the Comité Départemental, 1 June 1891, in AMF 575; report of annual meeting of the Comité Départemental, 2 December 1890, in AMF 579; report from departmental secretary, 15 March 1889, in AMF 579.

41. Report from secretary of the Ardennes, undated but 1888 or 1889, in AMF 574.

42. Report from secretary of the Meurthe-et-Moselle, 18 February 1884, in AMF 575; report from secretary of the Meurthe-et-Moselle, 6 May 1888, in AMF 575. For similar examples see Dupeux, *Aspects,* 588–89.

43. Report from secretary of the Hautes-Pyrénées, 3 April 1888, in AMF 582.

44. Dufeuille to Count of Paris, 4 October 1888, in AMF 631. Pierre Barral stresses the passion for exclusivity of the local royalist committees in *Le Département de l'Isère sous la troisième République* (Paris: Armand Colin, 1962), 399.

45. Minutes of meeting of Comité Royaliste of the Aisne, 19 October 1888, in AMF 578; prefect to minister of interior, 27 March 1886, AD Eure, 1M 208; report from secretary of the Nord, 19 February 1892, in AMF 583; Denis, *Les Royalistes,* 456–57.

46. Report from secretary of the Marne, 9 December 1890, in AMF 580; report from secretary of the Loir-et-Cher, 30 March 1889, in AMF 579; report from secretary of the Basses-Pyrénées, 18 April 1888, in AMF 582.

47. De Mun's circular of 19 April 1881 is cited in Dreux-Brézé, *Notes et souvenirs,* 463; Pierre Calla to Count of Paris, 4 November 1887, in AMF 621.

48. *L'Espérance de Nancy,* 31 August, 28 November 1888.

49. Prefect to minister of interior, 12 March 1888, AD Haute-Garonne, 4M 99.

50. Commissaire central to prefect, 18 September 1889, AD Charente-Maritime, 4M 2/40.

51. Emile Monnet, *Archives politiques du département des Deux-Sèvres: Histoire des élections législatives de 1789 à 1889* (Niort: L. Clouzot, 1889), 413–18.

52. Reports of prefects to Ministry of the Interior, 21 February 1884, AN F[7] 12431.

53. *Le Figaro,* 23 December 1874.

54. Pierre Albert, ed., *Documents pour l'histoire de la presse de province dans la seconde moitié du XIXe siècle* (Paris: CNRS, n.d.), 134.

55. The source for statistics on circulation is Albert, *Documents.* See also

Louis de Vaucelles, *Le Nouvelliste de Lyon et la défense religieuse* (Paris: Les Belles Lettres, 1971), 210.

56. Albert, *Documents,* 134ff.

57. Report from the Finistère, 28 February 1887, in AMF 575.

58. See Cordier's report on the press and the annual meeting of the Comité Royalist de la Gironde, 1 June 1891, in AMF 575; Edouard Lur-Saluces to Count of Paris, 29 April 1886, in AMF 603.

59. Minutes of meeting of the Comité Royaliste of the Charente-Maritime, 3 February 1890, in AMF 580.

60. Claude Bellanger, Jacques Godechot, Pierre Guiral, and Fernand Lenou, eds., *Histoire générale de la presse française,* 5 vols. (Paris: Presses Universitaires de France, 1979), vol. 3, 181.

61. Arsène Thévenot, *Souvenirs d'un journaliste* (Paris: Léon Frémont, 1901), 75–79.

62. Subprefect of Pont-Audemer to prefect, 20 March 1886, and subprefect of Andelys to prefect, 19 March 1886, AD Eure, 1M 208.

63. Prefect to minister of interior, 8 October 1888, AD Seine-Maritime, 4MP 4125. See reports from the *missi,* 23 January 1887, in AMF 581; Dufeuille to Count of Paris, 14 June 1889, in AMF 578.

64. Count d'Aymery to Count of Paris, September 1888, in AMF 582.

65. Report from secretary of the Saône-et-Loire, 4 April 1891, in AMF 583.

66. Dufeuille to Count of Paris, 23 January 1888, in AMF 623; subprefect of Bressuire to prefect, 8 June 1895, AD Deux Sèvres, 4M6 26. See Irvine, *French Conservatism,* 45–49, for comparable examples in the 1930s.

67. Report from secretary of the Gironde, 8 March 1891, in AMF 583.

68. Vicomte d'Adhémar to Dufeuille, 8 February 1889, in AMF 578; Testes, *Anatomie,* 195; Irvine, *French Conservatism,* 63–65.

69. Beauvoir to Count of Paris, 10 December 1886, in AMF 611; Beauvoir to Count of Paris, 14 and 17 November 1887, in AMF 621; Denys Cochin to Count of Paris, 26 December 1887, in AMF 622.

70. Report on the Ligue Populaire Royaliste, 12 January 1884 and 12 March 1884, in APP, B/a 405.

71. Hervineau to Edmond Boucher, 1 October 1883, in Boucher papers, AN 305 AP 3.

72. *La Gazette du Midi,* 2 May 1888.

73. Subprefect of Le Havre to prefect, 28 June 1899, AD Seine-Maritime, 4MP 4234.

74. Commissaire central to prefect, 14 November 1898, and commissaire spécial to prefect, 13 November 1898, AD Haute Vienne 1M 156.

75. Report from secretary of the Haute-Garonne, 4 August 1888, in AMF 579; commissaire central de police to prefect, 17 October 1889, AD Haute-Garonne 4M 99.

Chapter 3

1. La Ferronnays to Count of Paris, 27 June 1886, in AMF 604; Marquis de Montebello to Count of Paris, 29 December 1887, AMF 622.

2. On Dillon's pre-Boulanger years, see his dossier in APP B/a 906. Dillon had contacted the Count of Paris as early as 1873, professing his monarchist convictions and attempting to interest the pretender in various maritime inventions. See Dillon to Count of Paris, 25 January 1873, in AMF 485.

3. For the early meetings of royalists and Boulanger, the best source is the Count of Paris's own account entitled "Relations avec le général Boulanger: Récit sommaire" in AMF 634 (hereafter "Récit sommaire"). Appended to it are the firsthand accounts of one of the chief royalist conspirators, Edmond de Martimprey. Another account by Martimprey, dated August 1888, is in the Mackau papers, 102. By far the most accessible and best-informed secondary account of the high-level contacts is Levillain, *Boulanger*. In this section only those primary sources not consulted by Levillain have been cited.

4. Martimprey, a former officer and son of a distinguished imperial general, had been forced to leave the army for having protested while in uniform the expulsion of a Dominican congregation. Despite his Bonapartist roots he had rallied faithfully to royalism under the Count of Paris. See his dossier in APP, B/a 1174.

5. Beauvoir to Count of Paris, 5, 9 December 1887, and Duc de Chartres to Count of Paris, 9 December 1887, in AMF 622.

6. Beauvoir to Count of Paris, 4 February 1888, in AMF 624; Beauvoir to Count of Paris, 14 January 1888, in AMF 623.

7. *Le Journal du Loiret,* 29 February, 23 March 1888; *L'Union monarchique du Finistère,* 14 April 1888; *Le Messager de Toulouse,* 18, 22 March 1888; *Le Moniteur de la Saintonge,* 18 March 1888; *L'Avenir de la Haute-Marne,* 21 March 1888; *Le Nouvelliste de Rouen,* 16 March 1888; *Le Nouvelliste du Tarn,* 19–20 March 1888; *La Franche-Comté,* 17 March 1888; *Le Normand,* 17 March 1888; *Le Roussillon,* 16 March 1888.

8. *L'Eclaireur de la Dordogne,* 29 February 1888; *L'Espérance du peuple,* 8 March 1888; *Le Morbihannais,* 18 April 1888; *Le Messager de Toulouse,* 1, 6 March 1888; *Le Postillon du Seine-et-Oise,* 3 March, 14 April 1888; *L'Echo rochelais,* 10 March 1888; *Le Journal de l'Aveyron,* 22 March 1888; *Le Vrai Dauphiné,* 24 March 1888.

9. *Le Nouvelliste du Nord et du Pas-de-Calais,* 7, 14, 17, 18 March 1888; *Le Nouvelliste de Bordeaux,* 20 March 1888; *Le Charentais,* 25, 26, 28 February 1888; *La Gazette du Centre,* 28 February, 18, 28 March, 3 April 1888; *L'Espérance du peuple,* 7, 12, 30, 31 March 1888; *Le Nouvelliste de Rouen,* 23 March, 1, 10 April 1888; *Le Nouvelliste du Tarn,* 19–20 March 1888; *La Franche-Comté,* 1, 7, 10 April 1888; Le Roussillon, 12 April 1888; *L'Electeur des Côtes-du-Nord,* 31 March 1888.

10. *Le Nouvelliste de Bordeaux*, 16, 17 March, 12 April 1888; *L'Eclaireur de la Dordogne*, 21, 28 March 1888; *Le Journal de Rennes*, 27 March, 26 April 1888; *Le Journal du Loiret*, 11 April 1888, 31 March 1888; *Le Courrier des Ardennes*, 28 March 1888; *La Gazette du Midi*, 15 March, 13 April 1888; *Le Propagateur picard*, 18 April 1888; *Le Messager de Toulouse*, 6 March 1888; *La Défense de Seine-et-Marne*, 11 April 1888; *Le Journal de l'Oise*, 15 March 1888; *Le Nouvelliste de Cherbourg*, 12 April 1888; *Le Nouvelliste du Tarn*, 25 March 1888; *L'Espérance de Nancy*, 23 March 1888; *Le Progrès de l'Aisne*, 30 March 1888; *Le Roussillon*, 12 April 1888; *Le Courrier de l'Aude*, 15 April 1888; *La Gazette de Châteaux-Gontier*, 18 March, 12 April 1888; *Le Patriote de l'Ardèche*, 11 April 1888; *Le Normand*, 24 March 1888.

11. *La Revue de l'Ouest*, 1, 8 February 1888; *Le Morbihannais*, 22 March 1888; *L'Electeur des Côtes-du-Nord*, 22 April 1888; *La Gazette du Midi*, 21 March, 15 April 1888; *Le Nouvelliste de Rouen*, 5 March 1888; *L'Echo de la frontière*, 1, 20, 27 March 1888. The early enthusiasm for Boulanger exhibited by this last royalist newspaper might have owed something to the fact that its editor was the brother-in-law of Paul Lenglé, a Bonapartist and ardent supporter of Boulanger.

12. Tarlé to Porteu, 27 February 1888, in AMF 574; Porteu to Bocher, 2 March 1888, in AMF 585; *L'Anjou*, 5–6 April 1888.

13. Alexis Maréchal to Count of Paris, 17 April 1888, in AMF 626.

14. Count of Paris to Mackau, 5 April 1888, in Mackau papers 103. Beauvoir to Count of Paris, 16 March 1888, in AMF 625; Marquis de Breteuil, *La Haute Société: Journal secret, 1886–1889* (Paris: Marcel Jullian, 1979), 223.

15. Sources for these meetings are Martimprey, "procès verbaux," in Mackau papers, 102; Count of Paris, "Récit sommaire," in AMF 634; Levillain, *Boulanger*, 64–69; Breteuil, *La Haute société*, 231–32.

16. Jacques Néré, "Les Elections Boulanger dans le département du Nord," 3–18.

17. Dufeuille to Count of Paris, 23 October 1886, and Bocher to Count of Paris, 25 October 1886, in AMF 609; Charles Grimblest to Dufeuille, 24 November 1886, in AMF 610; Bocher to Count of Paris, 30 March 1888, and Beauvoir to Count of Paris, 31 March 1888, in AMF 625; J. J. Plichon to Count of Paris, 20 April 1888, in AMF 626; *Le Nouvelliste du Nord et du Pas-de-Calais*, 31 March, 4, 5, 7, 8, 9 April 1888; *L'Echo de la frontière*, 3 March, 3, 5 April 1888.

18. Breteuil, *La Haute Société*, 249.

19. Néré, "Les Elections Boulanger," 100–174.

20. J. J. Plichon to Count of Paris, 20 April 1888, in AMF 626.

21. *L'Espérance du peuple*, 13, 25 April 1888; *L'Espérance de Nancy*, 10, 15–16 April 1888; *Le Roussillon*, 17 April 1888; *L'Indépendant de l'Ouest*, 7 April 1888; *Le Moniteur de la Saintonge*, 19 April 1888; *Le Publicateur de la Vendée*, 18 April 1888; *La Franche-Comté*, 16 April 1888.

22. *Le Patriote de l'Ardèche,* 22, 29 April 1888; *Le Progrès de l'Aisne,* 17 April 1888; *Le Propagateur picard,* 20 April 1888; *Le Nouvelliste de Rouen,* 17 April 1888; *Le Journal d'Alençon,* 17 April 1888; *L'Echo de la frontière,* 31 March, 3, 5, 12 April 1888; *Le Journal de l'Aveyron,* 17 April 1888; *Le Normand,* 17 April 1888; *Le Messager de Toulouse,* 17 April 1888; *L'Avenir de la Haute-Marne,* 18 April 1888; *Le Courrier de l'Aude,* 18 April 1888; *Le Pas-de-Calair,* 16–17 April 1888.

23. Edouard Hervé to Count of Paris, 20 April 1888, in AMF 626; Duc de Deaudeauville-Rochefoucauld to Count of Paris, undated but May 1888, in AMF 627; P. Le Breton to Count of Paris, 22 April 1888, and Baron de Montagnan to Count of Paris, 21 April 1888, in AMF 626.

24. Mackau to Count of Paris, 30 March 1888, in AMF 625.

25. Sources for these meetings are: Count of Paris, "Récit sommaire," in AMF 634; Martimprey, "Procès verbaux," in Mackau papers 102; Levillain, *Boulanger,* 76–84; Breteuil, *La Haute Société,* 246–49.

26. Count Othenin d'Haussonville to Count of Paris, 27 April 1888, in AMF 626.

27. Count of Paris, "Conversations avec Dillon," in AMF 634.

28. *Le Figaro,* 25 April 1888; Duc de Broglie to Count of Paris, 14 May 1888, and Count of Paris to Broglie, 20 May 1888, in AMF 627.

29. Bocher to Count of Paris, 9, 20 April 1888, in AMF 626, and 14 May 1888, in AMF 627; Haussonville to Count of Paris, 17, 19 April 1888, 26 May 1888, and Beauvoir to Count of Paris, 28 April 1888, in AMF 626.

30. Mackau, Martimprey, de Mun, Piou to Count of Paris, 16 May 1888, in AMF 627; copy of same letter in Mackau papers 103.

31. Breteuil, Rochefoucald, de Mun, and de Maillé represented the Droite Royaliste; Mackau, Martimprey, Cassagnac, and Piou, the Union des Droites; and Jolibois, Chevreux, Delafosse, and Berger, the Bonapartist Appel au Peuple.

32. *L'Autorité,* 27 May 1888. On Auffray and the work of the league, see Bernard Auffray, *Un homme politique sous la IIIᵉ République, 1852–1916* (Paris: La Pensée Universitaire, 1972), 102–7. For his activities in Paris, see his dossier in APP, B/a 942. His correspondence with Mackau concerning his work with the league is in Mackau papers 110.

33. Dufeuille to Count of Paris, 11, 27 June 1888, in AMF 628; *L'Autorité,* 4, 5 June 1888; Count of Paris to Mackau, 3 June 1888, and Mackau to Count of Paris, 1 July 1888, the Mackau papers 103. Count of Paris to de Mun, Piou, and Breteuil, 17 June 1888; Piou, Breteuil, and de Mun to Count of Paris, 16 June 1889; Beauvoir to Count of Paris, 16 June 1888; Breteuil to Count of Paris, 20 June 1888; Count of Paris to Breteuil, 22 June 1888; Mackau to Count of Paris, 24 June 1888; Beauvoir to Count of Paris, 27 June 1888; Piou to Count of Paris, 30 June 1888; Chartres to Count of Paris, 27 June 1888—all in AMF 628. Martimprey to Count of Paris, 3 July 1888, and Beauvoir to Count of Paris 3, 4 July 1888 in AMF 629.

34. *Le Matin,* 21 May 1888; Duc d'Harcourt to Count of Paris, 27 May 1888, in AMF 627.

35. Dufeuille to Count of Paris, 6 May 1888, in AMF 627. On the increasing difficulties with Lambert de Sainte-Croix, see Bocher to Count of Paris, 17, 23 October 1888, in AMF 631, and 1, 28 November 1888, in AMF 632; Dufeuille to Count of Paris, 2 November 1888, in AMF 632.

36. Count of Paris to Edmond Boucher, 21 April, 12 May, 3 June, 16 June 1888, in Boucher papers, AN 305 AP2.

37. Broglie to Lavedan, 18 March 1888, in Boucher papers, AN 305 AP7; Broglie to Count of Paris, 14 May 1888, in AMF 627; Mackau to Count of Paris, 19 May 1888, in Mackau papers 103; Duc d'Aumale to Count of Paris, 18, 24 June 1888, in AMF 628, and 16 September 1888, in AMF 642; La Trémoille to Count of Paris, 24 May 1888, in AMF 627. The Count of Paris certainly sought to appease his uncle. Although he did not address his uncle's concerns about Boulangism, he suggested a number of ways in which he might facilitate the current proposals for exempting Aumale from the laws of exile. Count of Paris to Aumale, 19 June 1888, in AMF 628.

38. Edward Whiting Fox, *History in Geographic Perspective: The Other France* (New York: Norton, 1971), 141–42. The emphasis on the apparent resistance of Orleanists dates from Mermeix, *Les Coulisses,* 104.

39. As late as 1888 Lambert was still capable of disrupting royalist conferences by denouncing the classic Orleanist designation of the future sovereign as the "king of the French" rather than the "king of France." See his newspaper, *La Défense de Seine-et-Marne,* 28 April, 2, 6 June, 19, 24 August, 21 November 1888.

40. Calla to Count of Paris, 1 January 1889, in AMF 635; Breteuil, *La Haute Société,* 302; Mackau to Count of Paris, 31 October 1888, in AMF 631. Lambert de Sainte-Croix had a penchant for referring to the pretender's eldest son as the "Dauphin," which outraged Breteuil, Mackau, and the Count of Paris.

41. Beauvoir to Count of Paris, 26 October 1888, in AMF 634.

42. Bocher to Count of Paris, 1 October 1889, in AMF 645. Bocher began to play an active role in the intimate negotiations with Dillon and Boulanger at the end of July 1888: Bocher to Count of Paris, 27 July 1888, in AMF 629.

43. Piou to Count of Paris, 12 April 1888, and Beauvoir to Count of Paris, 28 April 1888, in AMF 626. Both Piou and his biographer subsequently managed to obscure his calculated support for Boulanger in 1888. See Joseph Denais, *Jacques Piou: Un apôtre de la liberté* (Paris: La Nef de Paris, 1958), 33; Jacques Piou, *D'une guerre à l'autre* (Paris: Editions Spes, 1932), 109.

44. Haussonville to Count of Paris, 2 October 1888, in AMF 631.

45. Piou to Count of Paris, 12 April 1888, in AMF 626; Haussonville to Count of Paris, 19 April 1888, in AMF 626; Breteuil to Count of Paris, 18 May 1888, in AMF 627; E. Boucher to Count of Paris, 20 April 1888, in

AMF 626. Cazenove de Pradine to Count of Paris, 23 May 1888; Harcourt to Count of Paris, 27 May 1888; Bocher to Count of Paris, 20, 22 May 1888; Henri Delbreuil to Count of Paris, 25 May 1888—all in AMF 627.

46. Bocher to Count of Paris, 22 May 1888, and Cazenove de Pradine to Count of Paris, 23 May 1888, in AMF 627; Mackau to Count of Paris, 13 September 1888, 20 October 1888, in AMF 631. See also Cassagnac in *L'Autorité,* 29 May 1888.

47. See his replies to the secretaries of these departments: Vienne (30 November 1888), in AMF 574; Tarn (2 September 1888) and Sarthe (1 October 1888), in AMF 577; Vosges (1 November 1888), Mayenne (2 November 1888), Sarthe (29 October 1888), Vienne (31 October 1888), and Haute-Garonne (8 February 1888), in AMF 578.

48. Dumas to Count of Paris, 1 September 1888, and Dufeuille to Count of Paris, 4 October 1888, in AMF 631. Auguste Boucher to Count of Paris, 2 April 1888; J. de Michon to Count of Paris, 29 April 1888; Harcourt to Count of Paris, 30 April 1888—all in AMF 626. Beauvoir to Count of Paris, 12 June 1888; Dumas to Count of Paris, 13 June 1888; J. de Michon to Count of Paris, 26 June 1888—all in AMF 628. Bocher to Count of Paris, 7 July 1888, in AMF 629. Boulangists considered the tone of Dumas's campaign to be a crucial index of the ability of the royalist leadership to overcome the scruples of local monarchists. "Our secret allies," noted Beauvoir, attached "a very high priority" to the election in the Loiret: Beauvoir to Count of Paris, 15 June 1888, in AMF 628.

49. Beauvoir to Count of Paris, 10, 14 May 1888, in AMF 627; "Récit sommaire," in AMF 634.

50. Count of Paris to Hirsch, 5 May 1888; Count of Paris to Rothschild, 5 May 1888; Beauvoir to Count of Paris, 10, 13, 14, 20 May 1888—all in AMF 627.

51. "Récit sommaire," in AMF 634; Beauvoir to Count of Paris, 16 June 1888, in AMF 628. The contributions of the duchess added leverage of another sort as well, since royalists hoped that her generosity would prompt comparable munificence from Hirsch and Rothschild: Beauvoir to Count of Paris, 12 June 1888, in AMF 628. Uzès's account of her role in her *Souvenirs* (Paris: Plon, 1938) suffers from having been written forty years later and is often inaccurate.

52. Steven Englund's dissertation on Déroulède ("The Origin of Oppositional Nationalism in France, 1881–1889," Princeton, 1981) demonstrates that Déroulède retained important links with the Bonapartist tradition. Even had this been widely appreciated, however, it would have done little to appease royalists.

53. *L'Electeur de la Dordogne,* 20 June 1888; *La Gazette du Centre,* 28 June 1888; *L'Espérance du peuple,* 18–19, 22 June 1888; *Le Patriote de l'Ardèche,* 20 June 1888; *Le Moniteur de la Saintonge,* 21 June 1888; *Le Nouvelliste de la Sarthe,* 20 June 1888; *L'Avenir de la Haute-Marne,* 29

June 1888; *L'Echo de la frontière*, 21 June 1888; *Le Bonhomme percheron*, 1 July 1888.

54. André Siegfried, *Géographie électorale de l'Ardèche sous la IIIe république* (Paris: Armand Colin, 1949), 79–81.

55. Beauvoir to Count of Paris, no date but beginning of July 1888, in AMF 629.

56. Secretary for the Ardèche, report of 15 April 1888, in AMF 575.

57. Count of Paris, "Récit sommaire," in AMF 634. Dufeuille to Count of Paris, 10, 12, 20 July 1888; Mackau to Count of Paris, 15 July 1888; Chartres to Count of Paris, 13 July 1888—all in AMF 629.

58. *Le Patriote de l'Ardèche*, 13, 17, 18, 20, 22, 25 July 1888; *L'Avenir du Lot-et-Garonne*, 25 July 1888; *Le Moniteur de la Saintonge*, 29 July 1888; *Le Pas-de-Calais*, 21 July 1888; *Le Nouvelliste de Bordeaux*, 21 July 1888; *La Gazette du Midi*, 11, 16–17 July 1888; *Le Nouvelliste de Rouen*, 28 July 1888.

59. Duchesse d'Uzès to Count of Paris, 23 July 1888, and Albert de Mun to Count of Paris, 23 July 1888, in AMF 629.

60. See report of royalist secretary, 31 July 1888, in AMF 579. Siegfried contends that Boulanger did not obtain 100 republican votes (*Géographie*, 82). Report from secretary for the Ardèche, 20 July 1888, and "Procès verbaux de la réunion du comité central conservateur de l'Ardèche," 16 July 1888, in AMF 576.

61. Dufeuille to Count of Paris, 27 June 1888, in AMF 628. Beauvoir to Count of Paris, 24 July 1888; de Mun to Count of Paris, 23 July 1888; Bocher to Count of Paris, 28 July 1888; Uzès to Count of Paris, 23 July 1888—all in AMF 629.

62. Count of Paris to Blin de Bourdon, 3 August 1888, in AMF 634; "Récit sommaire," in AMF 634.

63. *L'Echo de la Somme*, 7–8 August 1888; Uzès to Count of Paris, 9 August 1888, in AMF 630.

64. Report from Ernouf-Bignon, 30 August 1888, and Ansart to Count of Paris, no date but late August or early September 1888, in AMF 579.

65. The cautious tone of the royalist press troubled some royalists in the department who thought the party ought to have supported Boulanger more enthusiastically: Ernouf-Bignon, report of 30 August 1888, in AMF 579.

66. Police reports of 13, 14, 17 August 1888, AD Nord, M 37/22; prefect to minister of interior, 13 October 1888, AD Nord M 154/20; Ernouf-Bignon, 30 August 1888, in AMF 579.

67. Charles Thèze to Baron Eschasseriaux, 9 July 1888, Eschasseriaux papers, AD Charente-Maritime 1Mi 38, B8.

68. Marchand to Eschasseriaux, 26 July 1888, Eschasseriaux Papers, B10; Beaussant to Eschasseriaux, 20 April 1888, Eschasseriaux papers, B5; Bonhomme to Eschasseriaux, 13 July 1888, Eschasseriaux papers, B9.

69. Eschasseriaux papers, B10. (Unless otherwise indicated, the reference refers to an undated diary entry.)

70. Eschasseriaux papers, B10.

71. Ibid., B10–11.

72. *Le Moniteur de la Saintonge,* 2, 9 August 1888; Lambert de Sainte-Croix to Count of Paris, 3 August 1888, in AMF 630.

73. *L'Echo rochelais,* 4, 8, 22 August 1888; Baron Oudet to Eschasseriaux, 9 August 1888; Emile Lucaseau to Eschasseriaux, 11 August 1888—all in Eschasseriaux papers, B11–12.

74. Beauvoir to Count of Paris, 8 August 1888; Dufeuille to Count of Paris, 19 August 1888; E. de Dampière to Count of Paris, 12 August 1888; A. Porteu to Count of Paris, 22 August 1888; A. Dufaure to Count of Paris, 30 August 1888—all in AMF 630. Dufeuille to Count of Paris, 4 October 1888, in AMF 631.

75. Néré, "Les Elections Boulanger," 195–269.

76. Beauvoir to Count of Paris, 24 October 1888, in AMF 631.

77. An exception is Michael Burns (*Rural Society,* 57–117), who emphasizes Boulanger's appeal among the peasantry. He examines in detail the way in which propaganda destined for the peasantry was uniquely suited to the culture of rural society. His otherwise excellent discussion overlooks, however, the fact that Boulangist propaganda was generally effective only among those peasants who traditionally voted for conservatives. As his analysis of the by-election of April 29–May 13 in the Isère clearly reveals, the only pockets of support for Boulanger in this predominantly republican department were the traditionally conservative regions. He is wrong to conclude, however, that the election in the Isère was "the Nord . . . in reverse" (p. 97). In both departments the bulk of Boulanger's support came from conservative peasants; the difference was that in the Nord there were more of them.

78. Commissaire spécial to prefect, 1 May 1889, and subprefect of Lorient to prefect, 21 August 1889, AD Morbihan M3445; prefect to minister of interior, 21 July 1889, AD Morbihan M4447; commissaire spécial to prefect, 9 October 1888, AD Charente-Maritime 2M 4/22; commissaire spécial to prefect, 5 July 1889, AD Finistère 3M 1889(el). Commissaire spécial to prefect, 21 March, 2 May 1888, and subprefect of Domfront to prefect, 28 October 1888, AD Orne 1228. Prefect to minister of interior, 13 September 1889, AD Orne 414; subprefect of Fougères to prefect, 27 April 1889, AD Ille-et-Vilaine 1M 142; commissaire spécial to prefect, 6 November, 24 December 1888, AD Nièvre 4M 1143/1; prefect to minister of interior, 16 May 1889, 14 August 1889, AD Vendée 1M 375.

79. Subprefect of Béziers to prefect, 14 December 1888, AD Hérault, 39M 291; subprefect to prefect, 4 May 1889, AD Hérault, 15M 40; subprefect of Béziers to prefect, 2 February 1889, AD Hérault, 39M 291; subprefect to prefect, 24 June 1889, AD Hérault, 39M 277; Viple, *Sociologie politique de l'Allier,* 196–97.

80. Prefect to minister of interior, 29 November 1888, 19 March 1889, AD Hérault, 39M 291; commissaire spécial to prefect, 13 August 1889, AD Rhône, 4M 250. Of course a Boulangist might attract working-class votes for

different reasons. In the thoroughly republican Côte-d'Or, the conservative-Boulangist Darcy nearly won a seat in 1889, because he attracted votes from a number of workers who usually voted for the Radicals. He did so, however, because he owned a large factory complex and mobilized his foremen to ensure the support of his employees. Subprefect of Châtillon to prefect, 2 October 1889, AD Côte-d'Or, 20M 1181.

81. "Procès verbaux de la réunion du comité royaliste de la Charente-Inférieure," 3 February 1890, in AMF 580.

82. *La Cocarde,* 12 November 1888.

Chapter 4

1. *L'Ere nouvelle,* 1–2 January 1889; "Récit sommaire," in AMF 634.
2. Duc de Chartres to Count of Paris, 25 October 1888, in AMF 631.
3. Report from secretary of the Tarn, 21 September 1888: report from Vicomte d'Adhémar, 25 September 1888; report from secretary of the Sarthe, undated but September 1888—all in AMF 577. Secretary of the Vosges, 31 December 1888, in AMF 579.
4. *Le Nouvelliste du Nord,* 22 March 1888.
5. *Le Nouvelliste du Bordeaux,* 18 August 1888.
6. *L'Espérance du peuple,* 20–21 August 1888.
7. *Le Courrier de la Champagne,* 20 August 1888.
8. *L'Eclaireur de la Dordogne,* 2 June 1888; *Le Moniteur de la Nièvre,* 26 May 1888; *Le Journal de Rennes,* 21 August 1888; *Le Charentais,* 16 December 1888; *Le Courrieur des Ardennes,* 20 March 1888; *La Revue de l'Ouest,* 21 June 1888, 30 October 1888; *L'Océan,* 2 May 1888; *L'Avenir du Lot-et-Garonne,* 8, 9 May 1888; *La Gazette du Midi,* 20 October 1888; *Le Nouvelliste du Tarn,* 11, 16–17 April 1888; *La Franche-Comté,* 12 April 1888; *L'Espérance de Nancy,* 28 November 1888; *Le Normand,* 29 May 1888; *Le Progrès de l'Aisne,* 14 March 1888, 12 July 1888; *La Revue bourguignonne,* 13 March 1888; *Le Roussillon,* 27 June, 6, 13, 21, 31 August 1888; *Le Journal d'Alençon,* 23 April 1888; *Le Conservateur du Gers,* 21 March 1888; *Le Propagateur picard,* 30 August 1888; *Le Nouvelliste de Rouen,* 13 August 1888.
9. Prefect to minister of interior, 18 April 1889, AD Vendée 1M 375.
10. Report from Pradelle, 31 October 1888, in AMF 576. On the comparative appeal of portraits of Boulanger and the Count of Paris in the Mayenne, see Denis, *Les Royalistes,* 481.
11. Count of Paris to the *missi,* 29 October 1888, in AMF 648.
12. Count of Paris, "Récit sommaire," in AMF 634.
13. *L'Anjou,* 27 September 1888; *La Gazette de France,* 5 October 1888. Dufeuille to Count of Paris, 2, 4 November 1888; Adhémar to Count of Paris, 15 November 1888; Lur-Saluces to Count of Paris, 15 November 1888—all in AMF 632.
14. The most notable example of a zealous but maladroit royalist convert

to Boulangism was Count Adrien de Lévis-Mirepoix, deputy from the Orne. Count of Paris to Lévis-Mirepoix, 7 October 1888; Lévis-Mirepoix to Count of Paris, 3 October 1888; Dufeuille to Count of Paris, 4 October 1888—all in AMF 631. The pretender did at least quash an attempt by royalists in Bordeaux to hold an anti-Boulanger conference.

15. The Count of Paris did, with perfect disingenuousness, disavow some of the text of Breteuil's speech, even though he knew in advance of its general tenor and had given his approval: Count of Paris to Tristan Lambert, 25 November 1888, in AMF 596. He also assured Edouard de Lur-Saluces that the speech had been unauthorized: minutes of general meeting of the royalist committee in the Gironde, 16 November 1888, in AMF 578.

16. Breteuil to Count of Paris, 7 November 1888, in AMF 632; Breteuil, *La Haute Société*, 302. For the text of the address, see *La Gazette du Midi*, 12–13 November 1888.

17. Report from secretary of the Bouches-du-Rhône, 30 November 1888, in AMF 574.

18. Report from secretary of the Ardèche, 18 November 1888, in AMF 574.

19. Haussonville to Count of Paris, 20 November 1888; Duc de Chartres to Count of Paris, 22 November 1888; Dufeuille to Count of Paris, 20 November 1888—all in AMF 632.

20. Report from secretaries of the Finistère, 28 November 1888, and of the Vienne, 27 November 1888, in AMF 574; Vicomte de la Villarmois to Count of Paris, 14 November 1888, in AMF 632.

21. Cornelius de Witt to Count of Paris, 21 November 1888, in AMF 632.

22. *Le Figaro*, 25, 28 October 1888. Beauvoir to Count of Paris, 25 October 1888; Dufeuille to Count of Paris, 25 October 1888; Duc de Chartres to Count of Paris, 25 October 1888; Haussonville to Count of Paris, 29 October 1888—all in AMF 631.

23. Breteuil, *La Haute Société*, 312–13.

24. Beauvoir to Count of Paris, 19 November 1888, in AMF 632.

25. *Le Figaro*, 4 December 1888.

26. *La Cocarde*, 14 November, 8, 17, 21 December 1888.

27. La Trémoille to Count of Paris, 1 November 1888, in AMF 632; Breteuil, *La Haute Société*, 305; *Le Moniteur du Puy-de-Dôme*, 27 October 1888. The newspaper knew that Martimprey, Meyer, Breteuil, and de Mun were in contact with Dillon and that a "Duchesse d'U——" had offered her fortune to the Count of Paris at Ems. It also hinted at the financial role of a "Baron H." The many inaccuracies in the account, however, suggest that its source was imperfectly informed. Royalist efforts to discover the source of the indiscretion failed. Chartres to Count of Paris, 1 November 1888, in AMF 632. Numa Gilly was a Radical deputy from the Gard who publicly declared that many deputies were every bit as corrupt as the notorious Daniel Wilson. His charges created a sensation, as did his subsequent revocation as mayor of Nîmes.

28. Boulanger to Naquet, 27 December 1888, Bibliothèque Nationale (hereafter BN) NAF 23783.

29. Beauvoir to Count of Paris, undated but first week of December 1888, in AMF 634.

30. *La Presse,* 6 December 1888; *La Cocarde,* 7 December 1888.

31. *Le Figaro,* 5, 6 December 1888.

32. *La Presse,* 8 December 1888.

33. *La Presse,* 8 December 1888.

34. The receipt for this transaction is preserved in AMF 633.

35. *L'Espérance du peuple,* 7 December 1888.

36. A point made by Dufeuille in his letter to the Count of Paris, 8 December 1888, in AMF 633.

37. Auffray did present figures to show that his relative performance in the industrial regions of the department was rather better than it had been in 1885. This might suggest that he derived some electoral advantage from his Boulangist image, but he also admitted to Dufeuille that Boulangist support, or lack thereof, would make a difference of no more than 500 votes in the Ardennes. Auffray to Count of Paris, 11 January 1889, and Dufeuille to Count of Paris, 1 January 1889, in AMF 635.

38. Beauvoir to Count of Paris, 9 December 1888, in AMF 633; Breteuil, *La Haute Société,* 314, 318; Beauvoir to Count of Paris, 26 December 1888, in AMF 633. English in the original.

39. Reports of the Commissaire spécial des chemins de fer, 11, 18 December 1888, AD Charente-Maritime, 2M4/22; Beaussant to Eschasseriaux, 1 November 1888, and Ossian Pic to Eschasseriaux, 23, 27 December 1888, in Eschasseriaux papers, AD Charente-Maritime, 1Mi 38, B17–22. See also the Eschasseriaux narrative of events in same collection, 1Mi 38, B13–26; Beaussant to Dufeuille, 8 January 1888, in AMF 635.

40. Count of Paris, "Récit sommaire" and "Conversations avec Dillon," in AMF 634; Beauvoir to Count of Paris, 24 October 1888, in AMF 631; Montaudon to Count of Paris, 28 November 1888, in AMF 632.

41. Count of Paris, "Récit sommaire," in AMF 634; Martimprey to Count of Paris, 20 December 1888, in AMF 633; Beauvoir to Count of Paris, 2, 12 January 1889, in AMF 635; *Le Mémorialiste d'Amiens,* 16, 19, 29 December 1888 and 3, 7, January 1889; *Le Temps,* 23 January 1889; *Le Messager de la Somme,* 6 January 1888.

42. *La Presse,* 8 December 1888.

43. Mayol de Lupé to Count of Paris, 10 February 1889, in AMF 578. The official leader of Parisian royalists, Ferdinand Duval, owed his rank as senior *missus* exclusively to his status as former prefect of the Seine. His lethargy and exclusive concern for his own political fortunes were so legendary that even the prefecture of police was aware of it. See APP, B/a 1062, 22 April 1887, 3 December 1888.

44. Count of Paris, "Conversations avec Dillon," in AMF 634.

45. Beauvoir to Count of Paris, 1 March 1887, in AMF 614. On the atti-

tude of the "milieux d'affaires," see Bocher to Count of Paris, 4 January 1889, in AMF 635.

46. Pierre Calla to Bocher, 4 January 1889, in AMF 635; Calla, "Notes et observations sur l'élection legislative dans le département de la Seine," 1 January 1889, in AMF 578.

47. Edouard Hervé to Count of Paris, 2 January 1889, in AMF 635.

48. This was the explicit intention of Ferdinand Duval, who also declared that he hoped for Montaudon's defeat in the Somme in order to undermine royalist-Boulangist cooperation in Paris. Beauvoir to Count of Paris, 12 January 1889, in AMF 635.

49. *Le Figaro*, 5 January 1889.

50. Beauvoir to Count of Paris, 12 January 1889, in AMF 635.

51. *Le Temps*, 16 January 1889.

52. Beauvoir to Count of Paris, 12 January 1889; Bocher to Count of Paris, 12 January 1889; Duc de Chartres to Count of Paris, 12 January 1889; de Mun to Count of Paris, 16 January 1889—all in AMF 635.

53. *Le Temps*, 7, 13 January 1888.

54. Englund, "Oppositional Nationalism," 626, 666; Sternhell, *La Droite révolutionnaire*, 58–60. On Boulangist organization and the attitude of various elements on the Left, see APP, B/a 497. By far the best discussion of the Ligue des Patriotes, its role in Parisian Boulangism, and the socioeconomic composition of its members is Englund, "Oppositional Nationalism." Englund has a particularly able dissection of the distinction between the petit bourgeois and proletarian elements in the capital. Although both supported Boulanger in January, the former did so more consistently.

55. For the dismay of provincial royalists at the "abdication" in Paris, see *Le Normand*, 15 January 1888; *Le Roussillon*, 5, 15 January 1889; *Le Nouvelliste de Bordeaux*, 31 December 1888 and 5 January 1889; *La Revue de l'Ouest*, 22 January 1889; *L'Océan*, 18 January 1889; *Le Publicateur de la Vendée*, 13, 16, 18, 20, 27, 30 January 1889; *Le Nouvelliste de la Sarthe*, 5 January 1889; *L'Espérance du peuple*, 28 December 1888 and 9, 10, 11, 12, 14–15, 18, 20, 24, 25, 26, 27, 28–29 January 1889; *Le Morbihannais*, 17 January 1889; *L'Indépendant du Pas-de-Calais*, 19 January 1889; *Espérance de Nancy*, 7, 13–14, 17 January 1889; *Le Courrier de l'Aude*, 27 January 1889.

56. *L'Echo de l'Oise*, 29 January 1889.

57. The most detailed recent study of these elections concludes that Boulanger received 85,000 conservative votes. Louis Girard, "Les Elections à Paris sous la IIIᵉ République" (thèse pour le doctorat de IIIᵉ cycle de sociologie, Université de Dakar, 1968), 92. For assessments of the fluctuation of the conservative electorate, see *Le Figaro*, 24 January 1889; Beauvoir to Count of Paris, 13 September 1889, in AMF 644. For royalist assessments of their support for Boulanger, see *La Gazette de Château-Gontier*, 31 January 1889; *L'Electeur des Côtes-du-Nord*, 3 February 1889; *Le Journal de l'Oise*, 29 January 1889; *Le Moniteur de la Saintonge*, 31 January 1889; *Le Propa-*

gateur picard, 27 January 1889; *Le Normand,* 26, 29 January 1889, 16 February; *Le Nouvelliste de la Sarthe,* 5 January 1889; *L'Avenir de la Haute-Marne,* 6, 20 January 1889; *Le Charentais,* 30 January 1889; *Le Patriote de l'Ardèche,* 29 January 1889; *L'Avenir du Lot-et-Garonne,* 9, 17 January 1889; *Le Messager de Toulouse,* 8, 29 January 1889; *La Defense de Seine-et-Marne,* 30 January 1889; *Le Courrier du Var,* 31 January 1889.

58. Histories of the affair from Mermeix to Dansette all insisted on the "coup d'état manqué," but Seager, *The Boulanger Affair,* 203–10, effectively refutes this claim; see also Levillain, *Boulanger,* 142–43. Englund, "Oppositional Nationalism," 669–72, examines the conflicting evidence concerning Déroulède's intentions, concluding that he *probably* had no plans for a coup at that time.

59. Count of Paris, "Récit sommaire," in AMF 634; Levillain, *Boulanger,* 143–44.

60. See the letter to his son, 6 March 1889, to be read after his death, in AMF 708.

61. Breteuil, *La Haute Société,* 336. Bocher to Count of Paris, 17 February 1889; Breteuil to Count of Paris, 5 February 1889; Beauvoir to Count of Paris, 14 February 1889—all in AMF 636. Beauvoir to Count of Paris, 15 March 1889, in AMF 637.

62. Lambert de Sainte-Croix to Count of Paris, 14 February 1889; Dufeuille to Count of Paris, 16 February 1889; Beauvoir to Count of Paris, 26 February 1889—all in AMF 636.

63. Mackau to Beauvoir, 11 February 1889, in AMF 636.

64. *l'Indépendant de l'Ouest,* 20 March 1889; *L'Espérance de Nancy,* 20 March 1889; *Le Pas-de-Calais,* 18–19 March 1889; *Le Publicateur de la Vendée,* 20 March 1889.

65. Dansette, *Boulangisme,* 265.

66. *L'Echo du Pays d'Auge,* 24 March 1889; *Le Charentais,* 23 March 1889; *Le Journal d'Alençon,* 19 March 1889.

67. Keller to Count of Paris, 23 February 1889, and Beauvoir to Count of Paris, 24 February 1889, in AMF 636. Bocher to Count of Paris, 25 March 1889; Dufeuille to Count of Paris, 10, 26 March; Beauvoir to Count of Paris, 15 March 1889—all in AMF 637.

68. Dufeuille to Count of Paris, 23 February 1889, and Beauvoir to Count of Paris, 18, 26 February 1889, in AMF 636. Beauvoir to Count of Paris, 15 March 1889, in AMF 637.

69. Dufeuille to Count of Paris, 2, 19, 23 February 1889; Bocher to Count of Paris, 17, 19 February 1889; Breteuil to Count of Paris, 5 February 1889—all in AMF 636.

70. La Trémoille to Count of Paris, 23 October 1888, in AMF 631; 1, 21 November 1888, in AMF 632; 29 January 1889, in AMF 635. Hirsch to La Trémoille, 30 January 1889, in AMF 634. The other members of the committee were Mackau, de Mun, Breteuil, Beauvoir, Deaudeauville, and Prince Léon. The committee was purely decorative, insisted upon by Hirsch

so that the circle of royalists aware of his generosity might be enlarged. In practice the real decisions as to allocation were made by Bocher in consultation with La Trémoille. La Trémoille to Count of Paris, 2, 19 March 1889, in AMF 634, and 15 September 1889, in AMF 642.

71. *Le Figaro*, 6 December 1888.

72. On Constans, see L. Bruce Fulton, "The Political Ascent of Ernest Constans: A Study in the Management of Republican Power" (Ph.D. dissertation, University of Toronto, 1971).

73. Beauvoir to Count of Paris, 30 March 1889, and Bocher to Count of Paris, 29 March 1889, in AMF 637; Dufeuille to Count of Paris, 2 April 1889, in AMF 638.

74. Bocher to Count of Paris, 4 April 1889, in AMF 638; *Le Pas-de-Calais*, 6 April 1889. Even the Duchesse d'Uzès was momentarily embittered. "Well, gentlemen," she reportedly exclaimed to the royalist leaders, "we just saved ourselves 1,100,000 francs" (Uzès, *Souvenirs,* 92).

75. Beauvoir to Count of Paris, 4 April 1889, in AMF 638.

76. Bocher to Count of Paris, 14 April 1889; Beauvoir to Count of Paris, 11 April 1889; Jacques Piou to Count of Paris, no date but 10 or 11 April 1889—all in AMF 638.

77. Royalists overestimated the efficiency of the police. Although they were making a serious effort at uncovering the source of Boulanger's support, by the spring of 1889 they still had little more than unsubstantiated rumors. Uzès was on their list of possible financial backers, but it was a long list. See the report of 28 April 1889 in APP B/a 977. The police had heard about Dillon's visit with the Count of Paris in the fall of 1888, but attached no special significance to it. See report of 19 March 1889 in APP B/a 906. On this issue there was little in their files that could not be gleaned from a close reading of the press.

78. Bocher to Count of Paris, 20 April 1889, and Beauvoir to Count of Paris, 29 April 1889, in AMF 638.

79. Mackau to Count of Paris, 22 April 1889, in AMF 638. As Mackau characteristically put it, "we had the rifle on our left shoulder; now we must shift it to our right."

Chapter 5

1. Ménard to Croissy, 8 February 1889, in Mackau papers 109. For a similar evolution on the part of the deputy from the Deux-Sèvres, La Rochejacquelein, see La Rochejacquelein to Mackau, 18 July, 2 September 1889, in Mackau papers 110.

2. APP, B/a 977, 28 April 1889.

3. Auffray to Count of Paris, 23 May 1889, in AMF 640.

4. Martimprey to Count of Paris, 25 May 1889, in AMF 640.

5. The "professions de foi" of these (defeated) candidates are in Mackau papers 105.

6. For example Count Adrien de Maggiolo, former secretary to the Count of Paris, in *La Franche-Comté,* 26 April 1888, 5 September 1889.

7. *La Presse,* 5, 6, 7, 8, 9, 10, 11, 12 September 1889.

8. Ibid., 5 September 1889.

9. *La Cocarde,* 6 September 1889. Not all Boulangists were as sanguine about the lack of "exclusivism" in the official list. Boulanger himself had opposed its publication because of the preponderance of royalists and Bonapartists. Mackau to Count of Paris, 25 July 1889, in AMF 642.

10. See the snide observations of some "rallied republicans." Chassaigne-Goyon to Croissy, 12 September 1889, and Prax-Paris to Croissy, 9 September 1889, in Mackau papers 110.

11. De Batorre to Mackau, 20 July 1889, in Mackau papers 107; de Vallée to Croissy, 18 August 1889, in Mackau papers 109; Violet to Croissy, 2 September 1889, and Vermont to Croissy, 22 June, 6 September 1889, in Mackau papers 110.

12. Sûreté Générale (minister of interior) to prefect, 12 September 1889, AD Finistère, 3M 1889 (el); de Grilleau to Mackau, 23 July 1889, and de Grilleau to Auffray, 8 September 1889, in Mackau papers 108; dossier on Béllisen in Ariège folder in Mackau papers 107; subprefect of Béziers to prefect, 1 July 1889, AD Hérault, 39M 291; Olivier to Croissy, 13 August 1889, in Mackau papers 108; LeGuen to Croissy, no date but September 1889, in Mackau papers 109.

13. Leblanc to Croissy, no date but September 1889, in Mackau papers 109.

14. *Le Temps,* 8, 9, 12, 17, 19 September 1889; *Le Figaro,* 27 September 1889.

15. Piou to Mackau, 8 September 1889, in Mackau papers 108.

16. Beaussant to Croissy, 5, 23, 28 September, 21 October 1889, in Mackau papers 107. Charles LaChambre to Mackau, 15 September 1889; Bonneval to Auffray, 10 September 1889; Chevilotte to Croissy, no date but September 1889—all in Mackau papers 108. Prefect to minister of interior, 5 September 1889, AD Calvados, M2339; prefect to minister of interior, 23 May, 27 July, 11 September 1889, AD Calvados, M2874; Desloges to Mackau, 9 September 1889, and Desloges to Auffray, 13 September 1889, in Mackau papers 107.

17. Desjardins to Croissy, 8 September 1889, and Godelle to Croissy, 5 September 1889, in Mackau papers 107.

18. *La Presse,* 14 September 1889.

19. Auffray to Count of Paris, 23 May 1889, and Dufeuille to Count of Paris, 26 May 1889, in AMF 640; Bocher to Count of Paris, 11 May 1889, in AMF 639, and 9 June 1889, in AMF 641.

20. *La Gazette de France,* 19 September 1889; Bocher to Count of Paris, 10 September 1889, in AMF 644; Boulanger to Naquet, 10 September 1889, BN, NAF 23783.

21. Even a historian as well informed as Philippe Levillain takes the pretender's charges of Boulangist infidelity at face value (*Boulanger*, 162).

22. On the chaos in the Boulangist ranks, see especially Maurice Vergoin, "Notes sur le mouvement républicain révisioniste et le boulangisme," in Archives Nationales, F⁷ 12445, and Verly, *Le Général Boulanger*.

23. Subprefect of Béthune to prefect, 21 September 1889, AD Pas-de-Calais, M 100; subprefect of Montreuil to prefect, no date but September 1889, AD Pas-de-Calais, M 98. Gentès to Croissy, 17 July 1889; Albert Desmythère (president of the local royalist committee) to Croissy, 28 June, 3 July, 17 July, 12 August, 22 August 1889; Adam to Mackau, 23 July, 7, 23, 26 August, 5 September 1889—all in Mackau papers 109.

24. Georgi to Croissy, no date but July or August, and Paul de Cerq to Croissy, 18 August 1889, in Mackau papers 109. See also the report of the Commissaire spécial des chemins de fer, 5 July 1889, which describes Georgi as a "clerical reactionary factory owner," AD Pas-de-Calais, M97; Desmythère to Croissy, 12 September 1889, Mackau papers, 109. Georgi led on the first ballot but lost on the second, despite efforts to bribe a socialist candidate. Georgi to Croissy, 27 September 1889, in Mackau papers 109; *L'Express du Nord et du Pas-de-Calais*, 15, 16–17, 20, 21 September 1889.

25. Rudelle, *La République*, 261; Siegfried, *Tableau politique*, 488; prefect to minister of interior, 5 September 1889, AD Calvados, M2339; Bocher to Count of Paris, 1 October 1889, in AMF 645.

26. Prefect to minister of interior, 20 July, 19 August 1889, and subprefect of Chateaubriant to prefect, 7 June 1889, AD Loire-Atlantique, 1M 520.

27. Mackau to Dillon, 31 August 1889, in Mackau papers 102. Vivier to Martimprey, 11 May 1889; Princeteau to Croissy, 9 May, 31 July, 3, 6 September 1889; Froim to Martimprey, 18 May 1889; Vivier to Croissy, 11 June 1889—all in Mackau papers 108. Hervé to Count of Paris, 25 July 1889, in AMF 642.

28. Subprefect of Sarlat to prefect, 8 May 1889, and subprefect of Ribérac to prefect, 16 April 1889, AD Dordogne, 1M 81; prefect to minister of interior, 30 March 1889, and subprefect of Nontron to prefect, 1 September 1889, AD Dordogne, 3M 66. Vivier to Croissy, 22, 24, 26, 28, 29, 30, and 31 May 1889; Maréchal to Mackau, 2 July 1889; Bosredon to Croissy, 24 August 1889; Couteleau to Croissy, 2 September 1889—all in Mackau papers 108.

29. Commissaire spécial to prefect, 17 July 1889, AD Indre, 1M 266; commissaire spécial to prefect, 30 September, AD Indre, 3M 1328.

30. Report on La Manche, 29 July 1889, in Mackau papers 109.

31. Benazet to Mackau, 21 July 1889, in Mackau papers, 108; subprefect of Blanc to prefect, 30 March, 31 August 1889, AD Indre 3M 1328.

32. Prefect to minister of interior, 30 November 1888, AD Vendée, 3M 255; prefect to minister of interior, 2 June 1889, AD Vendée, 1M 375.

33. Subprefect of Arcis-sur-Aube to prefect, 28 August 1889, AD Aube, M 193; Armand to Croissy, 12 September 1889, in Mackau papers 107.

34. Subprefect of Saint-Gaudens to prefect, 2 August 1889, AD Haute-Garonne, 2M 45; Maribail to Croissy, 19 June 1889, in Mackau papers 108.

35. Subprefect of Montélimar to prefect, 12, 26 August 1889, AD Drôme, 3M 68.

36. Subprefect of Reims to prefect, 24 June, 30 June 1889, AD Marne, 30M 41; Auguste Paille to Duchesse d'Uzès, 17 July, 12 August 1889, in Mackau papers 109.

37. For a comparison with later periods, see Irvine, *French Conservatism,* chapter 5.

38. Commissaire de police of Périgueux to prefect, 17, 19, 25 September 1889, AD Dordogne, 3M 66; commissaire de police to prefect, 3 June 1889, 2 November 1890, AD Dordogne, 4M 189.

39. Vivier to Croissy, 26 May 1889, in Mackau papers 108; subprefect of Bergerac to prefect, 29 August 1889, AD Dordogne, 3M 66; subprefect of Ribérac to prefect, 16 April 1889, AD Dordogne, 1M 81.

40. See for example the sponsorship of the "rival" radical Boulangist Robert Martin by the royalist Charles Le Cour in Nantes. Prefect to minister of interior, 20 July, 19 August, AD Loire-Atlantique, 1M 520; commissaire spécial to prefect, 2 February 1889, AD Loire-Atlantique, 1M 521; Le Cour to Mackau, 12 August 1889, in Mackau papers 109.

41. Hattu to Croissy, 10 July 1889, and Koechlin to Croissy, 14, 31 July, 29 August, 6, 7, 10, 14, 23 September 1889, in Mackau papers 108; subprefect of Montbéliard to prefect, 29 September 1889, AD Doubs, M 787.

42. Courtès to Martimprey, 22 June 1889; Amaz to Croissy, 24 September 1889; Ballière to unknown, 31 August 1889—all in Mackau papers 110. Beauvoir to Count of Paris, 13 September 1889, in AMF 644; *Le Var,* 5, 8, 12, 15, 22 September 1888.

43. Turcos to Croissy, 6, 9, 17 September 1889, in Mackau papers 109.

44. Steenackers's interminable correspondence is in the folder on the Haute-Marne in Mackau papers 109. From the same source see also the general report on the department, 25 June 1889; Bourlon de Rouvre to Croissy, 10 September 1889; Hedouville to Croissy, 11 September 1889. See also Auffray to La Trémoille, 3 December 1889, in AMF 587; Dufeuille to Count of Paris, 9 July 1889, in AMF 642; *Le Révisioniste de la Haute-Marne,* 8, 15, 21 September, 6 October 1889.

45. Commissaire spécial to prefect, 12 September 1889, and prefect to minister of interior, 2 September 1889, AD Nièvre, 3M 1126/5 (1889). Hattu to Croissy, 27 June 1889; Albert Déspeuilles to Croissy, 29 September 1889; Jaladoude le Sarre to Croissy, 9, 17 September 1889—all in Mackau papers 109. Auffray to Dillon, 13, 20, 31 August 1889, and Mackau to Count of Paris, no date but July 1889, in Mackau papers 102; Bocher to Auffray, 12 September 1889, in Mackau papers 110. On the political background in the Nièvre as well as Laporte's venality, see Alfred Massé, "Les Partis politiques dans la Nièvre de 1871–1906," *Les Cahiers nivernais,* no. 19 (April 1910), especially 45–63.

46. *Le Patriote du Centre,* 7, 8, 11, 13, 15, 19 September 1889; *La Gazette de l'Allier* (*Organe du parti républicain national*), 14, 15, 17 September 1889.

47. Nyvenheim to Dufeuille, 30 January 1889, in AMF 578.

48. Guen to Croissy, 26 March 1889, and de la Gorce to Croissy, 28 March 1889, in Mackau papers 107.

49. Philoprat to Croissy, 12 September 1889, and Nyvenheim to Croissy, 29 August 1889, in Mackau papers 107; *L'Autorité,* 28 August 1889; *Le Limousin et Quercy,* 15 September 1889.

50. Nyvenheim to Dufeuille, 18 October 1889, in AMF 568.

51. De Mun to Count of Paris, 1 May 1888, in AMF 627; report from the royalist secretary, 29 December 1888, in AMF 577; Commissaire spécial des chemins de fer to prefect, 28 May 1889, and prefect to minister of interior, 10 May 1889, AD Morbihan, M4447; prefect to minister of interior, 4 April 1889, AD Morbihan, M4711; subprefect of Lorient to prefect, 21, 29 August, 1889, AD Morbihan, M3445.

52. *Le Morbihannais,* 18 June, 11 July, 8, 9, 22 September 1889; Fiquet to Martimprey, 14 July, 10 September 1889, and Lamarzelle to Mackau, 29 July 1889, in Mackau papers 109; de Mun to Mackau, 16 August, 4 September 1889, in Mackau papers 110.

53. See the campaigns of the republican Boulangists Caillat and Pontoise in the Niort. Report on that department, 21 May 1889, in Mackau papers 110. From same source, Poinsigny to Croissy, 22 July 1889; Noirot to Croissy 17, 22 August, 11, 27 September 1889; de la Chevrelière to Count of Paris. Report from the royalist secretary, 31 October 1889, in AMF 568; Monnet, *Archives politiques,* 370ff.; *La Revue de l'Ouest,* 14, 19 September, 1, 3, 5 October 1889; *Le Mémorial des Deux-Sèvres,* 5 September, 1 October 1889.

54. Beauvoir to Count of Paris, 25 July 1889, in AMF 642.

55. La Trémoille to Count of Paris, 3 October 1889, in AMF 634.

56. Auffray to La Trémoille, 3 December 1889, in AMF 587; Auffray to La Trémoille, 5 November 1889, APP B/a 942.

57. Although of the right order of magnitude, these figures are, for the reasons given, necessarily approximate. There is no telling exactly how the Count of Paris allocated the 500,000 francs under his exclusive control, although some of it certainly went to Boulangists. The same is probably true of the substantial sums assigned to Dufeuille. On the other hand some of the money assigned to Mackau for Boulangists did end up in conservative hands. The tabulation of election expenses is from La Trémoille to Count of Paris, 3 October 1889, in AMF 634. (The date, of course, assures that this was not a definitive accounting.)

58. Mackau to Count of Paris, 25 August 1889, in AMF 643.

59. Raiberti to Croissy, 15 August, 7, 13 September 1889, in Mackau papers 107. Later on Raiberti would make a point of reminding everyone of his scruples: *Le Paris,* 23 September 1890.

60. Beauvoir to Count of Paris, 2 October 1889, in AMF 645. In this instance the government had particular reasons for monitoring the cable traffic. Two weeks previously one of Susini's supporters had been arrested for fabrication of fake telegrams between Constans and the prefect, which he had published in *La République nationale* (*Le Temps*, 21 September 1889).

61. Doty, *Cultural Rebellion*, 56; Patrick Hutton, "Popular Boulangism and the Advent of Mass Politics in France, 1886–1890," *Journal of Contemporary History* 11, no. 1 (1976), especially 90 and 98. It must be acknowledged, however, that his excellent and as yet unpublished doctoral dissertation gives a thorough and perceptive account of the role of Bonapartists and royalists in the Boulangist movement in Bordeaux: "The Boulangist Movement in Bordeaux Politics," Ph.D. diss., University of Wisconsin, 1969, especially 270–338.

62. Welche to Croissy, 28 July 1889, in Mackau papers 109; prefect to minister of interior, 17 November 1885, 6 February 1886, AD Meurthe-et-Moselle, 1M 636; Michaut to Dufeuille, 18 February 1884, in AMF 575; report from Poirel, 1 October 1888, in AMF 577; *L'Espérance,* 3 August, 8 November 1888.

63. *L'Espérance,* 23 March, 10, 15–16, 27 April, 30 May, 4 June, 14 July, 12–13, 21 August, 14 November 1888, and 3, 7, 13–14 January 1889; *Le Journal de la Meurthe et des Vosges,* 17, 25, 29 March, 10, 16, 19, 20 April, 22 May, 25 July, 18, 21 August, 1, 15 November 1888.

64. Report from Poirel, 1 March 1889, in AMF 574.

65. Gentès to Croissy, 21 June 1889, in Mackau papers 109.

66. His note was attached to the secretary's report of 1 June 1889, in AMF 578.

67. *Le Courrier de l'Est,* 27 October, 3 November 1889; commissaire spécial to prefect, 12 January 1890, 30 June 1889, 18 March 1890, AD Meurthe-et-Moselle, 1M 647; Gentès to Croissy, 6 July 1889, in Mackau papers 109.

68. Doty, *Cultural Rebellion*, 117–52.

69. Commissaire spécial to prefect, 5 May 1890, AD Meurthe-et-Moselle, 1M 647.

70. Report from Martimprey, no date but May or June 1889, in AMF 578; Gentès to Croissy, 21 June 1889, and Pierrot to Croissy, 17 July 1889, in Mackau papers 109. Arthur Meyer also praised his "moderation" in *Le Gaulois,* 10 September 1889.

71. Welche to Croissy, no date but July 1889, and Mondel to Auffray, 19 August 1889, in Mackau papers 109.

72. Hattu to Barrès, 18 September 1889, and Croissy to Bocher, 28 August 1889, in Mackau papers 104; Mackau to Count of Paris, 25 August 1889, in AMF 643.

73. Croissy to Barrès, 30 September 1889, in Mackau papers 104.

74. Barrès justified Adam's presence in the race by insisting that Welche needed a "diversion" to force a second ballot. This reasoning convinced both

Mackau and the prefect, but not Welche. Mackau to Dillon, 13 August 1889, in Mackau papers 102; Welche to Croissy, 26 August 1889, in Mackau papers, 109; prefect to minister of interior, 9 September 1889, AD Meurthe-et-Moselle, 3M 83. The disillusioned Boulangist Vergoin subsequently insisted that Welche had remained the "occult" candidate of the Boulangist committee in Paris: Vergoin, "Notes," 74.

75. Report from Poirel, 1 June 1889, in AMF 578. Pierrot to Croissy, 16 July 1889; Welche to Croissy, 26, 27 August 1889; Renard to Croissy, 4 September 1889; Gentès to Croissy, 21 June 1889—all in Mackau papers 109.

76. Beauvoir to Count of Paris, 28 September 1889, in AMF 644; Bocher to Count of Paris, 1 October 1889, in AMF 645.

77. Welche to Croissy, 6, 8, 18, 19, 23, 24 August 1889, in Mackau papers 109.

78. Commissaire de police to prefect, 5 January 1889, AD Meurthe-et-Moselle, 1M 638.

79. Commissaire de police to prefect, 10 June 1895, AD Gironde, 1M 557; Olivier to Croissy, 10, 14 May 1889, in Mackau papers 108.

80. Olivier to Croissy, 14 May 1889, in Mackau papers 108.

81. Subprefect of Lesparre to prefect, 27 April 1889, and subprefect of La Réole to prefect, 30 April 1889, AD Gironde, 1M 412.

82. Burgeot to Croissy, 21 June 1889, in Mackau papers, 108.

83. Le Nouvelliste de Bordeaux, 13 April, 18 August 1888.

84. Ibid., 16, 20 March, 12 April, 1 October 1888; report from secretary of the Gironde, 11 February 1889, in AMF 579.

85. Subprefect of Libourne to prefect, 31 August 1889, AD Gironde 3M 237; Hélène Lacaze, "Le Boulangisme en Gironde," Revue historique de Bordeaux 16, n.s. (January–June 1967), 74.

86. Commissaire spécial des chemins de fer to prefect, 12, 23, 30 March, 19 April 1889, AD Gironde, 1M 513.

87. On the struggles between royalists and Bonapartists and the use of Boulangist labels by the latter, see subprefect of Blaye to prefect, 31 August 1889; subprefect of Libourne to prefect, 31 August 1889; subprefect of La Réole to prefect, 30 August 1889—all in AD Gironde, 3M 237; Olivier to Croissy, 14 May 1889, in Mackau papers 108.

88. Cordier to Croissy, 5 September 1889, in Mackau papers 108.

89. Olivier to Croissy, 14 May, 16 September 1889, and Cordier to Croissy, 5 September 1889, in Mackau papers 108.

90. Cordier to Croissy, 5 September 1889; Olivier to Croissy, 16 September 1889; Vivier to Martimprey, 5, 19 May 1889—all in Mackau papers 108. Croissy to Olivier, 13, 16 September 1889, in Mackau papers 104. Local Radicals alleged that Aimel had been implicated in the Wilson scandal and was attracted to Boulangism when his source of republican patronage began to dry up. Georges Grilhé, Comment on devient boulangiste: le dossier de M. Aimelafille (Paris: privately printed, 1890); Etienne Ginestous, Histoire politique de Bordeaux (Bordeaux: Editions Bière, 1946), 147.

91. Commissaire central de police to prefect, 3 September 1889, AD Gironde, 3M 237.

92. *Le Nouvelliste de Bordeaux,* 19 September 1889.

93. *Le Petit Boulanger,* 25 September 1889; Commissaire spécial des chemins de fer to prefect, 21 October 1889, AD Gironde, 1M 513. This era of good feeling reflected the magnitude of conservative support for Boulangism. Precise figures are impossible, but according to Patrick Hutton's careful estimate approximately 45 percent of those who voted for Boulangist candidates in Bordeaux had voted for conservatives in 1885, as compared to 38 percent who had then voted for advanced republicans and 17 percent who in 1889 were voting for the first time (Hutton, "The Boulangist Movement," 339).

94. *Le Nouvelliste de Bordeaux,* 2 November 1889. Cordier ran against the editor of *Le Petit Boulanger* and withdrew in favor of him on the second ballot. The newspaper remained favorably disposed to Cordier, acknowledging that on the first ballot a number of Boulangists had felt "a duty to vote for M. Cordier, who had so powerfully contributed to the success of our candidates" in the legislative elections. The mood changed abruptly when most of Cordier's royalist supporters abstained on the second ballot. *Le Petit Boulanger,* 6, 14 November 1889.

95. Duval to Count of Paris, 24 August 1889, in AMF 643.

96. Count of Paris to Mackau, 9 August 1889, in Mackau papers 103. In fact, he felt strongly about only five or six of the seats in Paris: "Récit sommaire," in AMF 634.

97. *La Cocarde,* 31 August 1889.

98. Duval to Count of Paris, 24 August 1889, in AMF 643.

99. Bocher to Count of Paris, 10 September 1889, and Beauvoir to Count of Paris, 13 September 1889, in AMF 644.

100. Beauvoir to Count of Paris, 10 September 1889, in AMF 644.

101. Deville to Count of Paris, 7 October 1889; Deprès to Count of Paris, 7 October 1889; Cochin to Count of Paris, 9 October 1889—all in AMF 645.

102. For examples of the government's use of administrative pressure, see L. Bruce Fulton, "L'Epreuve du Boulangisme à Toulouse: Comment les républicains manipulèrent les élections en 1889," *Annales du Midi* 88, no. 128 (July–September 1976), 329–43; Hutton, "The Boulangist Movement," 326–27.

103. Beauvoir to Count of Paris, 10 September 1889; Bocher to Count of Paris, 18 September 1889; Breteuil to Count of Paris, 25 September 1889—all in AMF 644. *L'Autorité,* 19 September 1889.

104. Pendrié to Boulanger, 21 July 1889, and Mercier to Croissy, 9 September 1889, in Mackau papers 107.

105. *Le Temps* of 14 September 1889 lovingly detailed his criminal record.

106. Commissaire central de police to prefect, 5 August 1889, AD Haute-Vienne, 1M 175.

107. Auffray to Dillon, 20 June 1889, reproduced in *Le Gaulois*, 12 October 1890.

108. Bocher to Count of Paris, 2 August 1889, and Beauvoir to Count of Paris, 2 August 1889, in AMF 643. The Count of Paris, not wanting responsibility for Boulanger's (possibly extended) incarceration, did not insist.

109. Bocher to Count of Paris, 31 August 1889, in AMF 643; Boulanger to Naquet, 20 September 1889, BN, NAF 23783.

110. Bocher to Count of Paris, 18, 25 September 1889, in AMF 644.

111. Godille to Count of Paris, 4 October 1889; Desjardins to Count of Paris, 4 October 1889; Lévis-Mirepoix to Count of Paris, 10 October 1889—all in AMF 645. Burns (*Rural Society*, 105–10) has a detailed account of the conservative manipulation of Boulangism in the Orne. He is surely incorrect, however, in stating that, in the two Domfront arrondissments of the department, republicans won because "Boulangist and Bonapartist candidates split the opposition vote" (109). In the first arrondissement of Domfront, where the republican triumphed by 1,500 votes, the Boulangist candidates obtained only 27 votes. In the second arrondissement there was no Boulangist candidate.

112. Croissy to Bocher, 7 August 1889, in Mackau papers 104.

113. *Le Journal de l'Oise*, 5 October 1889; unclassified dossier on the 1889 election in the M series in AD Oise; Roccofort (editor of *Le Journal de l'Oise*) to Count of Paris, 4 September 1889, in AMF 644.

114. *Le Courrier de l'Aube*, 15 October 1889; Fondi de Niort to Croissy, 18 July 1889, in Mackau papers 107.

115. Léon Marquisat (defeated royalist candidate in the Haute-Saône) to Count of Paris, 9 October 1889, in AMF 645. In the Cher the Marquis de Vogüé's public opposition to "the Boulangist adventure" lost him the support of the 600 Boulangists in his arrondissement and cost him the election. Vogüé to Mackau, 1 September 1889, in Mackau papers 107; Vogüé to Count of Paris, 10 October 1889, in AMF 645.

116. *L'Avenir du Lot-et-Garonne*, 26 September, 17 October 1889.

117. *Le Gaulois*, 8 October 1889.

118. De Mun to Count of Paris, 13 October 1889, in AMF 645; report from secretary of the Deux-Sèvres, 31 October 1889, in AMF 568.

119. Mackau to Count of Paris, 8 December 1889, in AMF 647. He stressed the close margins of many victorious republicans and the fact that the popular vote of conservatives (broadly defined) had increased in 51 departments and declined in only 36. His various ingenious computations are in Mackau papers 113. By his count, there had been 108 royalists, 42 Bonapartists, and 15 solutionists in the Chamber at dissolution, and 118, 32, and 17 respectively after the ballots had been counted. His calculations are in AMF 648.

120. Mackau to Count of Paris, 24 September 1889, and Count of Paris to Mackau, 27 September 1889, in Mackau papers 103.

121. For an informed, albeit partisan, account of republican electoral ma-

nipulation, see Paul Leroy-Beaulieu, *Un chapitre des moeurs électorales en France* (Paris: Imprimerie Chaix, 1890). For a classic example of the kinds of charges and countercharges made after a close election, see the dossier on the 1885 elections in the Ardèche in AN C 5301.

122. Auffray to Count of Paris, 31 October 1889, and Mackau to Count of Paris, 13, 17 October 1889, in AMF 645.

123. Constans certainly did receive the first 30,000 francs and possibly as much as 70,000. Auffray to La Trémoille, 5 November 1889, APP B/a 942; Dansette, *Boulangisme,* 336–37. Remarking on the continued efforts to ensure the validation of conservative deputies, the secretary general of the Union des Droites, the Marquis d'Auray, noted, "We buy validations with our silence." Auray to Count of Paris, 2 December 1889, in AMF 647. On invalidations see Jean-Paul Charnay, *Les Scrutins politiques en France: contestations et invalidations* (Paris: A. Colin, 1964), especially 92–96. In the end conservatives lost eleven deputies through invalidations, half the number of 1885. By contrast, fourteen Boulangists were invalidated. For examples of the collective embarrassment and mutual recriminations caused by the episode, see *Le Gaulois,* 9 December 1889; *Le Soleil,* 11, 26, 28 November 1889; *L'Autorité,* 27 November, 23 December 1889.

Chapter 6

1. Boulanger to Naquet, 20 October, 23 November, 9 December 1889, and 3, 10 January 1890, BN NAF 23783.

2. Naquet to Boulanger, 15 May 1890, BN NAF 23783.

3. Prefect to minister of interior, 14 January 1890, AD Morbihan, M4447.

4. Report of secretary from the Meurthe-et-Moselle, 29 February 1892, in AMF 582. Barrès assured royalists that the common platform would be acceptable to them and would be particularly strong on the religious question. Royalists, fearing excessive reference to "the social and political demands of the working classes," had reservations but, noting that an offer made by the Opportunists was far less generous, continued negotiations. The Count of Paris suggested that his followers pursue "the remarkable overture of M. Barrès." The alliance never materialized but in 1893 royalists again contemplated endorsing Barrès, demurring in the end because of the abuse heaped on the local leadership owing to their "benevolent" attitude in 1889. Report from the secretary, 31 January 1893, in AMF 585.

5. *Le Figaro,* 28 August through 7 October 1890. *Les Coulisses du Boulangisme* was later published in a slightly amended version (Paris: Léopold Cerf, 1890).

6. The commentary of the Count of Paris is in AMF 648. His irritation with Uzès led to a two-year rupture in their relationship, although she later protested that by the time she had talked to Mermeix, he "knew everything." Uzès to Count of Paris, 17 January 1893, in AMF 687. He may well have, since there were hints in later royalist correspondence that Breteuil had given

218 NOTES

Mermeix much of his information. See Duc de Chartres to Count of Paris, 15 April 1893, in AMF 690; also APP Ba/975, 9 September 1890. Martimprey was also suspected, although he offered the same defense as did Uzès; see his letter to Mermeix cited in *Les Coulisses,* 344.

7. For the debate about authorship, see APP Ba/975.

8. *L'Echo de Paris,* 17 September 1890; *Le Paris,* 11, 12, 13, 14, 16, 17, 18, 19 September 1890; *L'Egalité,* 6 September 1890; APP Ba/975, 6 September 1890.

9. Beauvoir to Count of Paris, 19, 23, 30 August 1890, and Bocher to Count of Paris, 24, 26 August 1890, in AMF 655; Bocher to Count of Paris, 23 May 1891, in AMF 664; Bocher to Count of Paris, 1 June 1891, in AMF 665; La Trémoille to Count of Paris, 3 October 1889, in AMF 634. The 6,000 francs were transmitted via Arthur Meyer without the knowledge of the Count of Paris. In the end "Les Coulisses" proved to be a good deal more expensive. For once Hirsch did not feel slighted that his generosity had gone unacknowledged, since he was terrified lest the exposure of his role result in his expulsion from France. Some 600,000 francs of his contribution went unspent in 1889, but royalists discovered to their dismay in 1893 that the baron had since exhausted what remained, in his efforts to buy the silence of the press. He might have saved himself (and royalists) the expense, since the authorities seemed quite aware of his role. Haussonville to Count of Paris, 5 February 1893, in AMF 688; Hirsch to Count of Paris, 14 April 1893, and Duc de Chartres to Count of Paris, 15 April 1893, in AMF 690; APP B/a 975, 13 September 1890. The police, having for years monitored the secret contacts between Mermeix and various royalists, fully expected Beauvoir to purchase the journalist's silence and even reported that he had done so. APP B/a 956, 3 September 1890.

10. For example *L'Echo de la frontière,* 30 September 1890; *La Chronique de Vaucluse,* 20, 27 September 1890; *La Gazette du Midi,* 1–2, 4, 11, 14 September 1890; *Le Messager de Toulouse,* 10 September 1890.

11. Report from secretary of the Var to Dufeuille, 30 November 1890, in AMF 581; secretary of the Charente, 1 October 1890, in AMF 580.

12. Report from secretary of the Isère, 5 November 1890, in AMF 582. On the eclipse of royalism in this department, as well as the absence of a significant Boulangist current, see Barral, *Le Département de l'Isère,* 402.

13. Beauvoir to Count of Paris, 5 October 1890; Bocher to Count of Paris, 5 October 1890; Dufeuille to Count of Paris, 6 October 1890—all in AMF 657.

14. *La Gazette de France,* 26, 29, 30 August 1890; 1, 5, 7, 9, 11, 12, 13, 14, 19, 26, 27, 28, 29 September 1890; 1, 3 October 1890.

15. Dufeuille to Count of Paris, 6 October 1890, in AMF 657.

16. *Le Monde,* 10, 13, 14, 15, 16, 17, 19, 20 June 1890; Marcel Barrière, *Les Princes d'Orléans* (Paris: Gallimard, 1933), 9–34; Arthur Meyer, *Ce que je peux dire* (Paris: Plon, 1912), 353–61; *Le Matin,* 15 September 1890.

17. On the health of the pretender and his relations with his obdurate son,

see a series of letters addressed to the Duc d'Orléans, to be opened after the writer's death, in AMF 708.

18. Barrière, *Les Princes,* provides an eyewitness account. For the reaction of royalists, see Dufeuille to Count of Paris, 5, 6 March 1891; Luynes to Count of Paris, 16 March 1891; Hulst to Count of Paris, 17 March 1891; Duc d'Orléans to Count of Paris, 27 March 1891—all in AMF 662.

19. On negotiations with the Pope, see Parseval to Paris, 2 March 1891, in AMF 662, and 14 April 1891, in AMF 663; Beauvoir to Paris, 14 April 1891, in AMF 663.

20. De Mun to Count of Paris, 13 October 1889, in AMF 645; Martin, *Count Albert de Mun,* 83–86. Piou to Count of Paris, 2 November 1889, in AMF 646; 9 January 1890, in AMF 649; 30 December 1890, in AMF 658. Dufeuille to Count of Paris, 6 March 1891, in AMF 662; Mackau to Count of Paris, 17 October 1889, in Mackau papers 103; Mackau to Count of Paris, 30 December 1890, in AMF 658; Breteuil to Count of Paris, 31 July 1891, in AMF 666.

21. On the *ralliement,* see Alexander Sedgwick, *The Ralliement in French Politics* (Cambridge: Harvard University Press, 1965).

22. Breteuil to Count of Paris, 8 August 1892, in AMF 682; Mackau to Count of Paris, 22 January 1892, in AMF 674, and 20 October 1892, in AMF 684.

23. *L'Autorité,* 15, 16, 17, 24, 28, 31 August 1892; 8, 12, 17 September 1892; 16 October 1892.

24. Haussonville to Count of Paris, 26 August 1891, in AMF 667.

25. Reports from the secretaries of the Vienne, 16 April 1891; the Lot-et-Garonne, February 1891; the Charente-Maritime, 26 February 1891; the Morbihan, 27 February 1891; the Loiret, 1 October 1890; the Aude, 15 December 1890—all in AMF 580. In private, Dufeuille was amused that the previously outspoken Haussonville was at last discovering the realities of the royalist organization. By 1891 there was so little life left in the party that Dufeuille cynically referred to "my seven remaining committees." APP B/a 984, 26 January 1891.

26. Haussonville to Count of Paris, 20 May 1891, in AMF 664.

27. Haussonville admitted that "the 'bonsoir messieurs' of the Church to the monarchy is extremely serious and greatly weakens us." Haussonville to Count of Paris, 22 January 1892, in AMF 673. See also Dufeuille to Count of Paris, 21, 23 January 1892, in AMF 673; 25 February 1892, in AMF 674; 23 March 1892, in AMF 675; report from secretary of the Nièvre, July 1892, in AMF 574.

28. The best survey of the Panama scandal is still Adrien Dansette, *Les Affaires de Panama* (Paris: Perrin, 1934).

29. Dufeuille to Count of Paris, 2, 24 December 1892, in AMF 686, and 2 January 1893, in AMF 687; Haussonville to Count of Paris, 2, 8, 24 December 1892, in AMF 686; Haussonville to Count of Paris, 26 January 1893, in AMF 687, and 13 February 1893, in AMF 688.

30. Haussonville to Count of Paris, 26 January 1893, in AMF 687; 13 February 1893, in AMF 688; 22 August 1893, in AMF 693. Given the vagueness of electoral labels and the ambivalence of many so-called *"ralliés,"* the electoral statistics quoted by authorities vary considerably. I have relied on the careful analysis of Sedgwick, *Ralliement,* 72.

31. The best recent account of fin-de-siècle royalism is B. Joly, "Le Parti royaliste et l'affaire Dreyfus, 1898–1900," *Revue Historique* 546 (April–June 1983), 311–66.

32. The details of this episode can be found in AMF 806 and APP B/a 1210.

33. Haussonville to Count of Paris, 11 January 1893, in AMF 687, and 31 July 1894, in AMF 702; Buffet to Count of Paris, 11 January 1893, in AMF 687; Calla to Count of Paris, 31 July 1894, in AMF 702.

34. Royalists knew about the police, of course. The pretender once sat up all night trying to make sense of a coded message only to learn, to his outrage, that it had been an intentionally undecipherable text designed to confuse the police: Buffet to Duc d'Orléans, 17 December 1898, in AMF 805. A copy of the pretender's angry letter is, naturally, in APP B/a 986. The various plans for entry into France are in AMF 804 and 806.

35. On the attempts by royalists to seduce generals like Verdière, Zurlinden, and de Sancy, see Lur-Saluces to Duc d'Orléans, 1, 6 January 1899; Thurot to Duc d'Orléans, 15 February 1889; de Grammont to Duc d'Orléans, report compiled between March and May 1899—all in AMF 806.

36. Peter M. Rutkoff, *Revanche and Revision: The Ligue des Patriotes and the Origins of the Radical Right in France, 1882–1900* (Athens: Ohio University Press, 1981), 117. By contrast, both the central committee and the thirty-three departmental branches of the Jeunesse Royaliste de France were dominated by counts, barons, and marquis. See the list of national and local leaders in the Almanach de la Jeunesse Royaliste de Bordeaux for 1889, AD Gironde, 1M577.

37. *L'Autorité,* 26 October 1889.

38. *Le Messager de l'Indre-et-Loire,* 27 March 1889; *L'Espérance du peuple,* 13, 25 April 1888, 19 May 1888.

39. *Le Publicateur,* 24 March 1889.

40. Jeannine Verdès-Leroux, *Scandale financier et antisémitisme catholique: Le Krach de l'Union Générale* (Paris: Editions du Centurion, 1969); Beauvoir to Count of Paris, 23 March 1892, in AMF 675.

41. *Le Var,* 15 December 1889.

42. Dufeuille to Count of Paris, 15 March 1886, in AMF 602; Count of Paris to Mackau, 10 November 1888, in Mackau papers 103.

43. Verdès-Leroux, *Scandale financier,* 118, 146; Dufeuille to Count of Paris, 24 March 1886, in AMF 602, and 23, 26 April 1886, in AMF 603.

44. Beauvoir to Count of Paris, 1 March 1887, in AMF 614, and 2 April 1887, in AMF 615.

45. Beauvoir to Count of Paris, 20 June 1889, in AMF 641; Dufeuille to Count of Paris, 8 November 1889, in AMF 646.

46. On the distress that Laur's campaign caused Alfred Naquet, see Boulanger to Naquet, 10, 17, 26 January 1890, 24 February 1890, 24 March 1890, BN NAF 23783.

47. Haussonville to Count of Paris, 21 January 1890, in AMF 649; Beauvoir to Count of Paris, 26 January 1890, in AMF 649.

48. Report of 7 August 1899, APP B/a 986. The claim was based on the recollections of a royalist from the Lot, Baron Alibert, whose correspondence the prefecture had stolen.

49. Haussonville to Count of Paris, 15 June 1893, in AMF 691; Dufeuille to Count of Paris, 4 July 1892, in AMF 681, and 10 June 1893, in AMF 691; report of 3 February 1893, APP B/a 1209.

50. For an exhaustive treatment of leftist anti-Semitism (and every other kind), see Stephen Wilson, *Ideology and Experience: Antisemitism in France at the Time of the Dreyfus Affair* (East Brunswick: Fairleigh Dickinson University Press, 1982).

51. Verdès-Leroux, *Scandale financier*, 56–57.

52. Claude Willard, *Les Guesdistes* (Paris: Editions Sociales, 1965).

53. Haussonville to Count of Paris, 21 January 1890, in AMF 649.

54. Cochin to Count of Paris, 2 January 1893, in AMF 687.

55. Report from secretary of the Landes, 4 April 1893, and from secretary of the Indre, April 1893, in AMF 585.

56. His replies are in AMF 585.

57. La Trémoille to Count of Paris, 21 December 1892, in AMF 686.

58. On the early attitude of royalists, see APP B/a 1058, 25 January 1898, 18 April 1898, 5 September 1898, 9 January 1899; APP B/a 1209, 20 July 1898.

59. APP B/a 1209, 22 December 1894; Dufeuille to Duc d'Orléans, 3 December 1897, in AMF 802; APP B/a 1058, 14 December 1897.

60. Lur-Saluces to Duc d'Orléans, 1 February 1899, in AMF 806.

61. Lur-Saluces to Duc d'Orléans, 6 February 1899, in AMF 806. Emphasis mine.

62. Buffet to Duc d'Orléans, 29 April 1898, in AMF 804.

63. The text of his February 22 address is in AMF 806.

64. *L'Action française*, 4 February 1922, in APP B/a 1164. His observations were made on the occasion of the death of Lur-Saluces.

65. The best recent synthesis is Jean-Pierre Rioux, *Nationalisme et conservatisme: La Ligue de la Patrie Française* (Paris: Edition Beauchesne, 1977).

66. Commissaire spécial to prefect, 15 September 1889, AD Nièvre, 3M 1126/51 (1889).

67. Doty, *Cultural Revolution*, 117–237.

68. The best recent accounts of these episodes are Rutkoff, *Revanche,*

125ff., and Joly, "Le parti royaliste." Further information on the royalist role is in AMF 804–6.

69. On the role of former royalists and Boulangists in the nationalist movement, see the detailed reports in AN F⁷ 12455–57.

70. Rioux, *Nationalisme,* 42, 94–98.

71. *L'Espérance du peuple,* 22 April 1900.

72. APP B/a 942, 13 April 1900, 10 June 1905. For a decidedly laundered account of the career of Jules Auffray, see Auffray, *Un homme politique.*

Conclusion

1. Charles de Freycinet, *Souvenirs* (Paris: Delegrave, 1913), vol. 2, 400.

2. See in particular Maurice Vergoin, "Notes sur le mouvement républicain révisioniste et le boulangisme," in Archives Nationales, F⁷ 12445, and Verly, *Le Général Boulanger.*

3. On continued contacts between royalists and Boulangists, see the reports in APP B/a 1331, especially 11 November 1888.

4. C. Stewart Doty, "Parliamentary Boulangism after 1889," *The Historian* 32, no. 2 (February 1971), 250–69.

5. For a sympathetic treatment of Barrès's socialism, see Doty, *Cultural Revolution;* for a more skeptical examination, see Robert Soucy, *Fascism in France.*

6. APP B/a 1275, 21 January 1898.

7. APP B/a 1288, 21 March 1898.

8. *La Gazette de France,* 8 October 1899. Ballière's lawyer, Nicolas Hornbostel, was another veteran of the Boulangist-royalist alliance, having run in Marseilles with royalist support.

9. APP B/a 1288, 10 April 1897, 16 August 1899, 26 March 1907.

10. Levillain, *Boulanger.*

11. Maurice Barrès, *L'Appel au soldat* (Paris: Nelson, 1920), 162.

12. On the leagues and their relationship to the traditional Right, see Irvine, *French Conservatism,* chapters 4, 5.

13. The classic statement of this position is René Rémond, *Les Droites en France* (Paris: Aubier, 1982). A more recent and explicit version is in Sternhell, *Ni droite ni gauche.* Soucy, *French Fascism,* presents a convincing rebuttal. See also William D. Irvine, "René Rémond's French Right Revisited: The Interwar Years," *Proceedings of the Fifth Annual Meeting of the Western Society for French History,* 1977 [1978], 301–9.

BIBLIOGRAPHY

Archival Sources

Private Papers

Archives de la Maison de France: Archives Nationales, Paris; 300 AP III,
    cartons 566–87, 596, 599, 601–702, 704, 708, 751, 795–801, 804–8.
Archives Mackau: Archives Nationales, Paris; 156 AP I, cartons 101–13.
Archives Boucher: Archives Nationales, Paris; 305 AP, cartons 2, 3, 7.
Archives Eschasseriaux: Archives Départementales de la Charente-Maritime,
    La Rochelle; microfilm strips 1Mi 38, 39.
Correspondance Boulanger-Naquet: Bibliothèque Nationale, Paris: NAF
    23783.

Official Documents

PARIS

Ministry of the Interior: Archives Nationales, Paris: series F^7, cartons
    12431–40, 12445–46, 12455–57.
Ministry of Cults: Archives Nationales, Paris: series F^{19}, cartons 5617–19.
Archives de la Préfecture de Police, Paris: series B/a, cartons 100, 101, 201,
    405, 411, 497, 611, 630–40, 906, 942, 956, 969, 975, 977, 984, 986,
    1000, 1058, 1062, 1138, 1174, 1209, 1210, 1275, 1288, 1289, 1292,
    1330, 1331.

DEPARTMENTAL ARCHIVES

Ardèche, 5M 43, 5M 44
Aube, M 193, M 1272
Bouches-du-Rhône, 6M 3381, 6M 3385
Calvados, M 2339, M 2874
Charente, M 204
Charente-Maritime, 2M 4/22, 4M 2/40
Corrèze, 1M 64
Côte-d'Or, 20M 496, 30M 1181
Côtes-du-Nord, 1M unclassified, prefect reports; 3M unclassified, 1889 elec-
    tions
Creuse, 1M 202, 1M 204, 3M 278

Deux-Sèvres, 3M 11/28B, 4M 6/26
Dordogne, 1M 81, 3M 64, 3M 66, 4M 189, 4M 191, 4M 199
Doubs, M 787
Drôme, 3M 68
Eure, 1M 138, 1M 187, 1M 208
Finistère, 1M 136; 1M 137; 3M 1889el; 1M unclassified, "opinion politique,"
    1890–1905
Haute-Garonne, 2M 45, 4M 99
Gironde, 1M 412, 1M 512, 1M 513, 1M 557, 3M 237
Haute-Marne, 27M 42
Haute-Vienne, 1M 156, 1M 175, 3M 150
Hérault, 15M 40, 39M 277, 39M 291
Ille-et-Vilaine, 1M 141, 1M 142
Indre, 1M 266, 3M 1328
Loire-Atlantique, 1M 102, 1M 520, 1M 521, 1M 522
Marne, 30M 40, 30M 41
Meurthe-et-Moselle, 1M 636, 1M 638, 1M 647, 3M 83
Morbihan, M 3445, M 4447, M 4711
Nièvre, 3M 1126/5 (1889), 4M 1143/1
Nord, M 154/9, M 154/10, M 154/16, M 154/17, M 154/20, M 37/22,
    M 37/24, M 37/25, M 37/26
Orne, M 414, M 1228
Pas-de-Calais, M 97, M 98, M 100, M 4850, M 4884, M 4887
Rhône, 4M 249, 4M 250
Sarthe, 6191(M), 3M supp. 16
Seine-et-Oise, 4M 2/62
Seine-Maritime, 4MP 4123, 4MP 4125, 4MP 4234
Somme, 81051Mb, 81052Mb, 8106Mb
Vendée, 1M 374, 1M 375, 3M 225, 4M 403

Newspapers

PARIS

L'Autorité, 1888–89, 1892
La Cocarde, 1888–89
La Croix, 1888–89
Le Figaro, 1886–90
Le Gaulois, 1888–89
La Gazette de France, 1888–90
Le Matin, 1888–89
La Presse, 1888–90
Le Soleil, 1888–90
Le Temps, 1885–90

DEPARTMENTS

Aisne: *Le Progrès de l'Aisne*, 1888–89

Allier: *La Gazette d'Allier*, 1889

Ardèche: *Le Patriote de l'Ardèche*, 1888–89

Ardennes: *Le Courrier des Ardennes*, 1888–89

Ariège: *Le Conservateur de l'Ariège*, 1888–89

Aude: *Le Courrier de l'Aude*, 1888–89

Aveyron: *Le Journal de l'Aveyron*, 1888–89

Bouches-du-Rhône: *La Gazette du Midi*, 1886–90; *Le Soleil du Midi*, 1886–88

Calvados: *L'Echo de pays d'Auge*, 1888–89; *Le Moniteur du Calvados*, 1888–89; *Le Normand*, 1888–89

Charente: *Le Moniteur de la Charente*, 1888–89

Charente-Maritime: *L'Echo rochelais*, 1888–89; *Le Moniteur de la Saintonge*, 1888–89

Corrèze: *Limousin et Quercy*, 1889

Côte-d'Or: *La Revue bourguignonne*, 1888–89

Côtes-du-Nord: *L'Electeur des Cotes-du-Nord*, 1888–89

Deux-Sèvres: *Le Mémorial des Deux-Sèvres*, 1889; *La Revue de l'Ouest*, 1888–89; *Le Républicain de l'Ouest*, 1889

Dordogne: *L'Eclaireur de la Dordogne*, 1888–89

Doubs: *La Franche-Comté*, 1888–89

Drôme: *Le Journal de Montélimar*, 1888–89

Eure: *Le Journal de Vexin*, 1888–89

Finistère: *Le Publicateur du Finistère*, 1888–90; *L'Union monarchique du Finistère*, 1888–89; *L'Océan*, 1888–89

Gers: *Le Conservateur du Gers*, 1888–89

Gironde: *Le Nouvelliste de Bordeaux*, 1886–90; *L'Union monarchique*, 1889; *Le Petit Boulanger*, 1889; *L'Espérance*, 1889; *Le Girondin*, 1889; *La Victoire*, 1889; *La France*, 1889

Haute-Garonne: *Le Messager de Toulouse*, 1886–90

Haute-Marne: *Le Révisioniste de la Haute-Marne*, 1889; *L'Avenir de la Haute-Marne*, 1888–89

Haute-Saône: *Le Réveil de la Haute-Saône*, 1888

Haute-Vienna: *La Gazette du Centre* (Haute-Vienne), 1888

Hautes-Pyrénées: *L'Ere nouvelle*, 1888–89

Hérault: *L'Eclair*, 1886–89

Ille-et-Vilaine: *Le Journal de Rennes*, 1888–89

Indre-et-Loire: *Le Messager de l'Indre-et-Loire*, 1888–89

Isère: *Le Vrai Dauphiné*, 1888–89

Landes: *L'Avant-Garde*, 1888–89

Loire-Atlantique: *L'Espérance du peuple*, 1886–90

Loiret: *Le Journal du Loiret*, 1888–89

Lot-et-Garonne: *L'Avenir du Lot-et-Garonne*, 1888–89

Maine-et-Loire: *L'Anjou*, 1888

Manche: *Le Nouvelliste de Cherbourg*, 1888–89

Marne: *Le Courrier de la Champagne*, 1888–89

Mayenne: *L'Indépendant de l'Ouest*, 1888–89; *La Gazette de Château-Gontier*, 1888–89

Meurthe-et-Moselle: *L'Espérance*, 1888–89; *Le Journal de la Meurthe et des Vosges*, 1888–89; *Le Courrier de l'Est*, 1899; *Le Journal de Lunéville*, 1888–89

Morbihan: *Le Morbihannais*, 1888–89; *Le Petit Breton*, 1888–89

Nièvre: *Le Moniteur de la Nièvre*, 1888–89; *Le Patriote du Center*, 1889

Nord: *Le Nouvelliste*, 1886–1890; *L'Echo de la frontière*, 1888–90; *L'Express du Nord et du Pas-de-Calais*, 1889; *La Vraie France*, 1888–89

Oise: *Le Journal de l'Oise*, 1888–89; *L'Echo de l'Oise*, 1888–89

Orne: *Le Journal d'Alençon*, 1888–89; *Le Bonhomme percheron*, 1888–89

Pas-de-Calais: *L'Indépendant du Pas-de-Calais*, 1888–89; *Le Pas-de-Calais*, 1888–89

Puy-de-Dôme: *La Dépèche du Puy-de-Dôme*, 1888–89; *Le Moniteur du Puy-de-Dôme*, 1888

Pyrénées-Orientales: *Le Roussillon*, 1888–89

Seine-et-Marne: *La Défense de Seine-et-Marne*, 1888–89

Seine-et-Oise: *Le Postillon*, 1888–89

Seine-Maritime: *Le Nouvelliste de Rouen*, 1888–89

Somme: *L'Echo de la Somme*, 1888–89; *Le Mémorial d'Amiens*, 1888–89; *Le Messager de la Somme*, 1889; *Le Propagateur picard*, 1888–89

Tarn: *Le Nouvelliste du Tarn*, 1888–89

Vaucluse: *La Chronique de Vaucluse*, 1888–89

Var: *Le Var*, 1889–90; *Le Courrier du Var*, 1888–89

Vienne: *Le Courrier de la Vienne et des Deux-Sèvres*, 1888–89

Vendée: *Le Publicateur*, 1888–89; *La Vendée*, 1888

Books

Albert, Pierre, ed. *Documents pour l'histoire de la presse de province dans la seconde moitié du XIXᵉ siècle*. Paris: CRNS, n.d.

Auffray, Bernard. *Un homme politique sous la IIIᵉ République: Jules Auffray, 1852–1916*. Paris: La Pensée Universitaire, 1972.

Barral, Pierre. *Le Département de l'Isère sous la troisième République*. Paris: Armand Colin, 1962.

Barrière, Marcel. *Les Princes d'Orléans*. Paris: Gallimard, 1933.

Bellanger, Claude, Jacques Godechot, Pierre Guiral, and Fernand Lenou, eds. *Histoire générale de la presse française*. Vol. 3. Paris: Presses Universitaires de France, 1979.

Berstein, Serge. *Histoire du parti radical*. 2 vols. Paris: Presses de la Fondation Nationale des Sciences Politiques, 1980.

Breteuil, Marquis Henri de. *La Haute Société: Journal secret, 1886–1889*. Paris: Marcel Jullian, 1979.

Burns, Michael. *Rural Society and French Politics: Boulangism and the Dreyfus Affair, 1886–1900*. Princeton: Princeton University Press, 1984.

Castellane, Marquis de. *La Politique conservatrice: Les cahiers conservateurs en 1889*. Paris: Plon, 1889.

Charnay, Jean-Paul. *Les Scrutins politiques en France: Contestations et invalidations*. Paris: Armand Colin, 1964.

Dansette, Adrien. *Les Affaires de Panama*. Paris: Perrin, 1934.

———. *Le Boulangisme*. Paris: Fayard, 1946.

Denais, Joseph. *Jacques Piou: Un apôtre de la liberté*. Paris: La Nef de Paris, 1928.

Denis, Michel. *Les Royalistes de la Mayenne et le monde moderne: XIXᵉ et XXᵉ siècles*. Paris: Klincksieck, 1977.

Denis, Pierre. *Le Mémorial de Saint Brélade*. Paris: Ollendorf, 1894.

Doty, C. Stewart. *From Cultural Rebellion to Counterrevolution: The Politics of Maurice Barrès*. Athens: University of Ohio Press, 1976.

Dreux-Brézé, Marquis de. *Notes et souvenirs pour servir à l'histoire du parti royaliste, 1872–1883*. Paris: J. Dumoulin, 1902.

Dupeux, Georges. *Aspects de l'histoire sociale et politique du Loir-et-Cher*. Paris: Mouton, 1962.

Elwitt, Sanford. *The Making of the Third Republic*. Baton Rouge: Louisiana State University Press, 1975.

Flers, Marquis de. *Le Comte de Paris*. Paris: Perrin, 1888.

Fox, Edward Whiting. *History in Geographic Perspective: The Other France*. New York: Norton, 1971.

Freycinet, Charles de. *Souvenirs*. 2 vols. Paris: Delagrave, 1913.

Gadille, Jacques. *La Pensée et l'action politique des évêques français au début de la IIIᵉ République*. 2 vols. Paris: Hachette, 1967.

Gautherot, Gustave. *Un demi-siècle de défense nationale et religieuse: Emile Keller, 1828–1909*. Paris: Plon, 1922.

Ginestous, Etienne. *Histoire politique de Bordeaux sous la IIIᵉ République*. Bordeaux: Editions Bière, 1946.

Godefroy, Eugène. *Quelques années de la politique royaliste, 1893–1900*. Paris: Librairie Nationale, 1900.

Goguel, François. *Géographie des élections françaises de 1870 à 1951*. Paris: Armand Colin, 1951.

Gouault, Jacques. *Comment la France est devenue républicaine*. Paris: Armand Colin, 1954.

Grilhé, Georges. *Comment on devient Boulangiste: Le Dossier de M. Aimelafille*. Paris: the author, 1890.

Harding, James. *The Astonishing Adventures of General Boulanger*. New York: Scribner, 1971.

Hutton, Patrick H. *The Cult of the Revolutionary Tradition: The Blanquists in French Politics, 1864–1893*. Berkeley: University of California Press, 1981.

Irvine, William. *French Conservatism in Crisis*. Baton Rouge: Louisiana State University Press, 1979.

Jones, P. M. *Politics and Rural Society: The Southern Massif Central c. 1750–1880*. Cambridge: Cambridge University Press, 1985.

Kayser, Jacques, ed. *La Presse de province sous la troisième République*. Paris: Armand Colin, 1958.

Laisant, Alfred. *Pourqoui et comment je suis boulangiste*. Paris: Librairie Populaire, 1887.

Leroy-Beaulieu, Paul. *Un chapitre des moeurs électorales en France*. Paris: Imprimerie Chaix, 1890.

Leusse, Paul de. *La Paix par l'union douanière franco-allemande*. Strassbourg: J. Busseniers, 1888.

Levillain, Philippe. *Boulanger, fossoyeur de la monarchie*. Paris: Flammarion, 1982.

Locke, Robert R. *French Legitimists and the Politics of Moral Order in the Early Third Republic*. Princeton: Princeton University Press, 1974.

Machelon, Jean-Pierre. *La République contre les libertés?* Paris: Presses de la Fondation Nationale des Sciences Politiques, 1976.

Martin, Benjamin. *Count Albert de Mun: Paladin of the Third Republic*. Chapel Hill: University of North Carolina Press, 1978.

Mazgaj, Paul. *The Action Française and Revolutionary Syndicalism*. Chapel Hill: University of North Carolina Press, 1979.

Mermeix (pseud. Gabriel Terrail). *Les Coulisses du Boulangisme*. Paris: Léopold Cerf, 1890.

Meyer, Arthur. *Ce que je peux dire*. Paris: Plon, 1912.

———. *Ce que mes yeux ont vu*. Paris: Olin, 1911.

Monnet, Emile. *Archives politiques du département des Deux-Sèvres: Histoire des élections législatives de 1789 à 1889*. Niort: L. Clouzot, 1889.

Néré, Jacques. *Le Boulangisme et la presse*. Paris: Armand Colin, 1964.

Nordmann, Jean Thomas. *Histoire des Radicaux*. Paris: Editions de la Table Ronde, 1974.

Osgood, Samuel. *French Royalism under the Third and Fourth Republics*. The Hague: Nijhoff, 1960.

Piou, Jacques. *D'une guerre à l'autre*. Paris: Editions Spes, 1932.

Rémond, René. *Les Droites en France*. Paris: Aubier, 1982.

Rioux, Jean-Pierre. *Nationalisme et conservatisme: La Ligue de la Patrie Française*. Paris: Editions Beauchesne, 1977.

Rothney, John. *Bonapartism after Sedan*. Ithaca: Cornell University Press, 1969.

Royer, J. P., R. Martinez, and P. Lecocq. *Juges et notabilités au XIXe siècle*. Paris: Presses Universitaires de France, 1982.

Rudelle, Odile. *La République absolue, 1870–89*. Paris: Publications de la Sorbonne, 1982.

Rutkoff, Peter M. *Revanche and Revision: The Ligue des Patriotes and the Origins of the Radical Right in France, 1882–1900*. Athens: Ohio University Press, 1981.

Seager, Frederick. *The Boulanger Affair*. Ithaca: Cornell University Press, 1968.

Sedgwick, Alexander. *The Ralliement in French Politics*. Cambridge: Harvard University Press, 1965.

Seignobos, Charles. *L'Evolution de la troisième République*. Paris: Hachette, 1922.

Siegfried, André. *Géographie électorale de l'Ardèche sous la IIIe République*. Paris: Armand Colin, 1949.

———. *Tableau politique de la France de l'ouest sous la IIIe République*. Paris: Armand Colin, 1964.

Simony, H. Rémy de. *Le Parti conservateur et son avenir*. Lille: Imprimerie Victor Ducoulombier, 1885.

Singer, Barnett. *Village Notables in Nineteenth-Century France. Priests, Mayors, Schoolmasters*. Albany: State University of New York Press, 1982.

Siwek-Pouydesseau, Jeanne. *Le Corps préfectoral sous la troisième et la quatrième République*. Paris: Armand Colin, 1969.

Soucy, Robert. *Fascism in France: The Case of Maurice Barrès*. Berkeley: University of California Press, 1972.

Sternhell, Zeev. *La Droite révolutionnaire*. Paris: Seuil, 1978.

————. *Maurice Barrès et le nationalisme français*. Paris: Presses de la Fondation Nationale des Sciences Politiques, 1972.

————. *Ni droite ni gauche: L'Idéologie fasciste en France*. Paris: Seuil, 1983.

Stone, Norman. *Europe Transformed, 1879–1919*. London: Fontana, 1983.

Teste, Louis. *Anatomie de la république, 1870–1910*. Paris: Librairie du XXᵉ Siècle, 1910.

————. *Les Monarchistes sous la IIIᵉ République*. Paris: n.p., 1891.

Thévenot, Arsème. *Souvenirs d'un journaliste, 1883–89*. Paris: Léon Frémont, 1901.

Uzès, Duchesse de. *Souvenirs*. Paris: Plon, 1939.

Vaucelles, Louis de. *Le Nouvelliste de Lyon et la défense religieuse*. Paris: Les Belles Lettres, 1971.

Verdès-Leroux, Jeannine. *Scandale financier et l'antisémitisme catholique*. Paris: Editions du Centurion, 1969.

Verly, Albert. *Le Général Boulanger et la conspiration monarchique*. Paris: Ollendorff, 1893.

Viple, François. *Sociologie politique de l'Allier*. Paris: R. Richon, 1967.

Willard, Claude. *Les Guesdistes*. Paris: Editions Sociales, 1965.

Wilson, Stephen. *Ideology and Experience: Antisemitism in France at the Time of the Dreyfus Affair*. East Brunswick: Fairleigh Dickinson University Press, 1982.

Zeldin, Theodore. *France, 1848–1945*. 2 vols. London: Oxford University Press, 1975–79.

Articles

Brustein, William. "Regional Mode of Production Analysis of Political Behavior: The Case of Western and Mediterranean France." *Politics & Society* 10, no. 4 (1981), 355–98.

Doty, C. Stewart. "Parliamentary Boulangism after 1889." *The Historian* 32, no. 2 (February 1970), 250–69.

El Gammel, J. "Un pré-railliement: Raoul-Duval et la droite républicaine, 1885–1887." *Revue d'histoire moderne et contemporaine* 29 (October–December) 1982, 599–621.

Fulton, L. Bruce. "L'Epreuve du Boulangisme à Toulouse: Comment les républicains manipulèrent les élections en 1889." *Annales du Midi* 88, no. 128 (July–September 1976), 329–43.

Hutton, Patrick. "The Impact of the Boulangist Crisis upon the Guesdist Party at Bordeaux." *French Historical Studies* 7, no. 2 (June 1974), 226–44.

————. "Popular Boulangism and the Advent of Mass Politics in France,

1886–1890." *Journal of Contemporary History* 11, no. 1 (1976), 85–106.

———. "The Role of the Blanquist Party in Left-Wing Politics in France, 1886–1890." *Journal of Modern History* 4, no. 2 (1976), 277–95.

Joly, B. "Le Parti royaliste et l'affaire Dreyfus, 1898–1900." *Revue historique* 546 (April–June 1983), 311–66.

La Caze, Hélène. "Le Boulangisme en Gironde." *Revue historique de Bordeaux* 16, n.s. (January–June 1967), 71–85.

Massé, Alfred. "Les Partis politiques dans la Nièvre de 1871 à 1906." *Les Cahiers nivernais* 19 (April 1910), 1–72.

Roberts, J. M. "La Commune considéré par la droite: dimension d'une mythologie." *Revue d'histoire moderne et contemporaine* 19 (April–June 1972), 187–203.

Sternhell, Zeev. "Barrès et la gauche du boulangisme à la Cocarde." *Le Mouvement social* 75 (April–June 1971), 77–130.

Theses and Dissertations

Bataille, Alain. "Les Droites dans la Sarthe, 1852–1914." Mémoire de maîtrise, Centre Universitaire du Mans, 1969.

Begliomini, M. "Le Boulangisme à Nice." Diplôme d'études supérieures, Université d'Aix-en-Provence, 1963.

Bournaud, Marie-Claire. "Les Elections dans le département de la Creuse de 1889 à 1914." Mémoire de maîtrise, Université de Paris, 1970.

Doustaly, Chantal. "La Droite à Nice à la fin du XIXe siècle." Mémoire de maîtrise, Université de Nice, 1974.

Englund, Steven. "The Origins of Oppositional Nationalism in France, 1881–1889." Ph.D. diss., Princeton University, 1981.

Fulton, L. Bruce. "The Political Ascent of Ernest Constans: A Study in the Management of Republican Power." Ph.D. diss., University of Toronto, 1971.

Girard, Louis. "Les Elections à Paris sous la IIIe République." Thèse pour le doctorat de IIIe cycle de sociologie, Université de Dakar, 1968.

Hutton, Patrick. "The Boulangist Movement in Bordeaux Politics." Ph.D. diss., University of Wisconsin, 1969.

Néré, Jacques. "La Crise industrielle de 1882 et le mouvement boulangiste." Thèse de doctorat ès lettres, 2 vols., Université de Paris, 1959.

———. "Les Elections Boulanger dans le département du Nord." Thèse complémentaire, Université de Paris, 1959.

Offen, Karen. "The Political Career of Paul de Cassagnac." Ph.D. diss., Stanford University, 1970.

Ryan, William Francis. "*La Croix* and the Development of Rightist Nationalism in France, 1883–1889." Ph.D. diss., University of Connecticut, 1970.

INDEX

Elections (1893), 165
Engels, Friedrich, 8–9
Engerand, Auguste, 133–34
Eschasseriaux, Baron Eugène, 101–2, 114, 159
Eudes, Emile, 5, 9, 158
Eure, 41, 61–62, 66–68
Eure-et-Loir, 67

Fascism, 13–16, 19–20, 181
  origins of, and Boulanger affair, 16–20
Ferrand, Pierre, 152
Ferronnays, Henri, Marquis de La, 38
Ferry, Jules, 8, 12, 27–28, 30–31, 74, 118, 121
Finistère, 129
Fiquet, Edmond, 140
Floquet, Charles, 12, 118, 122, 163
  changes electoral system, 125
  duel with Boulanger, 97
Fournier, Louis, 129
France juive, La, 168–69
Freycinet, Charles de, 34–36, 41–42, 75–76, 177

Gabriel, Alfred, 12, 142–46, 155, 158
  early radicalism of, 143
Galliffet, General Gaston-Auguste, 76, 172
Gambetta, Léon, 32, 57
Gaudin, Gabriel, 134
Gazette de France, La, 10, 131–32, 160, 165, 180
Georgi, Charles, 132–33
Gers, 26, 184
Gironde, 58–61, 65, 68, 108, 142, 146–48
Goblet, René, 36–37, 42, 114
Goguel, François, 41
Goirand, Léopold, 64
Grilleau, Baron de, 101, 129
Grévy, Jules, 31, 37, 42, 74–76
Guynet, William, 136

Harcourt, Count Emmanuel d', 52, 90
Haussonville, Count Othenin d', 63

and anti-Semitism, 169–70
becomes head of royalist organization, 163–66
opposes Boulanger alliance, 86, 88, 91–94
Haute-Garonne, 48, 65, 80, 136
Haute-Marne, 60, 138
Hautes-Alpes, 188
Haute-Vienne, 70
Hérault, 54, 129
Hervé, Edouard, 63, 83–84, 117, 150
Hirsch, Maurice de, 80, 95, 122, 169, 171–72, 218
Hude, Auguste, 116
Humann, General, 38
Hutton, Patrick, 7, 142

Ille-et Vilaine, 75
Indre, 60, 135
Isère, 61, 159, 202, 218

Jacques, André, 117–19
Jeromist Bonapartists, 24, 78, 134
Jollivet, Maurice, 141
Jourde, Antoine, 6, 142, 148–49, 179
July Monarchy, 23, 25–26, 43–44, 52

Keller, Emile, 63, 171
Koechlin, Nicholas, 137

La Rochejacquelein, Marquis Julien de, 68
Lacrouselle, Amédée de, 136
Laguerre, Georges, 101, 134, 146, 149, 152, 154, 158
  Auffray supports candidacy of, 112–13
  radical Boulangist, 5, 13, 36
  "rallied republican" label invented by, 128
Laisant, Charles-Ange, 5, 149
Lalou, Charles, 155
Lambert de Sainte-Croix, Charles
  dismissal, 121

in charge of propaganda, 25, 58
opposes Boulangism, 92, 110
Laporte, Gaston, 138–39, 175, 186
Lareinty, Baron Jules de, 35, 58
Laur, Francis, 5, 169
Lavigerie, Carlinal, 163–64
Le Hérissé, René Félix, 75, 79–80
Lecomte, Maxime, 138
Legitimists, 6, 32, 41, 75, 134–36, 168
and Boulangism, 89, 92–93, 110–11,
140, 143, 147
relations with Orleanists, 21–22, 24–
25, 46, 49, 58
Lenglé, Paul, 149, 197
Leo XIII, Pope, 163
Leusse, Count Paul de, 38
Lévis-Mirepoix, Count Adrien de, 204,
216
Ligue de la Consultation Nationale,
89–90, 112
Ligue de la Patrie Française, 175–76
Ligue des Patriotes, 5, 119, 122, 167,
175–76, 181
Ligue Populaire Royaliste, 69–70
Loir-et-Cher, 62
Loire-Atlantique, 35, 57, 58, 134, 176
Loiret, 94–95
Lot-et-Garonne, 154, 164
Lozère, 40
Lur-Saluces, Edouard, 172–74

Mackau, Baron Armand de, 39, 98, 148,
154, 158, 180
and Barrès, 144–46
on Boulanger's flight, 123–24
contacts with Boulanger, 9–10, 75–
76, 79–80, 113–15
and elections (1889), 131, 137,
140–42, 155
endorses Boulangist alliance, 84,
90–93
former Bonapartist, 24
parliamentary leader of conservatives,
42–43
rallies to republic, 162–63
Maine-et-Loire, 78
Maribail, Henri de, 136
Martimprey, Edmond de, 84, 86, 93

and elections (1889), 127–28, 140, 144
former Bonapartist, 9, 24
secret contacts with Boulanger, 75–
76, 79–80, 113, 115
foreign policy, 39
Maréchal, Aléxis, 136
Maurras, Charles, 174
Mayenne, 62, 84, 129
Mermeix (pseud. G. Terrail), 128, 149,
159, 177, 183, 199, 207, 217, 218
Meurthe-et-Moselle, 61, 143–46
Meyer, Arthur, 96, 113, 117, 155
Michelin, Henri, 5, 149
Millevoye, Jacques, 99, 152
Missi dominici, 57–58, 109, 165
Montaudon, General Jean-Baptiste,
114–16, 177
Morès, Marquis de, 169
Mun, Albert de, 10, 12, 37, 63, 98, 100,
144
and anti-Semitism, 168–70
and Boulangist alliance, 80, 84–86,
91–93, 95–96, 111–13, 115
and Catholic party, attempts to
create, 41
rallies to Republic, 162–63, 165

Nancy, 13, 63, 142–46, 152, 158
Napoleon III, 24, 75
Naquet, Alfred, 120, 149, 168, 177–78
and radical Boulangism, 5, 36, 111
relations with royalists, 113, 116,
121, 157–58
Nationalists
and Boulangism, 3, 16–18
royalist embrace at end of century,
18, 174–76
royalist hostility toward radical, 5,
31–34
Néré, Jacques, 7–8, 11, 82, 104
Newspapers, role of, in royalist
propaganda, 64–66
Nièvre, 105
Nolte, Ernst, 13
Nord, 8, 47, 62, 75, 79–84, 97, 99, 101,
104–5, 107, 129, 137
"Nouvelles couches sociales," 51, 57,
68, 168